OTHER MAGE TITLES BY WILLEM FLOOR

THE PERSIAN GULF SERIES

A Political and Economic History of 5 Port Cities, 1500–1750

The Rise of the Gulf Arabs, The Politics of Trade on the Persian Littoral, 1747–1792

The Rise and Fall of Bandar-e Lengeh, The Distribution Center for the Arabian Coast, 1750–1930

Bandar Abbas: The Natural Trade Gateway of Southeast Iran

Links with the Hinterland: Bushehr, Borazjan, Kazerun, Banu Ka'b, & Bandar Abbas

The Hula Arabs of The Shibkuh Coast of Iran

Dutch-Omani Relations: A Political History, 1651–1806

Muscat: City, Society and Trade

IRANIAN HISTORY

Agriculture in Qajar Iran

Public Health in Qajar Iran

The History of Theater in Iran

A Social History of Sexual Relations in Iran

Guilds, Merchants, and Ulama in Nineteenth-Century Iran

Labor & Industry in Iran 1850-1941

The Rise and Fall of Nader Shah: Dutch East India Company Reports 1730-1747

Games Persians Play: A History of Games and Pastimes in Iran from Hide-and-Seek to Hunting

ANNOTATED TRANSLATIONS

A Man of Two Worlds: Pedros Bedik in Iran, 1670–1675
translated with Colette Ouahes from the Latin

Astrakhan Anno 1770
Samuel Gottlieb Gmelin

Travels Through Northern Persia 1770–1774
Samuel Gottlieb Gmelin

Titles and Emoluments in Safavid Iran: A Third Manual of Safavid Administration
Mirza Naqi Nasiri

IN COLLABORATION WITH HASAN JAVADI

The Heavenly Rose-Garden: A History of Shirvan & Daghestan
Abbas Qoli Aqa Bakikhanov

Travels in Iran and the Caucasus, 1652 and 1655
Evliya Chelebi

WILLEM FLOOR studied development economics and non-western sociology, as well as Persian, Arabic and Islamology from 1963-67 at the University of Utrecht (the Netherlands). He received his doctoral degree from the University of Leiden in 1971. Dr. Floor was employed by the World Bank from 1983 as an energy specialist, however, after his retirement in 2002, he has dedicated his time to the study of the social and political history of Iran. He lives in the Washington DC area, where he is also an avid baker of bread.

Fig. 1: Tribal women baking bread in a tabun (Mage 1999).

HISTORY OF
BREAD IN IRAN

WILLEM FLOOR

MAGE PUBLISHERS
WASHINGTON DC

Copyright © 2015 Willem Floor

All rights reserved.
No part of this book may be reproduced
or retransmitted in any manner whatsoever,
except in the form of a review, without the
written permission of the publisher.

Library of Congress Cataloging-in-Publication Data
Available in detail at the Library of Congress

ISBN
1-933823-77-1
978-1-933823-77-5

Printed and Manufactured in the United States

MAGE PUBLISHERS

Washington DC
202-342-1642 • as@mage.com
Visit Mage Publishers online at
www.mage.com

CONTENTS

INTRODUCTION 10

CHAPTER ONE

THE BEGINNING OF BREAD
    The Beginning of Agriculture 11
    The Beginning of Bread Making 12
    Bread, What's in a Name? 14

CHAPTER TWO
BREAD GRAINS. 17
COMMON BREAD GRAINS 17
    Wheat 17
    Barley. 18
    Millet 19
    Rye 20
    Sorghum 20
    Maize 21
    Rice 22
PECULIAR BREAD INGREDIENTS 24
    Acorns 24
    Fishmeal 26
    Dried fruits 26
    Peas 26
    Hemp seeds. 27
    Manna 27

CHAPTER THREE
DOUGH PREPARATION IN RURAL AREAS 29
    Introduction 29
    Grinding and Sieving. 30
    The Group of the Millers – *tahhan*. 31
    Leavening 33
    Making the Mixture 34
    Flattening and Forming the Dough 36

CHAPTER FOUR
Bread Baking Methods ... 37
- Bread Baked in Hot Ashes and Embers ... 37
- Hot Stones ... 37
- *Saj* or *Taveh* ... 38
- Bread Baked in Ovens ... 41
- *Tabun* ... 41
- *Tanur* ... 43

CHAPTER FIVE
Urban Bread Making ... 49
- Commercial or home bakers? ... 49
- Bakers and Their Ovens ... 55
- Public sale of bread ... 58

CHAPTER SIX
Bread Types ... 63
- Introduction ... 63
- Breads Prior to 1600 ... 64
- Breads after 1600 ... 66
- Speciality Breads and Pastries ... 79
- Sweet breads ... 82
- 'Roller' bread ... 84
- Pizza-like bread ... 84
- Bread enhancements ... 85
- Sweetmeats, confections and pastries ... 85

CHAPTER SEVEN
Spiritual Aspects of Bread ... 89
- Bread, food fit for gods ... 89
- Bread, a sacred matter ... 90
- Bread distribution, a religious duty ... 91
- Bread, more than just a word ... 93
- Bread dos and don'ts ... 93
- Bread, don't leave home without it ... 94
- Bread and marriage ... 94
- Bread is to be shared ... 95
- Bread and salt ... 97
- Bread eating etiquette ... 98

CHAPTER EIGHT
Daily Bread or a Matter of Rizq 101
Urban Diets 101
- Imperial Period 101
- Medieval Period 102
- Safavid-Qajar period 103
- Twentieth century 104
- Rural Diets 109
- Persian Gulf littoral Diet 116
- Diet of nomadic groups 116

CHAPTER NINE
Bread, A Rizq Analysis 119
- Introduction 119
- Main problems of bread supply 123
- New but failed policy after the 1871 famine 128
- The First *Majles* and the Bread Problem 133
- The bread shortage of 1912 135
- The 1917-18 Famine 138
- The bread problem under Reza Shah 144
- The bread crisis during World War II 148
- Bread policy under the Islamic Republic 156

BIBLIOGRAPHY
- Archives 157
- Books and Articles 157

INDEX 170

ILLUSTRATIONS

Fig. 1: Tribal women baking bread in a tabun (Mage 1999). 2
Fig. 2: Beveled rim bowl (Goulder 2010, p. 357). 13
Fig. 3: Oven in the wall of a house, & Cupola oven in Sialk, 3200-3000 BCE (Währen 1967, p. 16). 14
Fig. 4: Tribal woman preparing the dough and baking bread (Mortesen 1993, p. 245). 28
Fig. 5: Wheat mill (Olmer 1908, p. 15). 32
Fig. 6: Mill to grind cereals and nuts (Tahbaz 1342, p. 117). 33
Fig. 7: Dough bowl (Feilberg 1952, p. 93) 34
Fig. 8: Baking implements (Mortesen 1993, p. 245). 35
Fig. 9: Baluch muleteer baking (Stratil-Sauer 1934, p. 121). 38
Fig. 10: Peasant baking on a convex iron plate or *saj* (Dieulofoy 1887, p. 649). 40
Fig. 11: Bakhtiyari women baking (Bird 1891, vol. 1, p. 159). 41
Fig. 12: *Tabun* (MacGregor 1879, vol. 2, p. 110). 42
Fig. 13: *Tanur* baking, Hamedan (Mage 2013). 44
Fig 14: Contemporary *taftun* bakery, Tehran (Mage 2013). 47
Fig. 15: Contemporary *barbari* bread bakery in Tehran, (Mage 2013). 48
Fig. 16: Beveled rim bowl (Goulder 2010, p. 360). 49
Fig. 17: Iranian baker in Baku with round bread (Schulz 1917, p. 86). 52
Fig. 18: Ambulant baker in front of druggist (Benjamin 1887, p. 95). 53
Fig. 19: Grain storage vessel or *kondu* (Horne 1994, p. 138). 54
Fig. 20: Brushwood supply (Dieulafoye 1888, p. 135). 56
Fig. 21: A *sangak* oven (Bolukbashi 1347, p. 37). 57
Fig. 22: Street baker and bakery shop in Shiraz (Weston 1921, pp. 455-56). 59
Fig. 23: Baker's sale slat and seal (Rowghani 1385, pp. 99, 100). 60
Fig. 24: Horse cart transporting bread (Rowghani 1385, p. 72). 61
Fig. 25: Various Iranian breads (Mage 1993). 62
Fig. 26: *Lavash* bread (Nader Souri, Mage 2013). 67
Fig. 27: *Sangak* oven (Rowghani 1385, p. 85). 71
Fig. 28: Schematic drawing of a *sangak* oven (Olmer 1908, p. 18). 73
Fig: 29: *Sangak* baking hook (Bolukbashi 1347, p. 33). 74
Fig. 30: Schematic drawing of a *taftun* oven (Olmer 1908, p. 20). 75
Fig. 31: Schematic view of a bakery (Bolukbashi 1348, p. 47). 75
Fig. 32: *Barbari* bread (Mage 2013). 77
Fig. 33: Schematic drawing of an oven for *nan-e rowghani* (Olmer 1908, p. 21). 80
Fig. 34: Rural baking implements (Homayuni 1371, p. 152). 83
Fig. 35: Mill to make rice flour (Rabino-Lafont 1911, p. 32). 87
Fig. 36: *Sangak* bread with a wedding blessing written on it on a ceremonial setting
 (Batmanglij 1986, p. 216). 88
Fig. 37: Kerman bread coupons (Sykes 1898, frontispiece). 131
Fig. 38: Stamps benefiting the Alimentation Service (credit: Behruz Nassre). 140
Fig. 39: Grain silo near Tehran (Shahri 1367, vol. 2, p. 405). 150
Fig. 40: The government's main problem BREAD (Shahri 1367, vol. 2, p. 404). 156

TABLES

Table 6.1: No. of persons employed in a large *sangak* bakery 73
Table 8.1: Monthly bread consumption in Tehran in 1887 104
Table 8.2: Urban middle-class household expenditures on food items 1936 (in %) . . . 105
Table 8.3: Typical Dietary Pattern in Urban Iran Province 1962-68 107
Table 8.4: Prices of articles of prime necessity in Tabriz in 1935-36 107
Table 8.5: Weekly menu of a middle-class farmer's family of 10 persons in Ahar 113
Table 8.6: Daily dietary pattern in villages in the Marvdasht plain (Fars) in the 1960s . . 114
Table 8.7: Dietary pattern among Feili Lurs in 1935 117
Table 8.8: Three days of diet of a group of Afshar (Kerman) ca. 1970 118
Table 9.1: Estimated daily expenses of a standard *sangak* bakery in Tehran 1930 . . . 146
Table 9.2: Cost of Living Index according to the Bank Melli Bulletin (1936-1947) . . . 153

MEASURES

WEIGHT	
the *man* (weight varies)	3 kg (except where stated)
batman	3 kg. (6.621 lb)
kharvar	300 kg.
sir	7.5 g.
cherek	0.25 *man*
girvanka	409.5 g.
mesqal	4.6 g.
kilogram	2.21 lbs
100 g	3.53 oz
16 oz	1 lb. (453 g)
2240 lb	1 ton (long)
CALORIFIC VALUE	
wheat	3580 kcal/kg (15 mj)

DISTANCE	
gaz	1 meter
meter	1.094 yard
cm	0,394 inch
inch	2.54 cm
foot (12 inch)	30.48 cm
yard (3 feet)	91.44 cm
mile	1,760 yard
mile	1,609 m
MONEY	
1 *tuman*	10,000 dinars
1 *qran*	1,000 dinars or 20 *shahis*
1 *riyal*	1,000 dinars
abbasi	200 dinars
1 *shahi*	50 dinars

INTRODUCTION

As a long time baker of my own daily bread I have always been interested in baking practices in other parts of the world, and, of course, in particular those practiced in Iran. Working for a living and writing books and articles about other interesting subjects prevented me thus far from delving into this issue. As usual, when I finally did, I found that I also did not know much about bread making in Iran and thus, the research for this book was a fascinating and rewarding experience.

Although certain types of bread were known to me, it soon became apparent that there was and is a large variety of regional or local breads throughout Iranian history that so far have received no attention. Even the informative article on bread making in the *Encyclopedia Iranica* basically limits itself to the five types of bread that everyone who is familiar with Iran is able to name. Nevertheless, old and knowledgeable Iran hands like Polak and Wills list only three types of bread.[1] This is surprising as the number and variety of breads baked in Iran was much larger.

Since ancient times, bread has been the staple diet of the peoples living in Iran and many other parts of the world. Bread was baked in various ways and produced in different forms, while it was made from a variety of grains and other products. Leaving aside the use of rice, as a general rule, the poorer you were the less wheat, or no wheat at all, was to be found in your bread.

Given the importance of bread in people's diets and in determining the rise or fall of governments and/or government officials, it is amazing that this issue has been ignored as a subject of study. There is only one monograph that mainly deals with the baking technique of *sangak* bread, while there are two articles that deal with the baking of *sangak* and *taftun* bread.[2] Even with food and/or social and economic studies dealing with Iran the importance of bread is not highlighted being lumped together with broader categories (food, caloric intake, income). The available information that is presented here, therefore, has been culled from a large variety of publications.

In this book I first look at the beginnings of agriculture and bread making and the early Iranian words used to denote bread. Next, I discuss the various grains and other products that were and are used to make bread. Third, I discuss the making of dough in rural areas, followed by an overview of village baking techniques in chapter four. In the fifth chapter I examine bread baking in towns and in chapter six the various kinds of bread that were and/or are still made in Iran, including some of their baking methods. In chapter seven an overview is given of the spiritual and social aspects of bread in Iranian society, and in chapter eight I assess the importance of bread to the people of Iran. In chapter nine I address how the 'bread issue' was dealt with by the state.

Dan Potter (Sydney) was kind enough to share his knowledge of the archeological literature with me, which facilitated my research enormously and Reza Khonsary (Tehran) brought me Rowghani 1385 from Tehran. Flemming Møller (Copenhaguen), a retired Kampsax engineer, was so very kind to do research in the Kampsax archives to see whether there was any interesting information concerning labor history in Iran, and Parisa Mohamadi, a Ph.D. student in Tehran drew my attention to three relevant Persian articles, while Keith Openshaw once again did a superb editing job. To all of them, many thanks.

---

1. Polak 1865, vol. 1, p. 110; Wills 1893, p. 334.

2. Rowghani 1385; Bolukbashi 1347; Ibid., 1348.

CHAPTER ONE

THE BEGINNING OF BREAD

The Beginning of Agriculture

The major input of bread is grain. In fact, without it you cannot bake bread. Thus, to determine approximately when the earliest bread was baked, first we need to establish when various grains became available to the people living in Iran. Although people were present in Iran (Kermanshah area) as early as 38,000 BCE that does not mean that they prepared bread, despite their consumption of various grains and plants growing in the wild. Grains were known to people when they were still living a peripatetic life of hunters and food-gatherers. However, to ensure that grains were available in predictable and growing quantities a more sedentary life was required. Archaeologists submit that domestication of plants and animals required fixed settlements. Furthermore, this meant the development of tools such as sickles, hafts, querns, and grinding stones was necessary to better harvest and process the cultivated grains. This was, of course, a slow process that proceeded by stages based on feedback from practice and experience. The final stage was true domestication, meaning that after grains were harvested, part was intentionally set aside as food and part as seed for next year's crop.

The first grains to be domesticated were wheat and barley, which grew side by side, a process that probably already started during the hunter-gatherer stage. Both plants occurred in the wild and were slowly selected and adapted to man's needs. These cereals occurred all over the settled areas of the Middle East (Levant, Turkey, Euphrates valley, Iran). The earliest and the most widespread of cultivated cereals was emmer (*Triticum dicocum*), probably the result of the domestication of wild emmer. In Iran its presence has been reported in Deh Luran from the seventh millennium (late Neolithicum) onward. The second and a somewhat later cultivated wheat variety is einkorn (*Triticum monococcum*); long-grain bread wheat (*T. aestivum*) came later and was found at Tepeh Sabz near Deh Luran (northern Khuzestan), Tell al-Sawan (Iraq) and Çatal Höyük (Turkey-Konya plain) in the sixth millennium. Recent studies have shown that *T. aestivum* was already a dominant grain in the southern Caucasus in the Neolithicum. Also, this may have been the case in Turkmenistan, where in Chagylly *T. aestivum* was found dating to 5700-4500 BCE.

The other important cereal in the Neolithic period was barley, of which two variants played an important role. The earliest cultivated variety was that of so-called two-row barley (*Hordeum distichum*), which probably was the domesticated form of its wild type. A variant barley type, the so-called hulled six-row barley (*Hordeum vulgare*) was cultivated later. In the Deh Luran plain its presence has been dated to around 5800 BCE. Rain-fed agricultural which implies seasonality, including winter grains is characteristic of wild cereals. This favored barley and bread-wheat, in some semi-arid areas such as Deh Luran furthered by irrigation, so that soft grains replaced the older harder grains.[1]

Although wheat and barley would remain the most important cereals in the diet of the peoples populating Iran, then as later other grains were found among Neolithic communities and used for

---

1. Lamberg-Karlovsky et al. 1970, pp. 30-32; Hole 1969, pp. 33, 35, 45, 53, 84, 91, 284, 288; Wright 1981, pp. 227-30; Helbaek 1969, pp. 383-426; Hole et al., 1969, pp. 43 (sickles), 182 (grain grinding); Miller 1992, pp. 39-58; Ristvet et al. 2011, pp. 18-19; Harris 2010.

bread making. For example, both rye (*Secale cereale* L.) and wild oats (*Avena fatue* L.) were found to be part of the diet of the people living in Deh Luran. Millet was not present until 3400 BCE, but was found at Dowlatabad.² In neighboring Iraq, for example, two-row barley, naked barley, millet, spelt or primitive wheat (*Triticum spelta*), einkorn and emmer were used as of the sixth millennium, and later other forms of wheat and rye also were used.³

Domestication of cereal plants was a real boon for the Neolithic population as more food became available. This was due to the fact that primitive wheats like emmer, einkorn, and spelt have in common a fragile, articulated head, which breaks into segments when threshed, while the ripe grain does not easily separate from its enveloping structure. In cultivated species such as *T. aestivum* the axis of the head is stout and not articulated, so that it resists breakage, when the ripe kernel breaks easily from its husk. This allows for more efficient harvesting and threshing.⁴

Roasted or as gruel, grains were eaten before bread making was known, or when none was available,⁵ and this type of consumption was known millennia later among nomadic groups who either still did not know how to bake bread or had just become acquainted with it. For example, around 1160, when trouble in Khorasan prevented Soltan Mahmud Saljuq from further advancing in Tabaristan, he was called *gandom-kub* or the wheat-crusher, "because his soldiers, finding no bread, used to cut and crush the ears of wheat which they found and eat them."⁶ Even in the 1930s, and most likely even to-day, among the Lurs, fresh wheat was grilled. The wheat 'ears' that were almost ripe were gathered with their branches in the form of a bouquet (*melisheh gandom*) and then grilled over the fire. Then the ears were rubbed over a metal plate so that the grains dropped out and then were eaten. They also grilled ripe wheat on a tray or *towa*, which was eaten with butter (*gandom beresteh ba kareh*).⁷

THE BEGINNING OF BREAD MAKING

The preparation of leavened bread seems already to have been practiced in Jericho ca. 6000 BCE, but there is more certainty about bread making one millennium later in Djarmo (NE Iraq) and later at other sites in the Middle East as well. Flat bread constituted the staple diet in the Neolithic period, as evidenced by cupola ovens, which coexisted in the Near East with cylindrical ovens (*tanur*).⁸ The earliest indication of bread making in Iran is from Tepe Sialk (4500-4000 BCE) where apart from grain silos also baking equipment was tentatively identified. There is more certainty about the practice of bread baking around 3200-3000 BCE in Tepe Sialk, when double cupola ovens are present at this site.⁹ At about the same time, there was a large circular oven that could have been used for baking bread in Deh Luran. In 3rd millennium Deh Luran there is no doubt about this, because circular or oval ovens with vertical or converging baked walls with a diameter of 0.40-1.95 m were present, just like those found in the same area today. Also, there were hearths with a baked floor and no definable sides. The bases were usually concave and the fill is often ash. They ranged from 0.40 to 0.95 m in length. Of course, beveled rim bowls for baking bread were not lacking either (see below).¹⁰

---

2. Lamberg-Karlovsky et al. 1970, p. 30.
3. Währen 1967, p. 10.
4. Matz 1992, p. 2; for a discussion of the development of the domestication process of hybrid wheats that later developed into bread wheat, see Helbaek 1969.
5. Wright 1981, pp. 65 (charred seeds); 190 (charred seeds found).
6. Ibn Isfandiyar 1905, p. 62; see also below chapter seven concerning the ignorance of nomadic groups in Central Asia about bread making as late as the mid-eighteenth century.

7. Feilberg 1952, p. 94.
8. Währen 1967, p. 11.
9. Währen 1967, pp. 11-12.
10. Wright, pp. 84-87, 128, 186.

Fig. 2: Beveled rim bowl (Goulder 2010, p. 357).

Iran was not exceptional in this respect as evidence of similar activities and types of oven were found all over the Middle East, in particular in neighboring Elam that controlled part of SW Iran. In 3400-2900 BCE, in Uruk bread was listed as one of the town's products; while bran bread was set aside for the prisoners of Elam and Susa.[11] At Ur III (2000 BCE) there were vessels for so-called beer-bread, which was a "combination unmalted grains and spices, made in an oven, which was combined with beer-mash, made with malted grain, in the making of bread."[12]

Bread was made from barley and emmer wheat; most of it was unleavened, shaped by hand and baked on a flat stone or dish over a fire or in an oven. Flat bread was found in the tomb of Uapi at Ur. Leavened bread, using sour dough or yeast, was made in molds of various sizes such as beveled rim bowls (coarse, thick-walled, conical ceramic bowls), which were very common in the 4th millennium BCE at Ur; they were discontinued by 3000 BCE. The cuneiform sign for bread resembles the shape of a beveled rim bowl (BRB). BRBs are found in many places in Iran, from the Tehran plain in the north to Pakistani Makran in the south-east. According to Goulder, who manually made BRBs and baked bread in them, BRBs were first heated, probably to produce rapid raising and speedier baking, then filled with dough and then placed in an oven.[13]

"Barley was the primarily preferred grain for human use in Babylonia and in the third millennium in northern Syria (Elba)."[14] According to Währen, in Babylonia "Loaves dated to the third millennium were made from barley, emmer, or wheat flour, and were round, concave, or triangular, or even ball- or ring-shaped."[15] This suggests that there was increasing diversification in the baking forms used, after the fourth millennium. This trend continued into the historic period, because, according to Xenephon, Iranians invented new breads and pastry.[16] This is also clear when Cyrus

---

11. Potts 1999, pp. 59, 137.
12. Potts 1997, pp. 141, 158, 163, note 5.

---

13. Renfrew 1994, pp. 191-202; Daniel 2009, pp. 2, 15-17; Goulder 2010, p. 357. This is exactly the same procedure that I use when baking my own bread.
14. Von Soden 1994, p. 100.
15. Währen 1967, p. 255; for a picture, see Ghirshman 1963, p. 327 (ill. 403).
16. Potts 2009; Briant 2002, p. 291.

 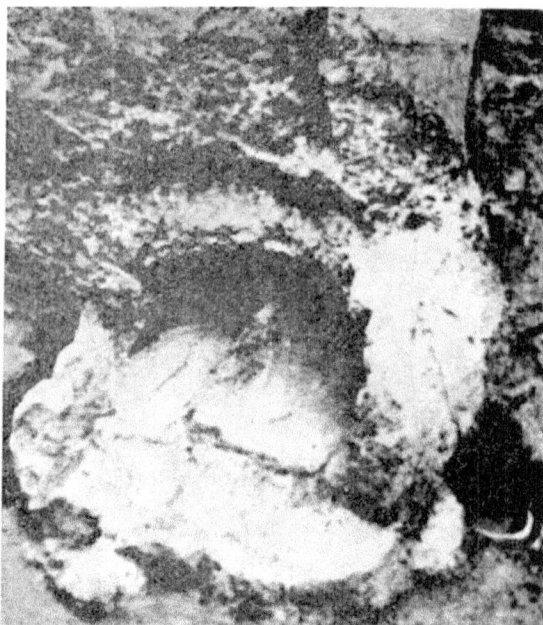

Fig. 3: *Left*: Oven in the wall of a house, & *Right*: Cupola oven with two baking surfaces in Sialk, 3200-3000 BCE (Währen 1967, p. 16).

on one occasion ordered wine and bread of the choicest kinds to be prepared.[17]

Bread, What's in a Name?

In the foregoing the advent of cultivated cereals, a necessary input for bread preparation, as well as the evidence of the first signs of the activity of bread baking was discussed. In this section the importance of the terminology used to denote bread as an indicator of the likely early distribution of bread baking methods over Iran is described.

In Iran two basic bread baking methods existed, to wit: in which bread dough was baked (i) in hot ashes and embers or (ii) in an oven or intermediate form thereof. These two methods are discussed in this section based on linguistic and in the next chapter based on factual corroborating evidence. Moreover, the question whether method (i) and (ii) correspond respectively to unleavened and leavened bread is addressed.

At present the common generic word for bread in Iran is *nan*, while there exist a large number of terms to denote various types of specialized and/or local breads, which may or not be qualified by the term *nan*. However, the earliest linguistic evidence shows that the Iranian tribes used three different words to denote bread, viz., **nikāna*, **nayna*, and **upakanta*.

According to Harmatta, who made a detailed study of these three words,**nikāna*, was used in proto-Iranian, as evidenced in Armenian *nkan[ak]*, 'bread baked in ashes' (a Parthian loanword) and in Brahui as *nkan*, "rations, food". Given this geographical distribution it is clear that this word and concept was used in the areas of both western and eastern Iranian languages, although the Brahui word may be a loanword from western Iranian languages. Harmatta and others argue that **nikāna* is derived from the verb *kan*, or 'to dig'; *nikān* in Middle Persian means 'buried' and thus is akin to

---

17. Herodotus 40, 59, 84, 117.

the meaning of 'baked in ashes'. The baking method consist in placing unleavened, unsalted dough on an iron, stone or ceramic plate with a handle that is baked on hot ashes or embers, being turned several times while baking. However, the word *nikān refers not only to dough being put on a stone slab, but also thereafter being baked, by covering with hot ashes and embers. This method was also known to the Greeks ('εγχρυφλασ) and Romans (*panis subcinerarius*). The fact that the most important feature of this type of bread baking was that the dough was covered with hot ashes and embers and then baked may have led Iranians to refer to this bread with a term that meant "dug in, covered". Based on linguistic analysis the word must have already occurred in Old Persian, and hence this technique must have been prevalent by the first half of the first millennium among the Iranian tribes. Although there is no linguistic evidence for its earlier use, this method must have been much older as baking in ovens was known and practiced already from the fourth, if not the sixth, millennium.

The second word to denote bread was *nayna that occurs in many east Iranian languages. Whereas *nikāna is restricted to western Iranian languages, words derived from *nayna are found throughout the Iranian linguistic area. The latter represented a more superior way of baking bread, and the modern version of this word, *nan*, always refers to any kind of bread baked in an oven. The term *nayna belongs to the primitive form of Iranian languages and therefore, must have been common to them all. It originally meant 'bare, naked, uncovered' as well as 'bread.' How can this be? Harmatta has suggested that like *nikān, which means both 'covered' and 'bread baked in ashes', *nayna must have meant 'bare' and 'uncovered bread' and that there could be no confusion in the meaning of either word. What gave rise to this new meaning was that the 'modern' bread was baked on the embers in either a clay vessel or oven. Closed baking equipment allowed the humidity of the dough to improve the baking process by allowing it to become lighter and more friable. Bread baked in an open oven or clay vessel could not be called *nikān or covered bread, and thus a new word had to be applied, one that denoted the bare, uncovered nature of the baking technique, and hence the use of *nayna. It was believed that the term *tanura* or oven was borrowed from the northern Semites, but the current thinking is that the term is a loan-word from the pre-Semitic or pre-Indo-European population of the area. It probably was already known in the Achaemenid period, while it also occurs in the Avesta (Vendidad VIII, 254).[18] The word as well as the new technique probably spread from the western Iranians to other Iranian peoples. Whereas in W. Iranian languages the meaning 'bare' became obsolete, in East Iranian languages this original meaning of the word was kept. However, *nayna did not indicate bread made with leaven and thus indicates the as yet low level of development of bread preparation.[19]

The third word was *pekend*, meaning 'bread baked under ashes,' of which the earliest occurrence is in Ibn Fazlan's Arabic travel account, where it is written as *bekend*. The word *pekend* goes back to Old Iranian *upakanta. *Upa* meaning 'under' and *kanta* meaning 'excavation' (originally part. perf. of the verb *kan* or to dig). Ibn Fazlan writes that an Oghuz nomad asked for bread or *pekend* by name in Khvarazmian. Thus, he did not use the word *nikān, which shows that there were different areas of diffusion for *nikāna and *upakanta. Although more recent work by Henning assigns the meaning of just simply 'bread' to the term *pekend* this does not invalidate Harmatta's argument.[20]

---

18. Jefferey 2007, pp. 93-95.
19. In the nineteenth century in in the Bust area of S.W. Afghanistan, the term denoted "the leavened cakes of wheat bread called *nan*." Bellew 1874, p. 181.
20. According to Henning, in Khvarazmian, the following relevant words occurred: 'kk pknd was dry bread, i.e. plain bread without condiment; 'kw'rk pknd is coarse, wholemeal bread ('kw'rk is coarse flour); Ffy'drc hy pcyd, 'he cooked it in the ashes'; Pknd = bread, food; m'dk = coarse; spydk = white;

The use of this Khvarazmian word proves that the early Iranian tribes had no common word for bread, not even for the most primitive form of it, i.e., the baking in hot ashes. Both *nikāna and *upakanta were used, and this means that *nikān cannot belong to the oldest, i.e. the Indo-Iranian period. Both words initially may not even have meant bread, certainly not in the proto-Iranian period. The fact that proto-Iranians and Iranians moved into the area now known as Iran in a staggered fashion over a long period with Iranian groups being wide apart due to the Caspian Sea implies that their linguistic ties had become looser. This also means that their contacts with the indigenous people living in that area,[21] who already knew bread making, occurred at different times. Since the various Iranian tribes have no common word for the primitive form of bread, they probably still did not know how to bake bread and, therefore, must have eaten grains roasted or as gruel. Once they were settled they became familiar with bread baking, hence the existence of two different words for baking bread in ashes. This means that the Iranian tribes possibly did not know bread baking before the first millennium.

It would seem that a variant of the baking method in hot ashes was the use of a baking pan. Middle Persian ta pak, 'a frying pan,' in Modern Persian tabeh or taveh, 'pan' was probably the word for the ancient bread baking pan. Middle Persian ta pak is derived from the stem *tap, "to burn, bake." It was also borrowed by Armenian (tapak; frying pan), Talmudic Aramaic (tpq': m`sh tpq', cakes baked on a hot plate) and Arabic (tabaq; big brick, tray, plate). In Baluchi t`afay means oven. As noted above, in most Iranian languages the term for oven is tanur, thus the Baluch word t`afay is a holdover from the Old Iranian period, may be in the intermediate period meaning baking pan.

The easy and rapid diffusion of the word *nayna to the area covered by E. Iranian languages was, therefore, facilitated by the use of another covered bread baking technique consisting of a kind baking pan. Harmatta has suggested that the Avestan term (8, 84) *χumbō zəmaini paičikō, meaning potter's oven, is further proof of that as well as indicating a method of a bread oven prevalent in Avestan society. The adoption of the tanur in Eastern Iran from the West was, therefore, no real break with existing practice, only a variant thereof.

Of the Iranian languages only Persian used nan, meaning 'bread', which word was formed in the 3rd-4th century CE, thus other languages that use this word as well must have borrowed it from Persian speakers. The Iranian peoples living within the confines of the Achaemenid empire as well as C. Asian and Siberian peoples borrowed the word *nayna – nan from the Persian speakers, but the Khvarazmians did not, nor the Iranian peoples north of Khvarazm.[22]

Because Turkic speaking tribes moved into Iran after the seventh century CE, they, in addition to using the Persian term nan nowadays, refer to bread as atmak or churak or dialectal variants thereof such as cherag or chorag (چُرَگ یا چِرَگ) by the Qashqa'i nomads.[23] The word was so prevalent in Turkic speaking areas of Iran that various nineteenth century authors noted that unleavened bread was called churak everywhere in northern Iran.[24]

---

pknd pcd = baked bread' 'y pknd f' trwn = parched (?) it in the oven. Henning 1971, pp. 26, 28, 38, 45.
21. Ghirshman 1977.
22. The entire discussion is based on Harmatta 1953, pp. 245-83.
23. Electronic communication by Mostafa Namdar in 2011 (Qashqa'i words); von Haxthausen 1854, p. 245 ("thin bread called tschoreki used as napkin"); Binder 1887, p. 352 (bread which they do not call lavash but chemek).
24. Bélanger 1838, vol. 1, p. 159; Soltykoff 1851, p. 63 (tschurek-murek); Gmelin 2007, p. 90 (thinly baked bread or tschurek).

CHAPTER TWO

BREAD GRAINS

Bread was made from a variety of grains and other plant products. The preferred grain was wheat, but that was often beyond the reach for most of the population. They, therefore, used other grains either singly, or, more usually, in combination to bake bread. Barley was the most important grain for bread making for the rural population, often mixed with wheat, millet and/or sorghum. Rice played a limited role as a bread grain, while acorns were a permanent staff of life for many migrant groups for part of the year. However, sometimes people had to eat inferior things, in particular in times of crop failure, famine or other natural or man-made disasters when people had to rely on a variety of products to survive. In this chapter I briefly discuss each of the various grains and plant products that were used in Iran to make and bake bread.[1] Furthermore, where possible a short historical background is offered to determine whether the use of certain products was of long standing, structural or incidental.

COMMON BREAD GRAINS

Wheat

Because bread was the staple for the people of Iran, wheat – *gandom* (*Triticum vulgare*) was the main cultivated cereal, because the best bread was made of wheat. It was almost exclusively used for bread preparation, and was planted both as a summer and winter crop. It was the principal cereal crop on which the peasants depended for their exchange in trade. Peasants hardly consumed any of it themselves, living almost entirely upon other grains, even if they had to be bought.[2] Of course, some wheat was also eaten in villages whenever they could afford it or when the occasion called for it. In the Caucasus, for example, "the bread eaten by the Ossetes is made of wheat or barley, unleavened and baked in the ashes,"[3] while in Sarvestan (Fars) bread was usually baked from excellent wheat flour, but sometimes also from barley or sorghum.[4]

Wheat is the indispensable ingredient for leavened bread. Therefore, wheat bread was and is the most desired bread in Iran, and the poorer you were the less chance you had to eat it. Only the rich could afford to eat pure wheat bread, and, therefore, more often than not 'wheat bread' contained many other ingredients. According to Adams, "their bread is made of wheat and rye, and some people who are poor use barley also."[5] In and by itself that was not necessarily a bad thing. For the addition of other grains to wheat enhanced the latter's color

---

1. For a detailed discussion of all these grains, see Floor 2003 a.
2. Polak 1865, vol. 2, p. 137; Aitchison 1890, p. 212; Sykes 1910, pp. 212-13.
3. Von Haxthausen 1854, p. 414.
4. Homayuni 1371, p. 148.
5. Adams 1900, pp. 153-54.

and flavor, reducing ingredient cost, and improving nutritional aspects.[6] Nevertheless, in the tenth century, Moslem physicians advised people to eat wheat bread and abstain from all other.[7]

In Iran wheat flour was usually mixed with barley and bran, and, therefore, wheat bread was never white. Moreover, around 1900, according to Lionel Olmer, a French physics teacher at the polytechnic school in Tehran in or about 1906, who made a special study of the bakeries in Iran, besides using mixed grain, to further cheat customers, the bakers made bread that was always badly leavened and almost always badly baked, because it was sold by weight. The bakers always mixed barley with wheat flour, and this reached as much as 50% by the end of spring, when stocks ran low and when wheat was expensive. To increase their profits even more, bakers might add other things, about which more in chapter nine.[8]

In the tenth century, according to Ibn Hawqal, a well-known Arab geographer, most bread was wheaten flat bread. However, he meant that it was consumed by the well-to-do, because wheat bread was mostly for the wealthy; less well-to-do people ate bread made of a mixture of wheat and barley, while the very poor ate barley bread.[9] The salaried class in the Middle Ages also consumed wheat bread.[10]

There were differences between wheat breads, because the wheat of certain localities was considered better than elsewhere. Allegedly, Merv had the best bread of Khorasan in the tenth century,[11] while Saghaniyan in Transoxiania also had excellent bread, and, moreover, it was cheap. However, the bread of Aveh, a town near Saveh, was very bad,[12] while that of Qazvin was "vile" and that of Hamadan poor.[13] In the nineteenth century, the bread of Tehran and Kashan was exceedingly good, but Yazdikhvast, a town located about halfway on the old road between Isfahan and Shiraz, was the best place in Iran to get bread.[14] Those who could afford it were very particular about what kind of wheat their bread had to be made of, and the same held for bakers (see chapter six). For example, the Qajar shahs only ate bread made from wheat that came from the village of Chardeh Kalateh.[15]

Barley

The cultivation of barley – *jow* (*Hordeum hexastichum* and *H. vulgare*) was widespread, both for human consumption and for the use as fodder for horses, mules and buffaloes.[16] The barley that was eaten by people was *jow-shirin* (*Hordeum hexastichum*) and barley bread – *nan-e jow* was the common fare of villagers. Often, this was due to poverty and scarcity, but also because "Wheat and barley are often sown together in one crop and then reaped together and threshed and ground without being separated."[17] Lionel Olmer reported that in the villages he regularly ate a kind of bread where the dough was made with barley and millet flour, made while grinding the millet in a mortar. "This

---

6. Matz 1992, p. 23.
7. Ahsan 1979, p. 87.
8. Olmer 1908, p. 17.
9. Spuler 1952, p. 508; Mez, p. 430 (Iraq basically grew wheat).
10. Ashtor 1976, pp. 41-42.
11. Spuler 1952, p. 510

---

12. Le Strange 1966, pp. 211, 440; Mustawfi 1919, p. 66.
13. Mustawfi 1919, pp. 65, 75.
14. Binning 1857, vol. 1, p. 357; Ibid., vol. 2, pp. 46-47, 66-67, 189, 293-94; Ballantine 1879, p. 146 (Yazdikhvast).. Thevenot 1971, vol. 2, pp. 121, 126
15. E`temad al-Saltaneh 1367, vol. 4, p. 1924.
16. Perkins 1843, pp. 428-29; Polak 1862, p. 130; Polak 1865, vol. 2, p.137. In Kurdistan, barley was referred to as "shayeer." Mignan 1839, vol. 1, p. 272.
17. Benn 1909, p. 73.

bread is baked like lavash, it is not bad."[18] It was eaten from Dashtestan in the south to Khorasan and the highlands of the Caspian provinces in the north.[19] Barley bread – *nan-e jow* in Sarvestan is like a thin fritter or *nan-e tanok*, but with barley. It has a dark color and is unleavened (*bi mayeh*).[20] Barley bread could be really bad, such as near Besitun, where in 1872, according to the British army surgeon and ethnographer Bellew, the bread was "simply uneatable, so black, so gritty, and musty was it. Even our servants refused to it."[21] The low opinion in which barley bread was held is clear from the following story. The famous minstrel-bandit of northern Iran Kuruglu, according to the songs about him that Aleksander Chodzko collected in the 1830s, asked a shepherd for some bread, who told him that he only had some made of millet and barley made for his dog.[22] Barley bread, therefore, was the symbol of frugality of dervish life and thus is often mentioned in poetry.[23]

MILLET

Millet was widely cultivated and used as food.[24] Common or proso millet – *arzan* or *dokhn* (*Panicum miliaceum*) was a small millet, which was cultivated all over Iran, and much eaten as bread by the poor and also cooked, somewhat like rice.[25]

Pennisetum spicatum or spiked millet was a common field crop in Baluchistan and on the Helmand.[26]

Millet was used to bake bread all over Iran. In the tenth century it is mentioned that "The food of the inhabitants [of Kerman] is millet-bread."[27] In eastern Iran in the nineteenth century, the staple bread was made with the common flour of the lesser millets, wheat, and barley. However, in some areas (such as Bala-Morghab in Badghis in N.W. Afghanistan)) ordinary flour consisted of maize with sorghum, and that of the spiked millet.[28] In 1912, when cereals were twice as expensive as normal, the peasants in Yazd subsisted on millet, cotton seed, turnips, beetroot, etc.[29] In Qa'en, E'tesam al-Molk, an Iranian government official traveling in that area, wrote: "where the peasants were generally poor, their diet consisted of millet bread, which was not even as good as barley bread."[30] In Baluchistan the use of millet to make bread was not exceptional

---

18. Olmer 1908, p. 20.
19. Fraser 1984, pp. 72, 157; O'Donovan 1882, vol. 1, p. 149; Jahangiri 1367, p. 81; Bazin and Bromberger 1982, p. 81.
20. Homayuni 1371, p. 150.
21. Bellew 1999, pp. 436, 485.
22. Chodzko 1842, p. 46.
23. Polak 1865, vol. 1, p. 111.
24. Aitchison 1890, pp. 86, 187; Amanat 1983, p. 133 (Yazd); Zarrabi 1342, p. 163; Mirza Ebrahim 2535, pp. 121, 232, note 20/121 (*javras*; *gavras*).
25. Aitchison 1890, p. 147; Tahvildar 1342, p. 54; Polak 1862, p. 130; Amanat 1983, pp. 76, 133; Polak 1865, vol. 2, p.137; Aucher-Eloy 1843, pp. 351-352; Fraser 1840, vol. 1, p. 128; Binning 1857, vol. 1, p. 335; Atma`eh 1360, p. 34 (*nan-e jow*).

26. Aitchison 1890, p. 150 (called *bajra* in India).
27. Anonymous 1937, p. 123. This kind of bread was known as *arzanin*.
28. Aitchison 1890, pp. 35-36, 76, 134-135.
29. *DCR* 5048 (1913) Ispahan, p. 51.
30. E`tesam al-Molk 1351, p. 314. see also W. Iwanow, "Persian spoken as in Birjand," Journal and Proceedings of the Asiatic Society of Bengal (New Series), vol. 24/4 (1928), p. 293, n. 3.

either.³¹ The Minab population's staple diet was barley, millet bread with dates, fish and some rice.³² In Owruzan (east of Taleqan), they made bread from wheat, barley and millet, but not in an oven but on a *saj* or baking tray.³³ In Kandalus (Mazandaran) *klas* or millet bread was a regular item in people's diet.³⁴ In neighboring Eshkevar (Gilan) they also bake millet bread called *cuki*.³⁵ Around 1840, in Qara-tepeh (Ormiyeh region), people told the American missionary Justin Perkins: "We don't eat one morsel of wheat of wheat bread, and only eat millet bread due to oppression."³⁶ In the Kurdish mountains bread was "made of a species of millet, wheat was hardly cultivated."³⁷ The use of millet was also widespread in the Caucasus in the nineteenth century. The Cherkess, "resigned to black barley or millet bread, forget the bitterness of poverty" and the same held for Abkhazian tribes such as the Duch and the Soani who in winter eat barley bread, and in summer millet-potage.³⁸ A side effect of millet bread was constipation.³⁹

Rye

Rye – *chavdar* (*Secale cereale* L.) was only grown in some mountainous areas, at the 1,700-2,000 meter level. At lower elevations its productivity was rather disappointing.⁴⁰ It is used mainly to make a kind of bread which is consumed locally by villagers. For example, the Lors ate rye bread,⁴¹ while in W. Azerbaijan people also ate bread made of wheat and rye in the nineteenth century.⁴² These days rye bread loaves are made in large cities and promoted by some modern niche bakeries as 'diet' (*rezhimi*) or 'fancy' (*fantezi*) bread.⁴³

Sorghum

Indian corn – *zorrat* (*Holcus sorgum*) was less widely cultivated than other major cereals.⁴⁴ Fresh sorghum (*zorrat*) in Isfahan was very tender and tasty; the poor made dried sorghum to make bread; it was also fed to the animals such as cows and sheep.⁴⁵ Millet (*arzan*) or sorghum was a spring cereal. The French seventeenth century traveler Jean Chardin observed, "Whereof [sorghum] they make Bread in some Places, as in *Courdestan*, when their Corn happens to be spent before Harvest." In Shiraz, at that time, it was used as bread for the poor, or in general to adulterate bread flour.⁴⁶ Also

---

31. See Stratil-Sauer 1934, pp. 121 (photo), 166 (photo).
32. Sadid al-Saltaneh 1342, p. 55.
33. Al-e Ahmad 1333, p. 28.
34. Jahangiri 1367, p. 81.
35. Bazin and Bromberger 1982, p. 81.
36. Perkins 1843, p. 170.
37. Perkins 1843, p. 7.
38. Reineggs 1807, pp. 242, also the Duchi, pp. 207, 336.
39. Olmer 1908, p. 20.
40. Polak 1862, p. 130; Ibid. 1865, vol. 2, p. 137; Schlimmer 1970, p. 505.
41. Anonymous 1846, p. 39.

---

42. Adams 1900, pp. 153-54.
43. Desmet-Grégoire 1989.
44. Amanat 1983, p. 133 (Yazd); Binning 1857, vol. 1, p. 335.
45. Tahvildar 1342, p. 54.
46. Chardin 1811, vol. 4, p. 102; Ibid., 1927, p. 254; Kemp 1959, pp. 2, 20 (Darband; in general); Fryer 1909, vol. 2, p.

in later centuries down into the twentieth, Iranian peasants were satisfied with unleavened barley and sorghum bread, while their landlord got the wheat.[47] In Sarvestan (Fars), according to one of its native sons and local historian Sadeq Homayuni, they ate bread called *suleh*, a sorghum bread; it is a white and brittle bread and tasty. *Kolak* is another kind of sorghum bread in Sarvestan; it is leavened and is baked in a *sangak* bakery. It is round, small (about 20 centimeters in diameter) and a few centimeters thick. Although it is thicker than *sangak* it is very brittle, hollow, tasty and nicely colored. You think at first sight that it is a special cake or sweet bread, according to Homayuni.[48] In eastern Iran staple bread made with the common flour of the lesser millets, wheat, and barley, or, in the case of some areas (Bala-Morghab in N.W. Afghanistan) ordinary flour consisted of maize with sorghum, and that of the spiked millet.[49]

Maize

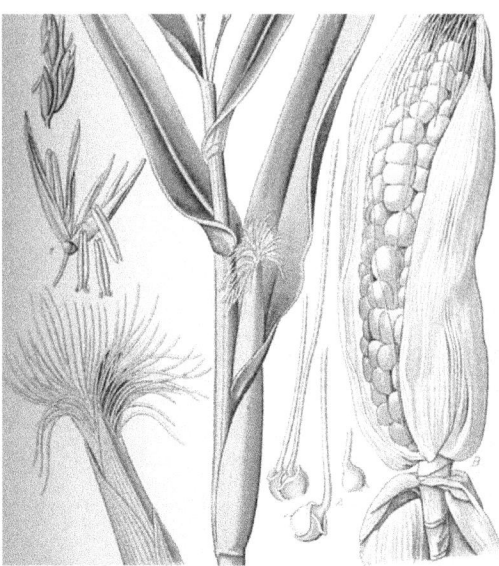

Corn or maize – *ballal, jowri, jowri-khordani* (*Zea mays*) was also cultivated in Iran, although its use as a grain for bread making is rather limited. "Corn is rarely raised. The only variety esteemed or grown is popcorn."[50] This statement by the American missionary James Bassett in the 1880s seems to be borne out by all other available information. Maize was grown in Baluchistan and on the Helmand flood plain only as an occasional plant, at large intervals through fields of cotton, melons and tobacco. It was planted as a luxury only. For eating, the cobs were roasted over the fire.[51] In Eshkevar (northern Talesh) people baked maize bread,[52] while in some areas (Bala-Morghab) ordinary flour consisted of maize with sorghum, and that of the spiked millet.[53] In the 1930s, the Feyli Lurs apart from wheat bread also made maize bread. It was served in yoghurt with pieces of this bread in it.

355; Olearius 1971, p. 566; Brosset 1849, vol. 2, p. 42; Asaf 1348, p. 311; Atma`eh 1360, p. 15 (*nan-e zurrat*).

47. Polak 1862, p. 130; Ibid., 1865, vol. 1, p. 111; Forbes-Leith 1973, pp. 39-40; Sykes 1910, pp. 210, 212-213; Perkins 1843, p. 170; Fraser 1840, vol. 1, p. 128, 131; Binder 1887, p. 352; Merritt-Hawkes 1935, p. 17; Rice 1923, pp. 60, 89.
48. Homayuni 1371, p. 150.
49. Aitchison 1890, pp. 35-36, 76, 134-135.

50. Basset 1886, p. 254.
51. Aitchison 1890, p. 223.
52. Bazin and Bromberger 1982, p. 81.
53. Aitchison 1890, pp. 35-36, 76, 134-135.

It was very tasty and nourishing, according to the Danish ethnographer Carl Gunnar Feilberg.⁵⁴

RICE

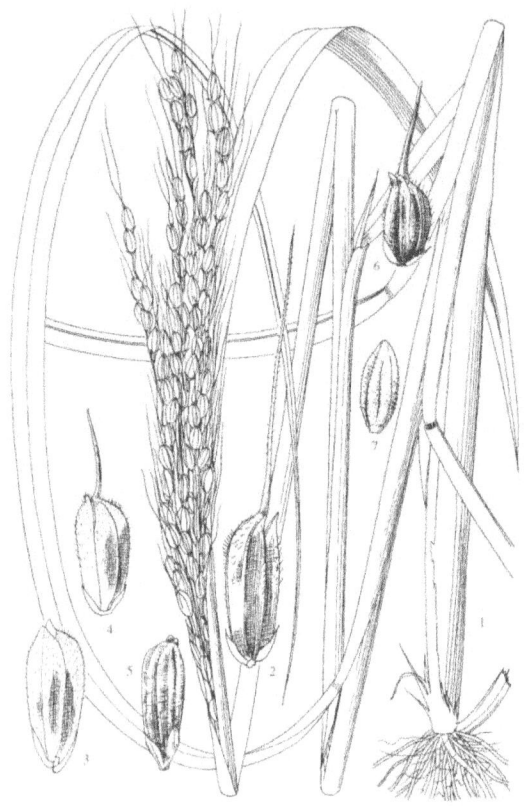

The rice plant – *shali* (*Oryza sativa*) yields the rice grain called *berenj*.⁵⁵ Rice cultivation in Iran was already practiced in Achaemenid times and continues up to the present.⁵⁶ It is mainly concentrated in Gilan and Mazandaran, with small patches of rice cultivation near a number of large towns. Until medieval times rice was also a major product of Khuzestan and in neighboring southern Iraq (Basra).

Not everybody ate wheat or barley bread; in southern Khuzestan and the Caspian provinces (where rice was the staple food), rice bread was eaten throughout the year. Some people were so accustomed to this rice that they became ill when they ate wheat bread. However, rice flour does not contain gluten proteins, which gives wheat flour its unique ability to form highly expanded, tender, white and flavorful yeast-leavened baked products.⁵⁷ Therefore, wheat flour was added to milled rice to produce flour from which bread could be baked.

Rice bread or *khubz al-aruzz* was eaten by the common people in Baghdad in the tenth century; several mills supplied the Baghdadis with its flour – hence rice must have been cheap.⁵⁸ Indeed, rice bread was the staple of the poor and al-Jahez (781-869), the prolific scholar from Basra, reports that it was the favored fare of misers, who offered it to their guests.⁵⁹ As with other kinds of breads, quality was a problem, for, according to al-Muqaddasi (945-1000) the famous Arab traveler, at Ahvaz, "the rice-flour bread on which the population fed was almost indigestible."⁶⁰ According to Yaqut (1179-1129), a renowned Syrian geographer, about 50,000 ovens were in daily operation in the vicinity of Ahvaz.⁶¹ Rice bread was not only a staple in the south, but also in the northern Caspian rice-producing regions, where in the tenth century

---

54. Feilberg 1952, p. 96.
55. Aitchison 1890, p. 146.
56. Canard 1959, pp. 113-131; Wulff 1966, p. 242; Bazin ad Bromberger et al. 1990; Ketabi 1364, pp. 459-66.

---

57. Matz, 1992, p. 33.
58. Ahsan 1979, p. 89; Spuler 1952, pp. 508, 510; Ebn Esfandiyar 1905, p. 76; Anonymous 1937, p. 134; Desmet-Grégoire 1989.
59. Waines 1987.
60. Le Strange 1966, p. 234.
61. Waines 1987.

Tabaristan, it is reported that "their food is mostly rice-bread and fish."[62]

al-Razi (d. 320/932), the famous Iranian polymath, physician and philosopher, held the view that rice bread was less digestible than wheat bread; hence it should be eaten with salty food or with a lot of fat or with milk or garlic in order to prevent ill side effects. Ibn Zuhr (d. 557/1162), a physician from Spain, adds that rice bread produces thick humour, causes obstructions in the intestines and has an astringent effect upon the stomach.[63]

Rice bread continued to be consumed in the centuries that followed. According to the famous Moroccan traveler Ibn Battutta, in S. Iraq rice-bread was eaten in the mid-fourteenth century.[64] In 1655, Evliya Chelebi, the well-known Ottoman traveler, reports that in the city of Umman, situated south of Basra, "Their food, bread, drinks and beer are all prepared from rice."[65] The same held for Northern Iran where in the mid-1470s Josaphat Barbaro, when ambassador to Iran, reported that "There growth litle wheate, wherefore they feede of ryse; of the which they make their breade."[66] Some 200 years later Jean Chardin observed that "There are several places in Persia where they eat very little Bread; whether it is from the great plenty of Rice as there is along the Caspian Sea, or from the scarcity of Bread-corn, as upon the Coasts of the Ocean; yet there is Bread to be found every where."[67] The same is true in the mid-eighteenth century, when the Scottish merchant Jonas Hanway reported that their food was "cakes of rice, and others of wheat flower, on which were sprinkled the seeds of poppies, and others of the like nature. ... these cakes are made thin, that they may be easily broken with the hand."[68]

The British Consul Charles MacKenzie in Rasht submitted around 1858 that "They are essentially rice eaters and it is a well-known fact, that the greater part of the villagers have never even tasted wheat or barley bread." It was only eaten in towns.[69] In Gilan, in 1809, Pierre Amadee Jaubert, a French orientalist who was sent as envoy to Iran in 1805, noted that in Gilan rice was eaten universally; bread was available only in the towns and in the households of the grandees.[70] Pierre Aucher-Eloy, a French botanist, noted in the late 1830s that near Enzeli no bread was to be found.[71] Aleksander Chodzko, a Polish diplomat who was the Russian consul in Rasht in the 1830s, reported that until recent times, the poorer classes of Gilan and Mazandaran not only didn't eat bread, "but consider it as a very unhealthy food. An angry husband there, scolding his wife, says, "Go! eat bread and die!" which is equivalent to our "Go, and be hanged.""[72] Lowland Gilakis called their mountain compatriots 'barley [bread] eaters.' Arthur Conolly (1807-42), a British intelligence officer, reported that "there is a saying among other Persians, 'An unruly Mazanderaun boy threatens his mother, that if his wish be not complied with, he will go into Irak and eat bread;'" thus a real punishment.[73]

Rice bread was also part of the diet in an unexpected area. The British Consul in Baghdad, Claudius James Rice (1787-1821), in the 1820s reported that the Chaldeans in the Hakkari (Kurdistan) were poor. "They are unacquainted

---

62. Anonymous 1937, p. 134.
63. Canard 1959, p. 122.
64. Ibn Battuttah 1958, vol. 2, p. 723.
65. Chelebi 2010, p. 252.
66. Barbaro and Contarini n.d., vol. 1, p. 83.
67. Chardin 1927, p. 228.
68. Hanway 1753, vol. 1, p. 224.
69. FO 248/191, (report dated 13/04/1860), f. 73, see also f. 77 recto; Sheil 1973, p. 379 ("bread is only procurable in towns.")
70. Jaubert 1821, pp. 337, 425.
71. Aucher-Eloy 1843, vol. 2, p. 414.
72. Chodzko 1842, p. 473, n. *; Rabino-Lafont 1910, pp. 139-40.
73. Conolly 1834, vol. 1, p. 25.

with wheat or barley, and cultivated only rice, of which they make bread." Rice praised the bread, "though the dust, straw, and ashes bore an equal proportion with the rice in the villainous composition which they denominated bread."[74]

Nowadays the bread eaten in the Caspian provinces is made of wheat and barley just like the rest of Iran, while rice bread is a pastry (see below chapter six).

PECULIAR BREAD INGREDIENTS

There were ingredients that normally were not used to bake bread, but due to circumstances, mostly to do with famine conditions, people had no choice but to resort to them. Three of them, acorns, fishmeal and dried fruit, were regular ingredients in bread making and had to do both with dietary preference (fishmeal, dates) and scarcity of grain (acorn, dried fruit). The other products mentioned below were only used in exceptional circumstances due to famine-like conditions.

ACORNS

In the deciduous forests, in particular in the Zagros mountain range stretching from Kurdistan to Fars and in the mountainous areas of the Caspian provinces the acorn producing *ballut* or oak (*Quercus sp.*) abounded. These acorns – *ballut* were collected, pounded and used to bake bread.

Eating acorn bread was not a new phenomenon, for the Greek historian and geographer Strabo (d. ca. 24 CE) referred to its consumption in that area when he wrote: "But though the rest of Media is extremely fertile, the northerly mountainous part has poor soil; at any rate, the people live on the fruits of trees, making cakes out of apples that are sliced and dried, and bread from roasted almonds; and they squeeze out a wine from certain roots;

and they use the meat of wild animals, but do not breed tame animals."[75] It certainly continued to be consumed in that area in the fourteenth century, when Ibn Batutta reports that in the Lurestan Mountains, "the trees on them are oaks, from the flour of them which they make bread."[76] And it remained that way until recent times. The Lurs, according to Lady Mary Sheil, wife of Justin Sheil the British envoy in Tehran between 1849 and 1853, "live for six months on acorn bread, steeped in mud to remove the acrid taste."[77] Although Carl Gunnar Feilberg in the 1930s reports that among the Lurs, acorn bread was something of the past, the well-known British traveler Freya Stark during the same period writes that "the people fed on acorn. They expected to do so this winter, because of their rainless cornfields."[78]

It was also consumed in Kermanshah province, where bread was made with "wheat, maize, and

---

74. Rice 1836, vol. 1, pp. 278-79.

75. Strabo, XI, 13, 12.
76. Ibn Batutta 1958, vol. 2, p. 288.
77. Lady Sheil 1973, p. 226; Najm ol-Molk 1342, p. 20; *DCR* 207 (1891), p. 4; Rivadeneyra 1880, vol. 2, p. 208; see also de Morgan 1895, vol. 2, p. 200, n. 2 (the Isavands who allegedly did not cultivate grain); Layard 1971, p. 338.
78. Stark 2001, p. 88; Feilberg 1952, p. 97.

ballotas, a kind of acorn. The dough is placed on sheet-iron and baked, but the dough is badly kneaded, badly fermented and therefore heavy and indigestible."[79] In fact it was consumed throughout the Zagros range (Baneh in Kurdistan to Larestan in Fars), where the rural population, in particular nomads, supplemented its food supplies with acorns. The women gathered the acorns as they dropped ripe from the trees. These were ground between two stones or rather pounded to pulp with the aid of a boulder rolled over a flat rock to extract the bitter juice. The flour obtained, sometimes mixed with wheat flour, was soaked in running water for several days, then dried in the sun and finally made into flat cakes. Or the paste was eaten raw. "It is not appetizing, but it keeps well, and people do not only survive but thrive," according to the American missionary in Tabriz, Samuel Wilson.[80]

The Boyer-Ahmadi and Bakhtiyari nomads in Fars, for example, made their bread from acorns, ground into meal, and they used acorn, too, in tanning leather. The bread made with a mixture of acorn and wheat flour was called *kalg* by the Bakhtiyaris.[81] Likewise, the Mamasani's "usual food is the acorn, which is first bruised between two stones, and made into flour, by being dried in the sun. The women bake cakes of this flour. The paste is likewise eaten raw, and is considered very nourishing."[82] In the valley called Dasht-e Burr, near the Kotal-e Pir-e Zan, people gathered acorns to make bread. In 1852, the British civil servant Robert Binning wrote: "The acorns are dried in the sun, peeled, and pounded into flour. This flour is soaked in water for two or three days, to take off the bitter astringent taste: then mixed with an equal quantity of barley meal, and baked in thin cakes."[83] However nourishing acorn bread may have been, eating it was a sign that those who did so were poor and destitute.[84]

Acorn bread thus was the ordinary food of the Bakhtiyaris, who actually found the raw paste "very palatable and nutritious." Clement baron De Bode (1777-1846), a Russian diplomat and traveler, further noted that a Bakhtiyari foot messenger whose "only provision for the journey was a bag filled with the moist flour or raw paste of the acorn, which he very obligingly offered me to taste, and was surprised at my not relishing it."[85] This observation by nineteenth century travelers was corroborated by twentieth-century anthropologists such as Lois Beck, who wrote: "Acorns were the single most important food resource gathered by [Qashqa'i] women in the past. Properly leached, ground, made into dough, and baked on convex iron griddles over open fires, acorns forced the staple until yields from irrigated fields replaced acorn bread with wheat bread, and, to a lesser degree, with rice." Due to shortages, various types of acorn bread were eaten until the 1960s. The gathering, processing and baking was women's work. They remembered with fondness their acorn gathering outings.[86]

Eating acorn bread was not limited to nomadic groups. T.S. Anderson, an employee of the Indo-Persian Telegraph Department in 1875 or thereabouts noted that the peasants were collecting acorns, which were turned into bread and eaten by them. Moreover, particularly in the area south of

---

79. Binder 1887, p. 352.
80. Wilson 1895, p. 166; Chirikov 1358, pp. 40, 104; Kinneir 1973, p. 55 (the nomads between Shiraz and Behbahan, subsisted on acorn bread); De Bode 1843, pp. 97-98; Koelz 1983, p. 89; Goldsmid 1876, vol. 2, pp. 30, 32.
81. Norden n.d. [1928]), p. 98; Digard 1981, pp. 191-92.
82. De Bode 1845, vol. 1, p. 283; it also was the main food for the Bakhtiyaris. Ibid, vol. 1, p. 395; see also Alexander 2000, p. 122.

83. Binning 1857, vol.1, pp. 196-197.
84. Layard 1971, p. 181.
85. De Bode 1843, pp. 97-98; Stocqueler 1832, vol. 1, p. 119; Beck 1991, p. 52 (collected acorn to make bread).
86. Nashat-Beck 2003, pp. 227-28 (acorn bread was not a favorite as it tasted bitter and caused constipation); Koelz 1983, pp. 97, 89.

Shiraz, in winter, villagers such as at Dasht-e Arjin subsisted on acorn bread and dried dates, a little goat's milk, and sometimes rice. "The bread is a most miserable, unpalatable kind; it is extremely bitter, about the thickness of a cowhide."[87]

Fishmeal

When Alexander's admiral Nearchus reached the Makran coast he observed that people "shewed them much meal made of fish dried, and ground to powder; but little of wheat or barley; for they made use of that powder of dried fish for bread, and if wheat-bread for meat."[88] The same custom, according to Herodotus, was practiced by three tribes in Babylonia.[89] This kind of fish meal bread was known in Safavid and earlier times as *mahi-yabah*, *mahi ashneh*, *mahiyaneh*, *mahyaveh* and *mahiyaveh*, which was prepared in Lar and Shiraz from small fish known as *mahi ashneh* that were brought from Hormuz.[90]

Dried fruits

In Elam and Babylonia bread was made from dates,[91] while in medieval Iran there was a type of dry bread known as *hashf* that probably was also made of dates. In the nineteenth century, in many parts of eastern Iran, the fruit of the wild pear (*Pyrus sp.*), as well as that of the *taghun* or *tokhm* (*Celtis caucasia*), a common indigenous tree in Khorasan, and of dried mulberries, were all converted into flour and mixed with ordinary flour to make into bread; so were the seeds of luffa (*tori*) and of some other members of the gourd family, according to surgeon-major Aitchison (1835-98), who made important contributions to the botanic knowledge of Iran, Afghanistan, and N.W. India. He further observed that the fruit of the ungrafted mulberry trees was not considered worth eating in a fresh state, but it was collected in immense quantities to be dried. The dried fruit, *tut-e-maghz*, was found in every household, for eating as a relish with their ordinary bread diet, or it was made into flour, *talkhan*, to be mixed with corn-flour and baked into bread.[92]

Peas

According to Marco Polo, between Kerman and Hormuz, the "wheaten bread is so bitter, owing to the bitterness of the water, that no one can eat it who is not used to it." It is also possible, as suggested by Oliver St. John, a British army engineer who was part of the team that managed the construction of the telegraph line in Iran in the 1860s, that the bitterness was due to acorn meal being added to wheat flour, or because a bitter leguminous plant growing in the wheat fields was not separated when the wheat was threshed.[93] It is also possible that Marco Polo mistook wheat bread for pea bread that was sometimes made in certain locations in Kerman province. The well-known British consul and traveler, Percy Sykes reported that around 1900, "In the Lalazar range the wild pea grows in great profusion to a height of about a foot. It resembles the sweet pea, and its pods are used as a relish. ... the Karru Kudi resembles the English pea, but it is very hard. Bread is occasionally made from it, and its value is lower, being the same as barley."[94] This was probably the same as *nan-e kashkin*, i.e.

---

87. Anderson 1880, pp. 94, 117 (not wanting to stop he ate "a piece of acorn bread and dates" in the fierce cold approaching Dehbid). According to Alexander 1827, p. 122, at Dasht-e Arjin, "Acorn bread is occasionally eaten by the villagers in this district."
88. Arrian 1812, ch. 28, p. 230; ch. 29, p. 231.
89. Herodotus, I. 200.
90. Borhan 1342.
91. Dandamaev and Lukonin 1989, p. 130.

92. Aitchison 1890, pp. 35-36, 76, 134-135.
93. Polo 1993, vol. 1, pp. 113, 126.
94. Sykes 1902, pp. 439-40.

bread made from beans, barley and wheat flour, which bread was known in medieval times.⁹⁵

Hemp seeds

In Kurdistan, people made a kind of thin flat bread from hemp-seed (which was eaten half dry).⁹⁶ In France this kind of bread is used as bird feed and as fish bait.

Manna – Persian: *taranjabin, shir-khesht*; Kurdish: *gezo* (*Lecanora esculenta*)

In 1828, during the war with Russia there was a grain deficit at Ormiyeh. The French botanist and plant collector, Aucher-Eloy, who was in that area in May 1837 reported that one day there was a violent storm and as a result the land was covered with lichens. The goats started eating these immediately; this gave people the idea to make flour from them and then make bread, which they found was very tasty and nutritious. The peasants ascribed this miracle to Imam Ali, because both before and after this event they had never seen these lichens, which therefore, must have been blown from a high mountain range.⁹⁷

---

95. Asadi Tusi 1336.
96. Binder 1887, p. 178. The Arabic term *fas* was used in medieval times to denote bread made with a certain herb in scarce times. Bread made from rape-root was called *yarabeh*.
97. Aucher-Eloy 1843, vol. 2, p. 399, n.1.

Fig. 4: Tribal woman preparing the dough and baking bread (Mortesen 1993, p. 245).

CHAPTER THREE

DOUGH PREPARATION IN RURAL AREAS

In this chapter I discuss the preparation of bread dough as practiced in villages and among nomadic groups. The same activity among urban dwellers is discussed in a separate chapter.

Introduction

The frequency of baking varied by ethnic or geographical group, family size, sedentary or non-sedentary living conditions, as well as by season and the type of bread baked. According to Youel Benjamin Mirza, an American educated Nestorian Iranian missionary from the Ormiyeh region, "In summer on account of the great heat, baking is done only occasionally. Some families on a cool day bake enough bread to last several weeks. To keep the loaves from getting moldy the bread is dried and stored away."[1] However, there were many variations on this seemingly general theme. Among the Lurs, for example, bread was baked almost every day,[2] while Turkmen, Sarhad Baluch and Afghan Hazarbuz women generally baked bread each morning and evening. The latter normally baked wheat bread, but maize was also used.[3] During the extremely busy migratory period, bread was only baked in the evening in such a quantity that enough remained for the next morning's breakfast.[4] Among Nestorians in the Ormiyeh area, "For large families they usually bake every day or every other day while some bake only once or twice a week,"[5] while among the Jews of Kurdistan it depended on the kind of bread; some were baked every day, others once a week.[6] It also happened that Bakhtiyari women baked a second batch, when members of the family had to make a trip that same day.[7]

Nevertheless, the predominant practice was that bread was not baked daily; women prepared it for a number of days or once a week. This required that the dough was unleavened – *fatir*; *bi mayeh*, so that the bread baked with it could be stored for a long time and thus be eaten at a later date.[8] This meant that on occasions, households were short of bread, for "It sometimes happens that guests come unexpectedly and there is not bread enough in the house to serve them. In such cases they borrow off their neighbors so many loaves and when they bake again pay them back."[9] However, it also happened that in villages, such as near Yazd, there was from time to time hardly any bread, as Napier Malcolm, a British missionary based in Yazd, experienced several times.[10]

Bread making, including the grinding, sieving, preparing the dough and baking it, was the task of women. For example, men of the Bakhtiyari Bamadi clan would never bake bread.[11] Therefore, as soon as a daughter was old enough she started sharing this task with her female relatives. In doing so they developed their skills gradually and girls or women were noted for their bread making skills.[12] Irrespective of the kind of baking technique used

---

1. Mirza 1920, p. 121.
2. Feilberg 1952, p. 94.
3. O'Donovan 1882, vol. 1, pp. 146 (evening), 148 (morning); Salzman 1994, p. 73; Frederiksen 1996, p. 116.
4. Salzman 1994, p. 73.
5. Knanishu 1899, p. 96.
6. Shwartz-Be'eri 2000, p. 46.
7. Beck 1991, 190.
8. Homayuni 1371, p. 149; Al-e Ahmad 1333, p. 29; Tahbaz 1342, p. 44; Bazin and Bromberger 1982, p. 81; Jahangiri 1367, p. 81.
9. Adams 1900, pp. 135-36.
10. Malcolm 1905, p. 32; see also Sheil 1971, p. 338.
11. Khurshid et al. 1346, p. 94 (with picture of baking on *saj*).
12. Nashat-Beck 2003, p. 232; Beck 1991, pp. 269 398-9; Rice 1923, p. 55; O'Donovan 1882, vol. 1, p. 146; Stark 2001, p. 131; Salzman 1994, p. 73; Conolly 1834, vol. 1, p. 172.

"the ladies woke up in darkness to bake bread: the embers of the fire, which had died down in the tent through the night, were piled with fresh oak branches to fight the chill," according to Freya Stark, a British female traveler who in the 1930s traversed Lorestan.[13] Women who were members of a migratory group "kept bread-making equipment in a tasseled bag that they hung by a braided cord from an animal's load (and otherwise tied to a tent pole)."[14]

In some cases men baked bread such as in the case of Baluch cameleers and other travelers. In 1876, Ernest Floyer, an employee of the Indian Telegraph Service remarked that the Baluch camelmen kept cooking oil or ghi (*rowghan*) "in a leather skin, and squeeze a little into his dough when making bread, or into anything else he may be cooking."[15] Other travelers also mention Baluch cameleers baking bread, even, in the case of Gustav Stratil-Sauer, a German geographer and traveler who explored eastern Iran in the 1930s, in a sedentary situation.[16]

Grinding and Sieving

Grain milling was an important activity, both in rural and urban areas, for domestic and commercial use.[17] The miller, therefore, was a well-known personage who, like other craftsmen, was the poetic target in the so-called *shahr-ashub* genre. In such a poetic outburst by a Safavid poet the miller – *daqqaq* was described as follows:

Ze daqqaq ruzam chunin tireh shod
Be daqqaqi sineh 'omran gozasht

ز دقّاق روزم چونین تیره شد
به دقاقی سینه عمرم گذشت

My days have been darkened by the miller
I have passed my life being thumped on the chest
(i.e. like grain in a mill)[18]

Grains were ground in the villages for their own use, or in the towns or by the owners who stored the grain until winter and the beginning of spring. It was not only the urban population that had their grain ground by professional millers (if they did not do it at home), but also part of the rural population. Their clients paid a fee (*asmoz* in Lari, Fars, dialect) as payment for grinding the grains into flour.[19] *As* is the term that denotes mill stone, but it also means the ground grain or flour.[20] Around 1300, the millstones quarried near the large village of Khollar (near Shiraz) were used throughout most of Fars. "The curious part is that in all Fars, they grind their corn with millstones from this village, but when the people thereof have to grind their own corn they go to some other village to do so," as there is no stream to turn a mill.[21]

In fact, in some cities bakers had to use particular millers, such as in Qom where they were obliged to have their grain ground at four mills that were crown property – *khaleseh*.[22] Isfahan in the 1890s represented the situation that was typical for most towns in Iran. Mirza Hoseyn Khan Tahvildar

---

13. Stark 2001, p. 64; O'Donovan 1882, vol. 1, p. 148.
14. Beck 1991, p. 180; Stark 2001, p. 131 ("and a handsome daughter sat down with the flour-bag to bake bread."); Salzman 1994, p. 79, among the Sarhad Baluch "the *gwal* was a large woven bag, used for storage or transport of bulky foodstuffs, such as grain, flour, and dates. A *shiakin* was a small, foldin textile with a large pocket for flour and was used for preparing bread and for keeping bread fresh once it as made."
15. Floyer 1882, p. 264-65.
16. Stratil-Sauer 1934, pp. 21 (bread baking in camel dung), 121, 166; Landor 1903, vol. 2, pp. 24, 259.
17. For a technical analysis of the various form of flour milling, see Wullf 1966, pp. 277-89.

---

18. Keyvani 1982, p. 279.
19. Mahmoodian 2007, p. 7 (*as-hal* is the miller in Lari dialect).
20. Sana'i 1380, p. 37.
21. Ibn Balkhi 1912, p. 54.
22. Arbab 2536, p. 118.

who has written a kind of social-geography in his hometown of Isfahan, which incorporates a short description of all its trades and crafts, included the following write-up of the millers around 1890.

THE GROUP OF THE MILLERS – TAHHAN.

There is a group of millers (other than the millers of the rural districts and dependencies), who bring the ground wheat of those parts to the city. There are many mills in this city. Some are moved by water, others by camel or donkey, some are hand or foot [mills] that are turned by human feet and hands.

First, the water mills: Many main irrigation channels – *madi* and streams – *nahr* have been branched off from the river and channel a huge volume of water through the city's quarters. These mills turn constantly, but during the four months that water is at its lowest mark, the mills being dependent on the motion of water, they sometimes work and sometimes they do not.

Secondly, those which are rotated by camels or donkeys: These are used of old especially in dry years and during the four summer months of water scarcity. There are many mills built in this city, which are rotated by camels and donkeys and are active for a third of the year.

Thirdly, those which are moved by hand and feet: In the past, the people of this city have known times of grave adversities and siege by rebels. Most houses have hand and foot mills, so that in unsafe times wheat can be ground by hand, and there is no need to go outside [the home].[23]

Indeed, in the villages they used millstones moved by donkeys, or camels (Kerman) or bulls (Yazd), or by water (*qanat* or stream) as well as hand-mills for domestic use. According to Dr. Jacob Polak, the shah's personal physician and careful observer of life in Iran from 1851 to 1860, the result was very coarse flour, for clay is only partly sifted from the flour.[24] In case use was made of a *qanat*, the mill was situated on a side channel that was closed and opened simply with an earthen wall.

Wheat or barley is placed in an elevated room (A) for milling. The grain runs slowly via a wooden tube into the center of a millstone (B), which is placed in a lower room. The mill-stone is put into motion by an iron pin that traverses the lower mill-stone and ends in four paddles that are turned by the water. The grinding is done slowly, and the stones are quite close to each other. This kind of grinding is different from the high-speed milling of Europe. In fact, the flour is not sifted at all; the bran and the sprouts remain mixed. One therefore is not interested in producing hulled grain. Mostly, the miller does not work for himself. It takes 24 hours to grind 10 *kharvar* (3,000 kg), and he charges 8 krans per kharvar of wheat, and 10 krans for barley, of which the shell is harder. One man always sees to it that one does not mix barley with wheat, or gypsum in the flour, nevertheless all flour that passed through my hands contained barley flour, visible with microscope, and often gypsum in the ashes at a much higher level than in Europe.[25]

---

upper one has a grip, the lower one a slit for ejecting the flour." Polak 1865, vol. 1, p. 111. According to Wills 1883, p. 360, "Flour is generally ground in a handmill by the poor." According to Höltzer 2535, p. 23 there were 51 millers (*asiyaban*) in Isfahan at that time. On sieving and milling, see also Rowghani 1385, pp. 95-98.

24. Olmer 1908, p. 14; Polak 1865, vol. 1, p. 111; Koelz 1983, p. 21. Despite these activities there still was sale of grain with impurities. Bonvalot 1889, p. 121.

25. Olmer 1908, p. 15.

---

23. Tahvildar 1342, p. 117. For more information on the construction of the various types of mills, see Wulff 1966, pp. 284-89; see also Floor 2003a, pp. 224-30. "In many houses a primitive hand-mill is used, consisting of two stones; the

Hand-mills were common among the rural population.[26] According to Mrs. Rice, a British missionary with many years of experience in Iran, "Most villages have a flour-mill worked by water within easy reach, but the women find it often easier to grind by the hand-mill in their own compounds than to carry heavy bags of grain and flour to and from the mill; expense too is saved, and there is not much current coin in the village."[27] It also happened that the grains, in the case of millet bread, for example, were ground in a mortar.[28]

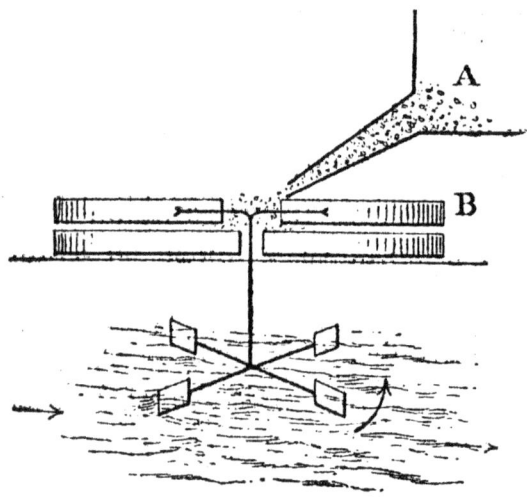

Fig. 5: Wheat mill (Olmer 1908, p. 15).

Indeed "A great deal of work falls to the women in the way of gleaning and grinding wheat and other grain."[29] According to Mahmoodian, describing the situation in Larestan (Fars):

> The millstone – *as*, is also called *haas*. It consists of a pair of circular stones four inches thick and fifteen inches wide one laced on top of the other. The top one rotate[s] over the bottom one which is fixed on top of a platform by a wooden rod, whose upper end hinges into a hole in the center of the top stone. A pencil like wooden stick, one inch thick and thirty inches long which pivots in a hole close to the edge of the top stone with its upper end being loosely fixed in a frame above the platform, enables a person, usually a woman, to grind the grains. The woman holds the stick and pushes around the upper stone with one hand while she pours the grain with the other hand into a hole in the center of the rotating top millstone, flowing into shallow grooves, known as channels, which radiate from the center of the stationary millstone. The channels lead the grain onto the flat grinding section, and to the edge, where it emerges as flour and gets accumulated in [a] concave area on the top of the platform. The miller usually sings but her voice cannot be heard due to the grating noise of the mill. Up to the late 1940s most houses in Larestan had an open room in which 'haas' and other household amenities were placed.[30]

Milling was a noisy affair, as the Irish journalist O'Donovan experienced, because before dawn "one is roused by the low rumbling of the hand-mills as the ladies of the community grind the flour for the morning bread. This is baked in cylindrical open-topped ovens, situated some yards from the entrance of the house."[31] With the introduction of modern mills, the old mills gradually faded away. In the 1930s, the municipality of Tehran issued rules for the milling of flour for different kinds of bread.[32] As of the mid-1960s there were even motor-driven mills in many villages, such as in Baluchistan where the migratory Sarhad-Baluch brought their grain.[33]

---

26. Kanishu 1899, pp. 162-63.
27. Rice 1923, p. 56.
28. Olmer 1908, p. 20.
29. Rice 1923, p. 55; O'Donovan 1882, vol. 1, p. 146.
30. Mahmoodian 2007, p. 6.
31. O'Donovan 1882, vol. 1, p. 148 (follows a description of the hand-mill and its operation).
32. Rowghani 1385, p. 65.
33. Salzmann 1994, p. 73.

Fig. 6: Mill to grind cereals and nuts (Tahbaz 1342, p. 117).

Sieving wheat and other grains was yet another of women's tasks.[34] The flour was sieved with a coarse sieve – *ardbiz* by pushing the flour by hand and rubbing it.[35] Because of this method the flour often contained all kinds of impurities. Soltykoff, for example, complained about bread containing sand near Tiflis,[36] while according to James Morier, this was sand from the threshing-floor that was found in all village bread.[37]

According to Koelz, an American zoologist:

> the bread here is good in taste. but gritty, and our companion said the grit is due to the millstones being made of gypsum. I think more likely they grind gravel with the wheat. When the winnowed grain is finally swept from the ground, many other things besides grain get swept up with it, and unless these extraneous items are cleaned out, their influence is felt in the bread. Weed seeds and gravel are the most common adulterants. The former are often so numerous and of such a sort that the bread tastes bitter or brings on a giddiness, and the latter so abundant that the bread is

gritty. Wheat is commonly rough-cleaned by the peasants before grinding. It may even be washed, but after such cleaning foreign ingredients remain, which can only be removed by hand, and I don't suppose hands are often employed in that way. If the seeds were cleaned before sowing and the worst weeds pulled in the fields, the one obnoxious element would be eliminated.[38]

Despite complaints about impurities in the badly sieved grain, rural people preferred their own grain and bread to that of urban areas. Lois Beck reported that when a Bakhtiyari tribesman had bought flour milled in town, his family considered the bread made from this flour to be "tough and stale."[39] Urban bakers also opined that modern machine milling of wheat reduced the particular attractive characteristics of certain types of wheat.[40]

Leavening

Natural yeasts exist everywhere, including in the air around us, and a warm paste will ferment spontaneously if left for a couple of hours. Therefore, it is likely that leavened bread is almost as old as unleavened bread, even if the leavening effect probably was 'discovered' by accident. In Iran, the leavening or 'sours' – *khamir-e torsh, khamir-mayeh, ab-e torsh, aji khamireh, owzima* usually was a small piece of dough that was kept over from a preceding baking kept for some days in water or it was "rolled up in the cloth or sheepskin on which the bread has been kneaded, and is put into the oven until the next baking day, perhaps three or four days off."[41] In ancient times, other forms of leaven were also used such a substance called *naga*, which was used in Mesopotamia in bread preparation; *naga* seems to have been the generic name of soda (Na_2CO_3) which was obtained from the ashes

---

34. Rice 1923, p. 55; Conolly 1834, vol. 1, p. 172. For a photo of a flour sieve, see Mortesen 1993, p. 245 (Fig. 6, 223 and Cat. Nos. 183 and 217-19).
35. Feilberg 1952, p. 94; the sieve was also known as *parvizan*. Sana'i 1380, p. 23.
36. Soltykoff 1851, p. 21.
37. Morier 1818, p. 290.

38. Koelz 1983, pp. 165-66.
39. Beck 1991, p. 215.
40. Rowghani 1385, p. 94.
41. Knanishu 1899, p. 95; Rice 1923, p. 55; Feilberg 1952, p. 94; Shwartz-Be'eri 2000, p. 46; Alberts 1963, p. 175; Tahbaz 1342, p. 44 (*owmiza*).

of Salsola kali.[42] Pliny reported that both ground bitter vetch – *gavdaneh* (*Vicia ervilia*) and chickpea – *nakhud* (*Cicer arientinum*) could be used as leavening agents; both plants were widely available in the Middle East.[43] Mr. Eton, a British gentleman who had visited Iran in the mid-eighteenth century reported the following:

The Persian method of making Yeast. This useful article, of which there is frequently a scarcity in this country, is thus prepared on the coast of Persia.

Take a small tea cup or wine glass ful[l] or split or bruised pease, pour on them a pint of boiling water, and set the whole in a vessel all night on the hearth, or any other warm place: the water will have a froth on its top the next morning, which will be good yeast. An English gentleman when in Persia, had his bread made with this yeast, and in the English manner, of good wheat flour.[44]

Until recently, in villages such as Kandelus (Mazandaran), the green skin of walnuts was dried and ground and its dust used to leaven bread, like soda (*jush-e shirin*) nowadays.[45]

Making the Mixture

The dough – *khamir* or *khabir* is prepared from flour, salt, water or oil – *rowghan*, and, if required or wanted, leavening. It is kneaded – *sarishidan* in a large wooden bowl, on a metal or wooden plate, or on a large stone. In Luri the basin is called *jofna*, but in Gilaki it is known as *majma*.[46] If the leavening has not been kept in water, but was hard, it was broken up and softened with hot water, and then added to the flour. Its mixture of wild yeasts and bacteria that had accumulated and stabilized during preceding baking inoculated the new batch, thus improving fermentation. This is due to the generation of carbon dioxide within the dough and which is the main leavening force.[47] Kneading was long and done carefully in the wooden bowl or on the flat metal sheet; later salt was added. One continued kneading and when the dough was ready it was covered and left to rise for some hours.[48] Time and good kneading is necessary to get fine dough. In 1885, the French traveler Henry Binder, noted in Kermanshah province that the dough was badly kneaded, badly fermented and therefore heavy and indigestible.[49] Sometimes, the dough was prepared a day in advance.[50] In the village of Yush, they knead the dough by hand in a vessel – *loak* and then put a fabric over it. It has to remain one hour like that to rise. Then they take bits from the dough and make these into balls – *bon*. They put these balls around the *loak* and put the fabric once again over it. The balls should not be touched as they would become unleavened – *fatir* and they also should not be counted, because this is a bad omen.[51]

Fig. 7: Dough bowl (Feilberg 1952, p. 93)

---

42. Potts 1997, p. 119.
43. Pliny 18.71.
44. Pybus 1810, p. 22. According to another English gentleman, some 60 years later, "Yeast is not procurable in Tehran." Eastwick 1864, vol. 1, p. 254.
45. Jahangiri 1367, p. 81.
46. Conolly 1834, vol. 1, p. 164; Feilberg 1952, p. 94; Shwartz-Be'eri 2000, p. 46; Bazin & Bromberger 1982, p. 81; Mobasheri 1389, p. 360; Mortesen 1993, p. 245 (a wooden bowl in which to mix the dough, Cat. Nos. 188-9 and p. 238).

47. Matz 1992, p. 53.
48. Knanishu 1899, p. 95; Rice 1923, p. 55; Feilberg 1952, p. 94; Mirza 1920, p. 121.
49. Binder 1887, p. 352.
50. Shwartz-Be'eri 2000, p. 46.
51. Tahbaz 1342, p. 45.

Dough Preparation in Rural Areas • 35

Fig. 8: Baking implements (Mortesen 1993, p. 245)

Flattening and Forming the Dough

When the leavened dough has risen sufficiently it is divided into small pieces the size of a bagel, which in medieval times was called *raghif*.[52] These balls are rolled out on a sheepskin, camel-hair cloth or on a floured plate with a very thin rolling-pin – Gilaki: *nanchub, vardaneh*; Luri: *tir*, into large round cakes; the women sprinkled flour over the dough to prevent the dough sticking to the roller or their fingers. These are tossed deftly, in making the bread the woman throws it from one arm to the other, letting it fall on the flat of her forearm. Every time it is thrown it becomes longer and thinner. According to the French diplomat Eustache de Lorey, they became large circular cakes nearly a yard across, as flat as Scottish oatcakes, while Norden describes them as thin sheets as big as a table napkin.[53] The bread was either round or stretched out, which the mystic poet Rumi referred to as *gerd va daraz kardan-e khamir*.[54]

And when the dough has taken its final shape, it is spread on a round wooden board or cushion with a handle – *nunaviz*, and slapped on the side of the *tanur* till baked. Then the bread was taken off the wall with a small scoop. This work was usually performed by two women: one who made the prepared the dough sheets and another who baked them.[55] Alternatively, if an open fire and/or no rolling pin was used, "A daughter flattened it with her hands into thin sheets as big as a table napkin; another baked each sheet quickly over a pan of coals and placed it on the pile already done. From this pile an old grandmother lifted each sheet of bread with a stick, waved it to and fro in the air until thoroughly dried, and then placed it on another pile."[56] In the case of one family, usually thirty or more of these sheets were baked every day, "and it is not an easy task, being over the hot furnace, preparing them."[57] The baking was done in a tent or inside the house, either in the courtyard, a special room, or in the female quarters – *anderun*, depending on the time of the year.[58]

---

52. Mobasheri 1389, p. 362.
53. Adams 1900, pp. 153-54; Knanishu 1899, p. 96; de Lorey 1907, p. 355; Rice 1923, pp. 55-56; Norden 1928, p. 277; Bazin and Bromberger 11982, p. 81; Beck 1991, p. 147; Feilberg 1952, p. 95; Mahmoodian 2007, p. 66 (*parsom* or the flour sprinkled over the dough). The term *vardaneh* is also used in Turkic speaking areas.
54. Mobasheri 1389, p. 361. For a breadboard on which to roll out the dough with a rolling pin, see Mortensen 1993, p. 245 (Cat. Nos. 184-85 and 220-21), see fig. 6..
55. De Lorey 1907, 355; Knanishu 1899, p. 96; Bazin, Marcel and Bromberger et al. 1982, p. 81.

---

56. Norden 1928, p. 177 (at Kenareh, village next to Persepolis); Mortensen 1993, p. 245.
57. Adams 1900, pp. 153-54.
58. Norden 1928, p. 177.

CHAPTER FOUR

BREAD BAKING METHODS

The linguistic evidence for the two baking methods discussed in chapter one is supported by facts on the ground. In this chapter the two main baking methods are discussed, to wit: in hot ashes and embers, or in an oven. Both these methods were usually used by all Iranians, whether a rural or urban dweller, depending on the circumstances, as is discussed below. Jewish villagers in Kurdistan, for example, made use of "two kinds of ovens in baking which was done in the house in winter and outside in summer."[1] This gave households flexibility, because if the oven was not available, bread was baked over an iron plate or in the hot ashes. Given this flexibility households were able to economize fuel.[2] Nevertheless, in some areas, such as in Gilan in the 1970s, there were three distinct bread baking zones: (i) in the plains, where bread was not baked at home; (ii) in the area of N. Talesh, E. Azerbaijan, and the Safidrud valley, where bread was baked in a domestic oven; and (iii) in case of migrant Shahseven, Talesh and Galesh, where bread was baked on a plate in embers or on hot stones.[3]

Bread Baked in Hot Ashes and Embers.

The baking of bread in hot ashes and embers may well be the oldest form of bread making and perhaps is derived from the practice of hunter and food-gatherer groups to roast the grains harvested from wild plants. Although the baking in hot ashes was mostly practiced by nomads, travelers, soldiers on the march and the like, its use was not limited to ambulant people. Several sources report the use of this method in sedentary communities. In medieval times this bread was called *sokarva*, *sokaru* and *tormus*. The tools used to bake bread in this manner were adapted to the kind of bread produced.

Hot Stones.

The simplest form of this baking method was described by the British painter and traveler Henry Savage Landor in 1901 as follows:

> The Baluch camel man first washed his hands, then flour and water, with great lumps of salt, were duly mixed together in a bowl until reduced into fairly solid paste. A clean cloth was then spread upon the ground and the paste punched hard upon it with the knuckles, care having been taken to sprinkle some dry flour first so that the paste should not stick to the cloth. When this had gone on for a considerable time the paste was balanced upon the knuckles and brought gaily bounding to where the hot cinder remained from a fire of camel dung which had previously been lighted. The flattened paste was carefully laid upon the hot ashes, with which it was then covered, and then left to bake for an hour or so.[4]

Landor reluctantly ate a piece of this bread so as not to hurt the man's feelings, but he is silent about whether he liked it or not. The German geographer, Gustav Stratil-Sauer, who provides a similar description of Baluch cameleers' bread baking art in 1934, commented that this crispy, warm, thin bread was marvelous.[5] The American anthropologist Philip Salzman offers a more detailed description

---

1. Shwartz-Be'eri 2000, p. 46. The Armenians of Jolfa/Isfahan baked paper thin bread, one and a half pace in diameter, on an iron plate or *saj* in the 1630s. Tavernier 1930, p. 283; as to its general use, see Chardin 1927, pp. 228-29.
2. Rice 1923, p. 178.
3. Bazin and Bromberger 1982, p. 80. In Larestan (Fars), *noo paukha* (in modern Persian *nan pokhteh*) "usually meant to bake bread at home, either over *bereza* or *tava*." Mahmoodian 2007, p. 310.

4. Landor 1903, vol. 2, pp. 24-25.
5. Stratil-Sauer 1934, p. 21.

of the baking method for this dense, hard-crusted, wheat bread called *wari*:

> To bake *wari*, the fire was burnt down to hot ashes, some of the ashes were swept aside, the dough was placed on the remaining layer of hot ashes, and then it was covered with the other hot ashes. The hot ashes thus acted as an oven, providing both the heat source and the heat container. After half an hour, the now baked *wari* was removed from the ashes, brushed off with the hand, and was ready to eat.[6]

Fig. 9: Baluch muleteer baking (Stratil-Sauer 1934, p. 121).

This method was not only used by Baluchis in general,[7] but also by Turkmen and others. "The Toorkmuns burn sticks or weeds to ashes, and cover up a cake of unleavened dough in them, turning it every now and then to prevent its burning: the bread thus prepared is excellent."[8] Talesh and Galesh pastoralists likewise put the dough in the embers to make what they called *nun-e atash*.[9] In various sedentary groups in the Caucasus and Mazandaran where bread baked in embers was called *kalva*.[10]

According to the British Indian official Edward Mitford, a variant of this technique was used by Afghan travelers in 1840. They baked bread "which is made in a peculiar way; some large round stones are first heated in the ashes, they are then covered with dough in the form of a dumpling and returned to the ashes until baked, when it makes a tolerable unleavened bread."[11] In the Bashagerd area in 1879, when Ernest Floyer, an employee of the British-Indian Telegraph Service, arrived at a Baluch camp, "the mother of the family was just preparing supper of thick slabs of unleavened bread baking on a broad, thin flake of sandstone."[12] In Central and southern Talesh and Gilan, the dough was also just placed on a heated stone and therefore was called *nan-e sang* or stone bread.[13] The same method was used by other nomadic groups such as the Lors.[14] The generic name for both these types of bread as well as for other types of village bread was peasant's bread- *nan-e dehati*, which is described as being unleavened bread that was pressed very thin and then baked on a stone or metal plate. "The entire preparation lasts at most half an hour."[15]

SAJ OR TAVEH

The more common method to bake bread in hot ashes and embers was with the use of a kind of tray, a method used throughout Iran. This tool was generally known as *saj*. Among pastoral nomads the dough was kneaded in a metal pan - *mazama*, *majama*, which in Safavid and earlier period was known as *lagan*.[16] In villages there also

---

6. Salzman 1994, pp. 172-73.
7. Salzman 1994, p. 78.
8. Conolly 1834, 1, 73, note.
9. Bazin and Bromberger 1982, pp. 57, 81; Bazin 1980, vol. 2, p. 57.
10. Klaproth 1814, p. 288; Reineggs 1807, pp. 45, 336 (half-baked in the ashes); Von Haxthausen 1854, p. 394 (Ossetes baked bread in the ashes); Jahangiri 1367, p. 81.
11. Mitford 1884, vol. 1, p. 94.
12. Floyer 1882, p. 200.
13. Bazin and Bromberger 1982, pp. 57, 81; Bazin 1980, vol. 2, p. 57.
14. Feilberg 1952, p. 95.
15. Polak 1865, vol. 1, p. 110.
16. Bazin and Bromberger 1982, p. 81; Desmet-Grégoire

existed receptacles made of sun dried, molded mud to bake bread in or on. They were known as *barzan* in Safavid and earlier times.[17]

The use of the *saj* was an old method and is mentioned around 1400 (although it dates from much earlier times), when the Castilian ambassador to Timur Leng, Ruy Gonzales Clavijo reported that "Their bread in these villages was indeed of a very bad quality, being made after a strange fashion. They take a little flour, knead it and make pan-cakes of the same. Then they take a frying-pan set it on the fire and when it has got hot throw the thin cake of dough into it, which as soon as it is heated and baked through they remove. This was the only bread that they supplied to us in the villages."[18]

In general, the *saj* was made of metal (iron, copper). In the 1930s, in Posht-e Kuh, bread was baked on a convex shield of metal called the *saj*; "the bread, warm and rather sodden, was ready in a minute or two."[19] The Turkmen also used the *saj* to bake bread[20] and likewise in Kermanshah province[21] and in the Caucasus. "Plates, from one to two inches thick, are used by the civilized mountaineers for the purpose of baking their bread; but if they incautiously heat them red hot, the plates fly into innumerable pieces, frequently to the injury of the bystanders."[22] The Shahsavan and pastoralists of the Talesh and parts of Gilan also used the *saj*, i.e. the dough is placed on the convex part or on the back of a baking platter (*posht-e gemej*) installed over a tripod.[23]

The *saj* was also known under other names, i.e., the *taveh* or *tabeh*, which is the modern form of Middle Persian *ta pak*, 'a frying pan,' as discussed in chapter one. Among the Sarhad Baluch the *saj* was known as *padink* and the long thin spatula used for removing bread from the *tin* griddle was called *nan gwah*.[24] Baking among the Lors was usually done on such an implement. The baking was done on its convex side, while the concave side was covered with wet ashes, probably to temper the effect of the fire. While the *taveh* was being heated, the woman prepared the bread on a wooden circular board, with a handle at one of its four corners called *khuneh*. The upper side of the *taveh* was sprinkled with water. Some flour was put on the board. The dough was rolled in the flour to envelop it, and then it was flattened on the board. Then the woman moved the dough from one hand to the other so that it became a soft and a large thin paste, which she placed on the *taveh*. The woman made three breads at the time in a production line: while one was baked on the *taveh*, another coming off the *taveh* was placed on a hot stone next to the fire and got a second baking; and the third one was being formed on the *khuneh* and/or in her hands. Whenever a loaf of bread was ready it was handed warm to those present.[25] Pastoralists residing in the summer quarters of the Kelashtar district of Gilan also covered the bread in the embers with a metal lid -*taveh*,[26] and the same held for the nomads in the Ormiyeh area. "Their oven or fire-place consists simply of a hole in the ground in the center of the tent. They bake their bread upon a concave plate of copper about two feet in diameter. The concave side is placed over the coals of the fire, while upon the convex or outer side they bake very thin, but very delicious loaves of bread."[27]

1980, p. 253; Borhan 1342. The *saj* was used both by urban and rural dwellers in Safavid Iran. Tavernier 1930, p. 383; della Valle 1664, vol. 2, p. 17.

17. Borhan 1342; Malcom 1905, p. 11.
18. Le Strange 1928, pp. 121-22.
19. Stark 2001, p. 61.
20. Amanat 1983, p. 39.
21. Binder 1887, p. 352.
22. Reineggs 1807, p. 23.
23. Bazin and Bromberger 1982, pp. 81-82.
24. Salzman 1994, pp. 72, 78-79.
25. Feilberg 1952, pp. 94-95 (in Lori the *taveh* is known as *towa*, as it is among the Bakhtiyaris, see Digard 1973, pp. 212-13); see also de Bode 1845, vol. 2, p. 263; Desmet-Grégoire 1980, pp. 254, 257 ("Other household items for food preparation include the following: a circular convex iron griddle for baking bread."); Mortensen 1993, p. 245 (Cat. Nos. 192 and 224).
26. Bazin and Bromberger 1982, p. 81.
27. Kanishu 1899, pp. 162-63.

Fig. 10: Peasant baking on a convex iron plate or *saj* (Dieulofoy 1887, p. 649).

In Sarvestan (Fars), *tova bargardun* denotes leavened dough. It requires a special *saj* or *taveh* that is smaller than the usual one. However, it has an iron handle covered with wood. When the dough is ready the fire is lit. Then a lump of dough is taken from the bowl and put on the inner somewhat hollow side of the *saj* and then directly placed over the fire. When the bread is ready it is taken off so that the other side may be baked. Then the frying-pan (*tabeh*) is taken up and with the *karunak* it is separated from the *saj*. Then the *saj* is strongly scraped with the *karunak* and another lump of dough placed on it.[28]

In Kurdistan, in Jewish families, the *saj* was known as *doqa*. It was used to bake a particular kind of bread, because for their regular bread they used the *tanur*.[29] The *saj* was not only in Jewish villages, but also in Moslem villages, and even in towns.[30] In the town of Lar, the *taveh*, which was "an iron, mildly concave circular plate of about 12 to 15 inches wide" was used "for baking bread specially *baala tava* on it."[31] In the large village of Sarvestan (Fars), next to the table cloth there is the hearth, a few stones sticking from the ground; here a fire is lit, then the *taveh* is put over it. Then the unleavened dough that beforehand was prepared in a large copper bowl is put to the left side of the bakery board, which is placed on the tablecloth. The board is 1 *gaz* or 1 meter long and 0.5 *gaz* or 50 centimeters wide and four fingers high and has small legs of a few cm so that it is over and not on the table cloth. The baker sits behind the baking board, and is assisted by two people, one who kneads the dough and puts it beside her; the other sits behind the *taveh* and with a smooth, black, elliptical rod of 0.5 *gaz* or 50 centimeters called a bread turner - *nun bargardun*, she lifts the bread from the *taveh*.

---

28. Homayuni 1371, p. 150, who notes that this is similar to the *nan-e do tepeh* of Baluchistan.
29. Shwartz-Be'eri 2000, p. 46
30. Basir al-Molk 1374, p. 134; Al-e Ahmad, 1333, p. 3.
31. Mahmoodian 2007, p. 92.

The baker takes a ball of dough, puts some flour on the baking board and makes the dough thin and round. She then puts it on a rod (*tir*) and places the flattened dough on the *taveh*; therefore, it is called *nan-tiri*. When the bread is ready she lifts the bread from the *taveh* with the bread turner and puts it on a platter (*kupuri* or *saleh*). This is very tasty bread; because it is unleavened (*fatir*) it can be eaten over a long period; each time they bake for a few days.[32] Hence this bread was known as *nan-e saj*, which was unleavened bread (*nan-e fatiri*).[33] This type of bread was either baked inside the tent or hut or outside.[34]

The fuel used for this type of baking depended on the circumstances and varied from dung cakes, to brushwood, while in Sarvestan (Fars) occasionally half-burnt - *nim-suz* charcoal was used, but only for sweet bread and *taveh-bardun*.[35]

Fig. 11: Bakhtiyari women baking (Bird 1891, vol. 1, p. 159).

Bread Baked in Ovens

Tabun

A simple kind of oven is known as *tabun*, which is basically a cement- or clay-lined or bricked hole in the ground of about 3-6 feet deep that widens out at the bottom.[36] According to the Nestorian priest Joseph Knanishu, in the Ormiyeh area around 1900, "A Persian stove or oven looks like a cylinder. It is built of clay and is about four feet deep by two and half feet in diameter. It is built in the ground near the center of the house, the top of it being on a level with the floor. They make a fire in it only once a day and at that time do their cooking and baking."[37] In this bricked hole a fire is lit and "when its walls are sufficiently hot the embers are taken out with an iron shovel, the flattened cake of dough is placed on the bottom of the hole, a steel plate or an earthenware dish is placed over it, and the whole is covered with the hot embers. After three to five minutes the bread is baked."[38] A variation of the *tabun*, in the form of a small domed one, was also used in Warmal (Sistan), where

> After sunset the women, with their heads wrapped in a sort of white chudder [*chador*], began to prowl about in a great state of excitement, carrying big balls of flour paste and small wicker work plates, like shields, covered over by a cloth. They lighted a big fire in one of the small domed ovens, and after beating the paste on the wicker shields till it had spread into a thin layer, they quickly took it up with their hands and, kneeling over the blazing furnace, struck the paste against the roof of the oven. They used long leather gloves for the purpose. While being baked the bread was constantly sprinkled with water from a bowl close at hand.[39]

32. Homayuni 1371, p. 149.
33. Wulff 1966, p. 291.
34. Stark 2001, p. 75.
35. Homayuni 1371, p. 153.
36. Belanger 1838, vol. 1, p. 159; Von Haxthausen 1854, p. 245; Morton 1940, pp. 121-22.
37. Knanishu 1899, pp. 95-96.
38. Wulff 1966, p. 292; see also della Valle 1664, vol. 2, p. 17.
39. Landor 1903, vol. 2, p. 259.

Similar domed ovens were used in Gorgan. "The oven consisted of a dome in section as above; the bread, which was of the usual blanket-like dimensions, being dabbed against the sides as shown in the accompanying section, the oven first being heated red hot by a fire beneath."[40]

A simpler version of this oven existed among the Lors as observed by Freya Stark in the 1930s. "A new hearth hastily made by scraping a hole in the middle of the floor... and a handsome daughter sat down with the flour-bag to bake bread."[41] An improved version of this type of oven is used among tribes of Khorasan and Baluchestan, who make an air hole (*badkesh*) in the earthen wall around the oven pit. Once the walls of the pit are hot, the flattened dough is pressed against the wall and

Fig. 12: *Tabun* (MacGregor 1879, vol. 2, p. 110).

baked.[42] Another version, used in the Caucasus, was a hole "dug in the earth, five or six feet wide and deep, and bricked; in this a fire is made; and when it is burned out, the ashes are removed, and the dough is thrown with a trowel against the heated sides of the oven. The hole is then covered up, and opened again in half an hour, when the bread is baked."[43] In case of the Turkmen, bread was baked in cylindrical open-topped ovens, situated some yards from the entrance from the house. "The ovens are ... short truncated cones of loam, hollow in the interior. ... In anything like a considerable village, long before the first blush of dawn is seen, the sky is red with the reflection of a hundred blazing ovens. The red cinders are then swept over it, and in this primitive manner the bread is baked."[44]

This type of oven was in particular used in northern Iran, probably because if the baking pit was not used to bake bread it served as *korsi* to keep the family warm during cold weather. Robert Speer, the secretary of the American Presbyterian Mission, who visited Iran in the late 1890s, reporting about people's domestic life said that:

The oven was an earthenware jar, about three feet deep and a foot and a half broad, sunk in the ground with the orifice level with the floor. In this a fire of dried cowdung or weeds heating the oven, heats the floor. The bread is baked in great flat cakes, two feet long and a foot broad, stuck against the inside walls of the oven. Over the mouth of the oven, in cold weather, a wooden frame two or three feet square is placed, and quilts are thrown over this so as to confine the heat, while the household creep under the quilts with the feet to the warmth and heads away. Where there is no oven, a pan of charcoal is placed under the frame, which the Persians call a *kursee*.[45]

The smoke escaped through the window.[46] This was also the case in other cold and mountainous zones in Iran, although the oven was often referred to as *tanur* rather than as *tabun*. In Mar Beshoo, a Nestorian village situated in the mountains near Ormiyeh, for example, "Some coarse rugs were spread around the great tandoor, a hole two or three feet in diameters and three feet deep. In this, in the morning, they build a great fire, and after an

---

40. MacGregor 1879, vol. 2, p. 110.
41. Stark 2001, p. 131.
42. Wulff 1966, p. 292.
43. Von Haxthausen 1854, p. 245.

44. O'Donovan 1882, vol. 1, p. 149.
45. Speer 1910, pp. 254-55; Fraser 1840, vol. 2, p. 200 (near Bisotun "The houses of the peasants in these parts are far ruder and less snug than any I have seen in other parts of Persia. They have no fireplaces, and are generally heated by a *courcy*, or a *tendoor*, in the floor, and which serves as well to bake bread as to warm the inmates of the habitation.")
46. Knanishu 1899, p. 94.

hour or two the stones become thoroughly heated and the fire dies away. The room will continue to be warm till the next day. In the cold winter frequently a circle of mountaineers will let their feet hang down inside. This tandoor is also their bake-oven, the dough being stuck in thin cakes to the smooth-side stones."[47] In a village outside Hamadan, the women had taken off the top of the *korsi* and two women were baking barley bread over a dung cake fire, "kneading their dough by beating it against the cobble stones that line the fire-hole".[48]

As the majority of the government's troops were drawn from nomadic groups the *saj* was also used by the military. In particular the more important people in the army had a portable version of the *tabun*. It consisted of two iron cones, each [the size of] a half-quart, which were equipped with large nails to hold the clay with which they have been covered. These two parts fitted together and thus formed one quart. They were narrower at the top than at the bottom. A large fire was made in it, over which they put the dough in the form of a round cake which stuck to the oven lining.[49] This oven, when used, was round and dug into the ground. Also, an entire sheep could be roasted in it. When the army camp moved the clay was broken off and the two semi-cones were loaded on the back of a beast of burden, one part on each side of the animal.[50]

The *tabun* method was not always a covered method of baking. According to Belanger, "In the morning women made dough that they rolled on a slab of granite to make it into a thin flat flap form of 2 feet. During that time her husband lit the oven in a hole dug into the soil. It resembled a jar that was about 4 feet deep. As soon as it was hot the women dexterously slapped the flans on the wall of the oven, the flan adhered to it and after a few minutes it was perfectly baked, then she took it off with a pointed stick."[51] In the town of Lar a type of *tabun* was used, known as *bereza*. It was built on, not in the ground, "the oven having a fixed convex circular pottery made top in the shape of a contact lens over which a variety of breads are baked."[52] The bread baked in the abovementioned manner was generally referred to as *nan- tabun*.[53]

Tanur.

For oven baked bread the most common kind of oven – *tanūr* – tanur was used both in rural (villages and by migrant groups) and urban areas (homes and bakeries). It has the advantage that unlike other baking methods many paste pieces could be stuck simultaneously to the inner wall of the oven.[54] The *tanur* (also called *tandur*, *tanir* or *taftun*) is basically an earthenware jar, often with an egg or conical form, "with an open bottom and a narrower top," which is built around a fireplace – *ateshgah*; called *ojaq* in Turkish speaking areas.[55] The *tanur* was either built by professionals (among whom there were women) or by the village and tribal women themselves.[56] In 1978, the cost of making a bread oven in the village of Baghestan (Khorasan) was riyals 300; in 1977, a daily worker

---

47. Marsh 1869, pp. 68-69. Binder 1887, p. 96 (*lavash* baked in an oven dug into the earth and fired with dried straw/Ormiyeh), 111 (in Kashkahn village, in the middle of the hut there was a hole where bread was baked), 159 (big hole in the middle of the room to bake bread/Armenian village in Kurdistan).
48. Dwight 1917, p. 279.
49. Richard 1995, vol. 2, p. 118. The quart, probably short for quartant, measured 68.5 liters, otherwise it means simply one-fourth of a measurement that it is not mentioned.
50. Bastiaaensen 1985, pp. 132-33; Chardin 1927, p. 272. For a picture of this oven in the Turkish *Surnameh* (ca. 1720-25) see Ettinghausen 1965, pl. 27.

51. Bélanger 1838, vol. 1, p. 159.
52. Mahmoodian 2007, p. 46.
53. Wulff 1966, p. 291.
54. Salzman 1994, p. 78.
55. Wulff 1966, p. 292; della Valle 1664, vol. 2, p. 16.
56. Safinezhad 1345, p. 65 (village women); Horne 1994, p. 141 ("Makers of ovens and the like were itinerant specialists, sometimes these were women"); Salzman 1994, p. 79 (tribal women); Desmet-Grégoire 1980, p. 255.

was paid 300-500 riyals/day.[57] Although there were and are differences between a village oven and one used in an urban bakery, as discussed below, the basic design was the same.

Depending on the situation and the wealth of the owner, a *tanur* could be made of pottery or of baked or dried mud (made on site from what was available). In the latter case the interior consists of a mixture of clay and animal hair (playing the role of binder). The *tanur* could be partly in the ground or entirely above ground,[58] while depending on the local situation different types of fuel were used. Ovens made in Khorasan were much larger and wider (1.5-2 m across the top, waist high, with a hole of 50-75 centimeters) than those built by Sarhad Baluch women (1 meter high, 60 cm wide). Also, there were ovens with other dimensions such as the *tanur* that was "a sort of amphora about four feet high [1.2 meters], made of baked clay, whose sides are three fingers thick, buried in the floor of the room."[59] These differences probably reflect the permanent character of village ovens as against the seasonal transhumant ones as well as local traditions.[60] In Khorasan, a village *tanur* was constructed as follows:

> To prepare for construction *gel-e sabz* for the oven's lining is dug up and soaked for three days, covered with a cloth in preparation of the arrival of the *ostad*, who will beat the clay and build the oven. The circular frame has a double wall of bricks filled in between with sand for insulation. The central hole is lined with *ghel-e sabz*, which bakes to ceramic hardness. Depressions on the top of the oven lets rainwater run off, and a hole at the bottom provides a draft.[61]

In the bazaar the design is the same as in villages, where bread is baked in a circular cone that widens out at the bottom, but in the bazaar

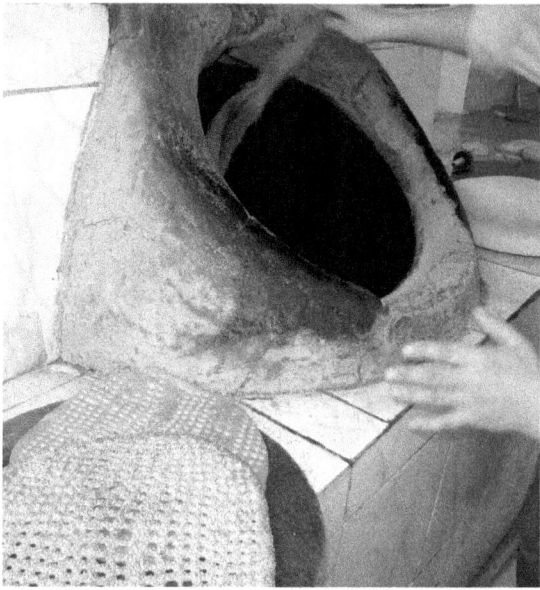

Fig. 13: *Tanur* baking, Hamedan (Mage 2013).

the position is reversed," i.e. the oven widens out at the top. [62] The British traveler Binning described a bakery oven in the bazaar as follows in 1852:

> The *tannoor* or oven is a large earthen jar, about four feet deep, shaped like an egg, and built into the *sukkoo* (platform) in front of the shop. The mouth, at the upper extremity of the jar, is about a foot wide, while the diameter of the middle or widest part is two feet or more. There is a smaller aperture at the bottom to admit a draught of air for the sake of the fire. The fuel used in this oven, consists chiefly of the small thorny plants

---

57. Horne 1994, p. 147; Desmet-Grégoire 1980, p. 255 (in the rural areas around Hamadan, the cost of a *tanur* made by a specialist was 15 to 20 *tumans*).
58. Bazin and Bromberger 1982, p. 81; Safinezhad 1345, p. 65 (The clay was mixed with goat hair and they made the interior smooth with a roller); Tahbaz 1342, p. 44 (The clay used for making the oven is reinforced with goat hair, and salt so that bread sticks well to the wall); Salzman 1994, p. 79; Rice 1923, p. 56; Bromberger 1974, p. 34; Desmet-Grégoire 1980, p. 55; Bromberger 1974, p. 34.
59. De Lorey 1907, p. 354.
60. Horne 1994, p. 145; Salzman 1994, p. 97.

61. Horne 1994, p. 145.
62. Morton 1940, pp. 121-22.

and shrubs, found in abundance in the plains.[63]

In villages and in camps of migratory groups ovens were often shared, "because not every household can afford to build one and because sharing saves fuel."[64] In Varamin, for example, some houses each had their own *tanur* while in other case 2-3 houses shared one. The *tanur*s, mostly made by the village women were commonly built into the soil and its sides filled like a platform to allow for seating of those who worked there. Usually, it was a space of 4-5 sq. meters. Its outer sides were smoothed with clay, and its top was covered with branches. Air ducts were made below the *tanur*, which are called *kholbar*; apart from facilitating air flow they also served to take the ashes out so as not to hinder air flow.[65] Likewise, in Kandelus (Mazandaran), each house or a number of houses jointly baked bread.[66] Sometimes the *tanur* was shared by a district of the village, like in Galdiyan (Gilan). The farmers supplied the flour and two old women made bread and were remunerated.[67] In Warmal (Sistan),

> Nearly each house has its own outer oven, but the one I was near seemed to be used by several families, judging by the string of clamouring women who impatiently- and they did not let the others know how impatiently!- waited with all necessaries in hand to bake bread for their men. The respective husbands and sons squatted around on their heels, languidly smoking their pipes and urging their women to be quick. … They [women] seemed much concerned if one piece got too much burnt or another not enough.[68]

During the summer, migratory groups such as Sarhad Baluch, who usually baked bread in hot ashes or on a *saj*, built a *tandur* in the camping ground outside one of the tents, in particular when large quantities of bread had to be baked.[69]

In most villages, the *tanur* was built in a separate room with a door and which had a hole in the roof, window, or pipe for evacuating the smoke.[70] This separate room for bread baking was in addition to the kitchen.[71] For bread baking in summer a *tanur* was constructed in a corner of the court-yard; in the mountain villages this is also used as a *korsi* during the cold season and is slept around. However, the winter *tanur* is of special importance, and is erected in the living room or a special dedicated room, which is turned into a *korsi* and around which the whole family sleeps.[72] Likewise, in the villages of the Talesh and the Gilani mountaineers the *tanur* is placed in a special building, next to the living quarters or in the courtyard. It is mostly used only for bread baking; hence it occupied no central place in the living space. Cooking was done on a tripod. The *tanur* opening was covered with tiles or rice stalks against the rain. In eastern Azerbayjan the *tanur* was mostly situated in the middle of the living quarters, which were not used in summer. This was done because in winter the *tanur* was the main heat source, while all year it was used to cook and bake.[73]

The baker first scrubs the oven well with a broom - *saza*, otherwise the bread will not stick properly to the wall. Then the hollow interior of the oven is filled with fuel, and is set on fire. Once the fuel has burnt down to cinders and the inside of the oven has become sufficiently hot, the ash is swept from the fuel feeder with a broom of tamarisk

---

63. Binning 1857, vol. 1, pp. 66-67.
64. Horne 1994, p. 145.
65. Safinezhad 1345, pp. 65-66; Desmet-Grégoire 1980, p. 255. The chimney was known as *dud-kesh* or as *tarma* in Turkic speaking areas.
66. Jahangiri 1367, p. 80.
67. Bazin and Bromberger 1982, p. 81.
68. Landor 1903, vol. 2, p. 259.

69. Salzman 1994, p. 79.
70. Safinezhad 1345, p. 65; Bazin and Bromberger, p. 81.
71. Gudarzi-nezhad 1352, p. 26.
72. Gudarzi-nezhad 1354, p. 33; de Lorey 1907, p. 354 ("in winter it heats the house and family; a rug is spread over it to keep the heat in.").
73. Bazin and Bromberger 1982, pp. 48, 81.

or other branches.⁷⁴ The dough that had been kneaded into balls was then flattened and the lower side moistened. It also happened that the woman baker takes each flattened bread ball and sprinkles sesame and rubs egg-white over them, in the case of *penjeh-kesh* bread baking (see below chapter 6), she would imprint the bread with her hand. Then the bread was pressed or slapped against the hot inner side of the oven, to which it adhered till it was baked. "A small cushion is the instrument used for this 'slapping' process." She puts 10-12 pieces in two rows, called *tanir sar zan* in Yush. The breads are not touched for a few minutes to avoid their falling off. She puts a fabric around her hand (which in the village of Yush is called *bal van*) to take off the bread.⁷⁵

The fire in the *tanur* was either lit by dry farmyard dung cakes, thorns, brushwood or firewood, depending on the local endowment of biomass. For example, for the Turkmen on the Caspian seaboard "rude brambles and morsels of decayed fishing boats" were used.⁷⁶ In Gilan and Talesh, fuel was practically always wood, only in special places (Ammarlu) brushwood and dung cakes were used, while in east Azerbaijan it is heated with pieces of dung cakes - *kerme*, *yappa*, and brushwood.⁷⁷ In most of Khorasan brushwood was used as a fuel.⁷⁸ In most parts of Iran, however, dung cakes were stored for baking and cooking. Camel thorns or *khar-e shotor* (Alhagi Adans spp.) were also collected.⁷⁹

It is easy to understand that in the Bronze Age the users of the *tabun* oven had no problem in making the switch to the modern *tanur*. Further, it is of interest to note that the *tabun* was not replaced by the *tanur*, which was used by sedentary or semi-sedentary groups in mostly mountainous and/or cold areas, where the *tanur* also functioned as a heating unit or *korsi*.

---

74. Desmet-Grégoire 1980, p. 254. In Larestan, the blaze of the heat of the *tanur* is called *bir*. The term *bir budeh* was used to indicate that the oven was blazing hot and ready for baking bread, while the term *bir kardeh* indicates that enough firewood had been put into the oven to ensure that its wall became really hot to be able to bake *gapok* in it. Mahmoodian 2007, p. 59.
75. Tahbaz 1342, p. 45; Rice 1923, p. 56; O'Donovan 1882, vol. 1, p. 149.
76. Rice 1923, p. 56; O'Donovan 1882, vol. 1, p. 149.
77. Bazin and Bromberger 1982, p. 81.
78. Horne 1994, p. 145.
79. Gudarzi-nezhad, 1352, p. 26; Ibid., 1354, p. 33; de Lorey 1907, p. 354; Adams 1900, p. 154; Desmet-Grégoire 1980, pp. 255-56. For the use of dung in general, see Floor 2003 a.

Fig. 14: Contemporary *taftun* bakery, Tehran (Mage 2013).

Fig. 15: Contemporary *barbari* bread bakery in Tehran, (photo Mage, 2013).

CHAPTER FIVE

URBAN BREAD MAKING

"The *Persian* Bread is generally thin, and like their broad thin Casks. There are several sorts of it. The ordinary Bread is bak'd in round Ovens, made in the ground, like a Hole about four or five Foot deep, and two Foot Diameter. They put the Bread against the Oven, and as the Bread is not so thick as one's Finger, especially in the Middle, it is bak'd in less than a quarter of an Hour." Chardin 1927, p. 233.

With the growth of settlements into towns and cities, a further distinction needs to be made between bread made domestically and commercially and what the latter meant.

Commercial or home bakers?

Initially there seems to have been no commercial urban bakers. At least in ancient Elba, according to von Soden, "No doubt bread was baked mostly at home: bakers, in contrast to millers and cooks, are mentioned only rarely."[1] However, in the case of Mesopotamia, Potts and others argue that from the fourth millennium onwards much bread was mass-produced by huge establishments, attested in cuneiform sources, attached to cities like Nippur or Umma as well as in Susa, Tal-e Malyan and Choga Mish, "where ca. 250,000 BRBs were found in just two seasons of excavation." The beveled rim bowls (BRBs) could be mass-produced by non-expert labor and made it possible to produce good bread efficiently. Although the BRBs went out of fashion by 3000 BCE this did not necessarily mean the end of the industrial production of bread. Potts and others have argued the fact that in the third millennium a great variety of breads, both as to the types of grain used as well as the shape of bread, suggests "increasing diversification in bread-baking," where BRBs were replaced by a greater number of ceramic forms.[2]

Fig. 16: Beveled rim bowl (Goulder 2010, p. 360).

By Achaemenid times, it looks as if commercial bread making was an established practice. This is suggested by the fact that some officials received revenues from several cities. "Each one had to provide him with bread, wine, fish, wardrobe, and part of the expenses of his house."[3] How could these cities provide these quantities of bread without having some form of non-domestic process, i.e. organized bread making infrastructure? Also, the fact that water mills existed suggests that large consumers were supplied with their flour needs.[4] This conclusion is supported by the fact that, according to Xenephon, there were markets in Babylonian towns such as Caenae on the Tigris that

---

1. Von Soden 1994, p. 101.
2. Potts 2009; Goulder 2010.
3. Briant 2002, p. 419; Dandamaev and Lukonin 2000, pp. 136, 318-19.
4. Pigulevskaya 1963, p. 155.

exported wheat, bread, wine, cheese as well markets in army camps where flour was sold.⁵ Moreover, there were institutional bakeries such as those attached to the royal palaces. In 501 BC, flour was ordered at Persepolis to bake bread for New Year enough to feed 10,000 people.⁶

At the same time it appears that urban households continued to bake bread for their own needs. For example, in 499/500, in Edessa, grains were distributed to bake bread, presumably using hand-mills to grind the grain. During the siege of Amida in 504-05 and the resulting famine in the city, the besieged Persian troops gave part of their rations to the women, because they were their mistresses and also because they needed them to mill and bake the bread. The women used hand-mills to grind the grain. The soldiers received one handful of barley per day.⁷

This hybrid situation where commercial and domestic baking existed side by side in towns and villages continued in Iran until recent times. Nevertheless, we are on firmer ground in the Islamic period, because more information is available. For example, in the ninth and tenth century, people in towns kneaded dough at home and brought it to the bakery (*farran*) to be baked.⁸ There were bakers such as a baker-poet in Basra in tenth century CE named *al-khubz aruzzi*, or the rice-bread baker.⁹ According to Muqaddasi, in Azerbaijan, the price of bread was quoted per 100 loaves, thus indicating that it was popular and bought in bulk, suggesting commercial baking.¹⁰ Also, speciality breads were exported from Iran, which implies commercial enterprises.¹¹ Nezam al-Molk mentions a chief of the bakers in the eleventh century, clearly indicating that this was a commercial group.¹² In medieval times commercial bakers were referred to as *khabbaz, nanva, nanba, nan-paz, nan-forush* and *khiri*, all of which, except for the last one, continued to be used after 1600. There also existed sellers of pieces of bread (*nan risheh-forsuh*), which suggests that he catered to the poor, who could not afford to buy an entire bread.¹³

Again, bread was baked in villages and transported to the neighboring city. The rules as laid down in the endowment deed of the Rashidi *vaqf* for Tabriz make it clear that bread was baked in villages and then supplied to the Rashidi hospice. The rules were that the village bakers had to be competent, the bread had to be made in accordance with the regulations and of good quality, and the work was not be given to others. The bakers had to deliver the bread in person to the hospice, which kept a reserve of grain in storage, viz. 60,000 *man* or about 50,000 kg.¹⁴ There also was institutional baking in case of large non-household establishments such as that of the castellan of Karish, who, in 1652, sent Evliya Chelebi's company, "about fifty sheep, about one thousand loaves of white bread, seven or eight mules loaded with fruit and cilantro mint sherbet." This means that he either had an enormous stock of baked bread (which is possible), or that the castle had its own bakery, which seems more likely.¹⁵ Even as late as the early twentieth century, there still existed situations like that in Iran. For example, because there was no bakery in the town of Tuyserkan, apart from one *sangak* bakery, villagers who baked bread brought *lavash* bread for sale to town; this bread was known as *deseleh-paz*. Townsmen who could not bake at home bought a large number of bread sheets and

---

5. Xenephon 1896, I. 5. 6, I. 8. 1, II 5. 28; III 2. 21, V.1.6.
6. Dandamayev and Lukonin 2000, p. 147.
7. Pigulevskaya 1963, p. 154.
8. Ahsan 1979, p. 88.
9. Ahsan 1979, p. 90.
10. Schwarz 1933, vol. 8, p. 1193.
11. Spuler 1952, p. 510.

12. Nizam al-Molk 1960, p. 48.
13. Atma`eh 1360, pp. 23, 74, 91, 131; Mobasheri 1389, pp. 257, 297.
14. Hoffmann 2000, p. 222.
15. Chelebi 2010, p. 6.

ate them over time.[16] The bakery situation was less enviable on the island of Qeshm in 1820, where the baker had just died, "so the only bread they could command was unleavened cakes from a very inferior flour, mixed with barley-meal purchased on the island."[17]

Hospices, shrines and other religious institutions that had funds to feed travelers, pilgrims and their own staff constituted a third category of city bakeries. In the case of the Rashidi hospice in Tabriz in addition to instructions about what kinds of bread needed to be baked (see chapter six) there was the instruction that all bread had to be made from grain that was cleaned and its flour sieved; the dough should not be too much salted and be well-baked. Only in case of emergency was it allowed to use lower-quality grains such as barley.[18]

The numbers of people fed in important religious centers such as the shrine of Imam Reza in Mashhad varied between 300 and 800 persons per day. Eastwick "saw the dinner served up—there was a goodly mess for every two persons, that is, four breads, four chops, and a platter of rice. Any stranger may dine for twenty days."[19] The bakeries in large establishments such as the royal court or that of a governor also belonged to this category. In Safavid times, the royal bakery was managed by a *churakchi-bashi*.[20] In the Qajar period, there was also a *churakchi-bashi* who made dough from the best wheat and baked it in a *sangak* bakery for the exclusive use of the inhabitants of the royal court.[21]

Finally, there were private households who baked their own bread and commercial bakers who supplied non-baking consumers with bread. It also happened that villagers and nomads bought bread in neighboring towns. The Qashqa'is did it occasionally in the 1960s, but the women did not like "modern, 'artificial' food such as bakery bread, which made them weak and sickly."[22] In the 1950s, in Davarabad (Khorasan) the villagers usually brought *sangak* bread with them that was available in a nearby market town, but they did not like modern European-types of bread.[23]

Unlike many other trades which tended to be concentrated in the bazaar, bakers were dispersed throughout various quarters of town.[24] In 1866, according to de Rochechouart, the number of bakery shops in Tehran was 100, which number, he reports, had remained unchanged since the days of Fath Ali Shah (1801-1834) when it had been fixed.[25] Whether or not these figures are correct for the 1820s, they are certainly wrong for the situation in 1866. A list of shops, drawn up for Naser al-Din Shah (1848-1896) in 1852/53 gives the number of bakery shops as 201.[26] In 1930 there were 295 bakery shops in Tehran employing 278 *ostad*s, 1,370 *shagerd*s and 226 *padu*s for a population of more than 220,000, so that there was one bakery per 760 persons.[27] In 1932 Tehran had a population of 257,000 and a total of 1,702 bakery workers.[28] Around 1890, there were 190 bakers in Isfahan, while in 1920 there were 120 bakers.[29]

Bakers formed a guild of which all the various bakery workers were members. The bakery guild was well organized and was firmly controlled by the

---

16. Gol Mohammadi 1371, vol. 1, p. 297. For a description of a village bakery, with "half-naked men making the same indigestible stuff," see Harris 1896, p. 124.
17. Fraser 1984, p. 32.
18. Hoffmann 2000, pp. 221, 291-92.
19. Chanykov 1862, p. 99; Bassett 1887, p. 226; Vambery 1867, p. 323; Goldsmid 1876, vol. 2, p. 364; Eastwick 1864, vol. 2, p. 213.
20. Asaf 1348, p. 100.
21. Mostowfi n.d., vol. 1, p. 403.
22. Nashat and Beck 2003, p. 226.
23. Alberts 1963, p. 176.
24. Fraser 1843, p. 33; see also Bleibtreu 1894, p. 57.
25. De Rochechouart 1867, p. 180.
26. Migeod 1990, p. 200, n. 2.
27. Baladiyeh-ye Tehran 1310, pp. 84-85 (*khabbazi*).
28. Baladiyeh-ye Tehran 1312, pp. 42, 138.
29. Höltzer 2535, p. 23; Janab 1303, p. 87.

Fig. 17: Iranian baker in Baku with round bread (Schulz 1917, p. 86).

nanva-bashi (head of the bakers' guild). In 1912 the bakers in Tehran only deviated from his instructions, because they were sure that the responsible authorities would not back their superior.[30] The bakers' guild formed a strong and tight-knit group, which, according to de Rochechouart, in Tehran had a guild fund with the aim "to help those of the colleagues, whose business is doing badly; in that case the debtor is obliged to redeem his debt out of his profit; on the other hand when a colleague was in business trouble because of his own fault and bad conduct, the guild would force him either to sell his business or to accept a manager being put in charge of his shop."[31]

This tightness of organization was understandable given the fact that the baking of certain types of bread was dominated by people from a specific town, area, or ethnic group. In the late 1800s, for example, many members of the baker's guild in Tehran seem to have been from Mashhad.[32] In the mid-twentieth century this picture had changed significantly due to the growth of Tehran and the arrival of many migrants. Then the *lavash* bakers mostly hailed from the Zanjan area; only a number of the *lavash-e zamini* bakers (see chapter six) came from other parts of Azerbaijan. The *sangak* bakers were mostly from Qom. The *barbari* bakery workers in Tehran were mostly from Khu'in and Sa`idabad and some from the villages around those places. The sweetmeat and confectionary shops were mostly in the hands of Yazdis and Azerbaijanis, but people from other provinces also started to get active in this branch in the 1970s. The people from the village of Shahrivar (near Ardabil) dominated the baking of *nan-e bulki*.[33]

Often, there were "no Christian bakers, butchers or fruit dealers in Persian cities, because in the case of vegetables, meat or anything that is moist, and sometimes in the case of dry articles of food, a Christian is not permitted to trade them," Wilson reported in 1896.[34] In fact, it seems that it also happened that only some bakeries served non-Moslems, according to Col. Sheil, the British envoy to Iran in the 1840-50s. "In Persia it sometimes happened, that they [Armenians] are not even allowed to purchase bread at the same shops as the Mohammedans."[35] This changed, at least in Tehran, towards 1900, when in that city there were "some Greeks who furnish a very good quality of European bread."[36]

Of course, there were urban households that baked bread at home. In the Safavid period, according to Chardin, "In Substantial Houses, they bake bread twice a-Day: It is the business of the Slaves to grind the Corn, and knead the Dough, and put it to the Fire."[37] The same was true for the

---

30. Mostowfi n.d., vol. 2, p. 398. On the role of guilds, see Floor 2009.
31. De Rochechouart 1867, p. 180. The strong organization of the bakers' guild was also due to the fact that it had some kind of *fotuvvat* initiation rite, see Rowghani 1385, pp. 233-41 and Bolukbashi 1347 b, pp. 47-48.
32. Mostowfi n.d., vol. 1, 400.
33. Zavosh 1370, pp. 251-53.
34. Wilson 1896, p. 280; Adams 1906, pp. 162-63."This debars the Christians from the following the trades of masons, tanners, painters, bakers, butchers, &c." Jones 1870, p. 417.
35. Sheil 1838, p. 72.
36. Wishard 1909, p. 141.
37. Chardin 1927, p. 223; according to Tavernier 1930, p.

Urban Bread Making • 53

Fig. 18: Ambulant baker in front of druggist (Benjamin 1887, p. 95).

Qajar period, where bakers came to the homes of the well-to-do to light the *tanur* and bake bread the whole day, which was then stored for the winter. In Tabriz, as recently as the 1940-50s, these so-called *churakchi*s or bakers performed their task in the fall in the households of the well-to-do.[38] In Tehran during the first decades of the twentieth century and likely earlier, the Armenians had "a big baking every few weeks, when they have a professional baker, generally a woman, in for a day or two."[39] In the 1970s in Gilan, on the occasion of big events, mostly religious, ambulatory bakers baked bread on the *saj*.[40]

However, in the big cities in general, baking at home seems to have been limited to wealthy households, a reality that already was observed in tenth-century Bagdad, as noted above. The reasons for doing so differed by town and period and socio-economic circumstances. In 1647, Evliya Chelebi reported on the situation in Tabriz as follows:

> There are twelve groups of ulama and other notables who cook at home. In the homes of all the other people it is less likely that they make a fire and cook food. But if they make a fire to prepare coffee, tea, fennel, salep, and *mahaleb* (St. Lucia cherry) cordial and for washing clothes they are not prevented from heating water. All servants and soldiers, the unemployed and unmarried ones buy and eat food from the bazaar. Therefore, the life of the uncouth Qizilbash [Iranians] is really bad in this respect, but it is cheaper and a man can eat whatever he wants.[41]

In Kerman, in the 1930s, people were so poor, "even judged by standards of a country where almost everyone is poor," and most did not even have "money to buy fuel even for cooking and food is commonly bought cooked."[42] In the 1960s, Shirazis bought "their bread from their regular bakery, Friday evening after worship."[43] In the 1970s Gilani bread eaters ate above all *lavash*, often also *barbari* that they bought daily or every other day from a bakery. In the large Gilani towns above all *sangak* was eaten like in Tehran.[44]

But even those that were able to bake at home did not necessarily do so. In the nineteenth century, the people of Kashan had wheat and barley at home the entire year, and bought bread from bakeries only part of the year.[45] This was not only true for Kashan. It was quite normal until recent times that each urban middle-class family at harvest time bought wheat for one year's needs, had it ground by the town's millers and then stored in the *kondu*,

---

282, people baked bread every day.
38. Hasan Javadi (oral communication in 2011).
39. Rice 1923, p. 178.
40. Bazin and Bromberger 1982, p. 80.

41. Chelebi 2010, p. 45.
42. Koelz 1983, p. 28.
43. Loeb 1977, p. 178.
44. Bazin and Bromberger 1982, p. 81.
45. Sepehr 2536, p. 437.

the special storage for flour.⁴⁶ The rich had grain brought from their estates to their town houses.

Kondus come in a variey of sizes, built to hold from 15 to 200 *mans* (about 45 to 600 kilograms) of unmilled wheat. Small

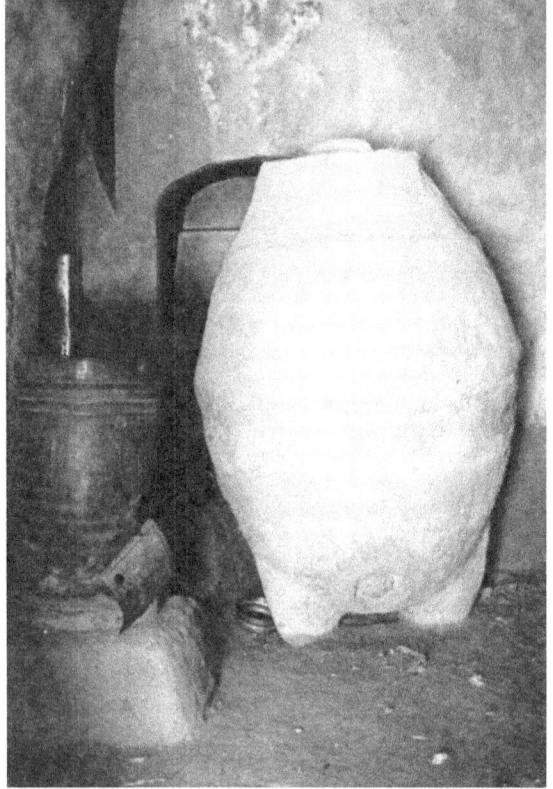

Fig. 19: Grain storage vessel or *kondu* (Horne 1994, p. 138).

ones tend to be spherical in shape and are designated by the number of *mans* they hold. Large ones are ovoid in shape and are designated by the number of clay rings with which they were assembled. Most are either footed or plastered to the floor and have an opening at the top that can be sealed by plastering the lid down and a plugged circular opening at the bottom through which the grain is removed. A five-ring *kondu* measures about 90 centimeters high and 65 centimeters in diameter; a 200-*man kondu* measures about 200 centimeters high and 100 centimeters in diameter. Some *kondus* are as much as 2 meters high. Some built twenty-five or thirty years ago are still in use. They once were made by the villagers themselves, but now are commissioned from a specialist from the area around Sabzevar who comes every two or three years and makers them on the spot. The rings are made out in the open, brought into the courtyard to be plastered together, and then installed in the storeroom.⁴⁷

Bakers also stored grain that they bought at harvest time, when grain was cheapest. Depending on their financial position they bought from 6-months to one-year's supply and stored this in a karavanserai. This had several other advantages. Grain that had been stored for six months required more leavening and less salt than grain that was taken from the threshing floor to the miller, and thus their bread became tastier and was more in demand. The stored grain also allowed them to have their grain milled in winter when mills were mostly idle and thus milled at a lower cost. Further, it allowed the baker to properly sieve his grain and make the right mixture of grains before it went to the mill. Finally, a large reserve of grain allowed them to sell it at the right time in the market.⁴⁸

There seems to have been no fixed rule as to the importance of home baking versus professional bakeries. There were towns like Tuyserkan where there was no bakery (apart from a *sangak* bakery) and, therefore, most houses had an oven and baked *lavash* bread every day. Those who did not bought bread from villagers who came to town to sell it.⁴⁹ The same held for Rey near Tehran. Most houses had their own *tanur*, and when they did not,

---

46. Zavosh 1370, vol. 1, p. 218.

47. Horne 1994, p. 143. In 1978, the cost of making a grain storage bin was Rls 100. A daily worker was paid 300-500 Rls/day in 1977. Ibid., p. 147.
48. Rowghani 1385, pp. 94-95.
49. Gol Mohammadi 1371, vol. 1, p. 297.

a number of families time-shared the oven. These ovens were constructed by local specialists, who made sure that both exterior and interior walls were smooth.⁵⁰ Those families that baked at home baked enough bread to last 2-3 months of the families' need. Once the bread was dry it was stored in a fixed placed known as *tabu* or *tapu*. As many bread flaps were taken from storage as needed and one hour before consumption each sheet was individually sprinkled with water to make them moist. Then they were put on the tablecloth.⁵¹

BAKERS AND THEIR OVENS

In case of professional urban bakeries a few artisans were involved, each having a specific task. The number of bakery workers varied per type of bread and size of oven, which became larger in the twentieth century. The oven or *tanur* that urban bakers used were similar to those used in large villages, which likewise were constructed by professionals either in the bakery or made elsewhere and later assembled in the bakery.⁵²

As in rural baking first the dough had to be prepared. To that end the *khamirgir* or doughmaker went earlier to bakery than the baker himself (*nanva*); usually at least 2 hours prior to the morning or dawn call to prayer (*adhan-e sobh*).⁵³ He mixed the ingredients of the dough in a trough (*toghar, tashtak, towghal*). Around 1900, he first mixed flour "with cold water and not with tepid water as in Europe, in proportions of 1 part flour to 6 parts of water.⁵⁴ Then one kneads it in a stone trough. Only then leaven is added, if required, about one-quarter of the weight of the dough. The latter, as in the rural areas, is made from left-over dough from the previous day, dissolved in water and kept in a warm spot." Because of that it is somewhat acidy and has a slight alcoholic smell. This is because fermentation in Europe is done at 30 degrees Celsius, while in Iran it is done at the coldest place that never exceeds 12-15 degrees. However in the 1930s if not earlier, urban bakeries "usually raised [dough] with a sourdough leaven, often with soda added."⁵⁵ Nowadays, *Torulopsis celluculosa* and *T. candida* are 'sour' or *torsh* starters used for the preparation of *sangak* bread.⁵⁶

Then salt was added, in the form of salted water, and one continued kneading. The dough was kneaded by hand and afterwards left to ferment in the trough for 2 hours, then the dough was brought towards the oven and one let it rest for another 2 hours at 25-30 degrees. Despite this time, which was four times more than in Europe in 1900, the preparation did not exceed that of Europe.⁵⁷

Prior to baking another bakery worker arrived, viz., the *atesh-andazi* as the stoker was called in case of the *sangak* bakery.⁵⁸ For other types of bakeries there appears not to have been a separate stoker. This was because the *tanur* needs to be "constantly fed with pieces of camel-thorn, which catch from the flames at the bottom, and keep the walls of the jar hot, as well as maintaining a high temperature

---

50. Rowghani 1385, p. 37.
51. Zavosh 1370, vol. 1, p. 218; Mirza 1920, p. 121; Shahri 1386, vol. 2, p. 388.
52. Shahri 1386, vol. 2, p. 388.
53. Shahri 1371, vol. 3, p. 280; Tahvildar 1342, p. 118. For detailed discussion of the dos and don't's of dough making, see Rowghani 1385, pp. 184-98.
54. I think Olmer made a mistake (or it is a printing error), because it should be 0.6 parts of water, because when you make bread, you do not add 6 parts of water per 1 part of flour.

55. Binning 1857, vol. 1, p. 66; Wulff 1966, p. 293; Koelz 1983, p. 166; Olmer 1908, p. 17. Soda, short for sodium bicarbonate is widespread used as a leavening agent, because of its low-cost, lack of toxicity, relative tasteless end products, and purity of commercial supplies. Matz 1992, p. 65.
56. Matz 1992, p. 62; see further the remarks by Rowghani 1385, pp. 200-02 concerning the quantity, preparation and use of 'sours.'
57. Olmer 1908, p. 17. Bakers bought large several kilos weighing rocks of salt straight from the mine and pounded this into small pieces in the bakery itself. Rowghani 1385, p. 107.
58. Shahri 1368, vol. 1, p. 282.

inside."⁵⁹ The fuel was "either withdrawn or allowed to burn out, before the bread is put in."⁶⁰

For *sangak*, brushwood was used.⁶¹ The *lavash* oven was constantly fed with pieces of camelthorn.⁶² Initially the bakers and households who baked their own bread used thistles collected by

Fig. 20: Brushwood supply (Dieulafoye 1888, p. 135).

villagers and some townsmen, who made a living with that (*khar-konan*). They had a few donkeys, a rope and an adze. They came to the *meydan* where their stuff was bought. Bakers bought 6 months reserve in mid-fall and stored that near their bakery. Since about 1940 fuel oil was used, although the taste of the bread changed. From a health point of view it was not good either because of the small oil particles that nestled on the bread, especially when the burning was not well controlled. The thistle cutters went out of business, which was good for the protection of the topsoil. Later instead of black fuel oil, bakers started to use so-called 'white oil' which was healthier. With the construction of the natural gas distribution network, ovens were gradually connected and then were 'fired' by gas.⁶³

Some time after the stoker, all other bakery workers arrived. The first to start working was the dough former (*chuneh-gir* or *chuneh-zan*), who takes pieces of the fermented dough and forms these into lumps (*chuneh, mosht*). Although in the twentieth century the law requires that they be weighed, the dough former knows from experience what the required quantity should be. The lumps are flattened by the dough flattener (*nan pahn-kon*) on a marble slab into 3/8 inch = 1 cm thick cake with the help of rolling pin (*vardaneh, khuneh, chub-e nan-paz*). When he has finished with a lump he throws it to the stretcher (*vavar, shater, nan dar-ar*), who places the flattened dough on a 35-50 centimeters wide cotton-stuffed cushion (*nan-bana, navan, navand*) and stretches the dough over it. In case of a *lavash* bakery a *kandeh-gir* or carver would print a pattern on the dough. Also, the *lavash* dough was not stretched, but the bakers tossed them "from one to the other and finally onto a convex plate."⁶⁴

---

59. Wills 1893, p. 335.
60. Rice 1923, p. 177.
61. Wills 1893, p. 334. On the various kinds of fuels used (*yushun, chaltaq, khar-e shotori, tarash, gaz,* and *gawan*) and their different qualities, see Rowghani 1385, pp. 101-07.
62. Wills 1893, p. 335.

63. Zavosh 1370, pp. 249-50.
64. Zavosh 1370, p. 252 (*kandeh-gir*); Hay 1937, p. 82. In the past, bread dough to be baked in the oven was put on an old cloth or pieces of cloth sewn together, which was called *kama, komayuk, rafideh, yuk,* or on a kind of tray called *kabuk*. In medieval times, bakers used a tuft of feathers or an iron wire brush called *menzaghat* or *mensaghat* to brush or make marks on their bread.

In the nineteenth century, according to Binning, when the fuel was burnt down to red embers at the bottom of the oven the baker "tied up his beard with a bandage to save it from scorching, and fastened a damp cloth round his right arm." In the mid-twentieth century the baker's forearms are bandaged to protect his skin against the oven heat. Next, the baker (*shater*) grabs the handle under the cushion and slaps the dough against the hot interior of the oven. He then puts another flattened piece of dough on the cushion, and so on, which is done with great rapidity. In case of a *tanur* the mouth of the oven is closed with a lid. When the bread is sufficiently baked and starts to become loose from the oven wall, which takes a very short time, the oven man (*vardas, nan-gir*) takes out the bread with an iron rod hooked at the end with a fork, pincers, or an iron hook (*sikh, nan-chin*) attached to a long wooden handle.[65] Others pieces of dough were then quickly placed into the oven until all was finished. "The introduction and the timely removal of the bread require a degree of care and dexterity which practice alone can teach."[66] Bakeries also employ a weigher (*tarazudar*), because the baked bread is sold by weight, who sells the bread. There is also a *padu* or a jack-of-all trade, who does all the odd jobs, hauling water, flour, fuel, cleaning etc.[67]

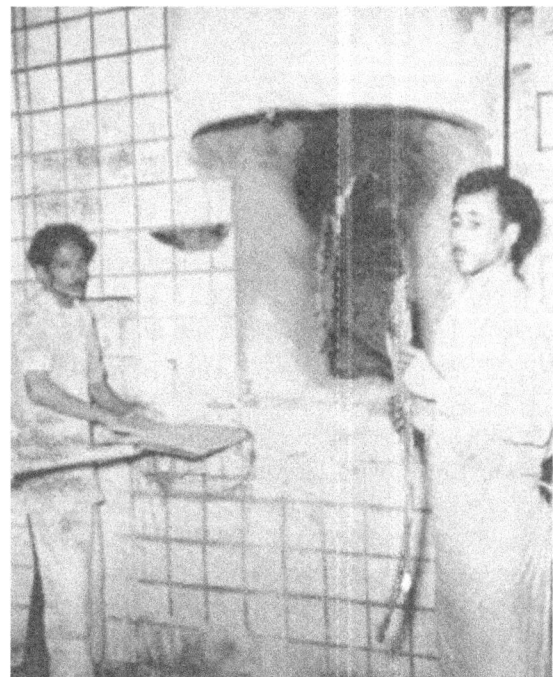

Fig. 21: A *sangak* oven (Bolukbashi 1347, p. 37).

Although initially there were two types of oven (*tanur* and the *sangak* oven) used in towns, by 1900 adaptations and specializations had taken place. For the period prior to 1890, Wills could still write that apart from the *sangak* oven, there was another oven mostly used "by the small bakers of the various suburbs of the towns, who have a slower sale. Your Persian likes his bread hot from the oven, save the thrifty Ispahani, who prefers it cold, thus gaining in the weight. This is the 'tannur' bread. The loaf is the same thickness as the 'sangak,' and about 2 feet by one, oval in shape."[68] This oven bakes *nan-e tanuri*, *nan-e taftan* and *nan-e lavash*. It is also used to bake *nan-e rowghani* or *khoshkeh* in which case the baker is called *khoshkeh-paz*, which is discussed in chapter six.[69]

---

65. In Safavid and earlier times this iron hook was called *sokar-ahanj, shekar-ahanj, gharanj, qolab,* or *kollab*. If bread had fallen from the side of the oven it was called *konjol* or *kolij*, the latter term also used to refer to bread baked in the ashes.

66. Binning 1857, vol. 1, p. 67.

67. The above description of the baking process is based on Wulff 1966, pp. 293-94; Tahvildar 1342, p. 118; Shahri 1368, vol. 1, pp. 282, 405; Ibid., vol. 4, 503; Zavosh 1370, p. 252 (*kandeh-gir*); Binning 1857, vol. 1, pp. 66-67; Wills 1893, p. 335 (fork); Benjamin 1887, pp. 95-96; Sykes 1910, p. 213; Collins 1896, p. 224 (pincers); Hay 1937, p. 82.

68. Wills 1893, p. 335.
69. Wulff 1966, p. 294.

Unlike in Europe and in Iran from the 1950s or so, "the processes of bread and sweetmeat-making are being carried on in full view."[70] Therefore, the first thing you noticed was "the glare from the bakers' furnaces" because "the oven, which was built into one of the corners opening on the street."[71] Likewise in modern times the bakers are dressed, but until the 1950s, bakers were doing their work while bare "save for loin cloths."[72]

The above description applies to bakery operations in larger towns. Elsewhere, bakery operations were more limited and basically the same as in a large village. Also, like in villages, the bakers tended to be women rather than men. This was even the case in a medium-sized town such as Semnan, a town well-known for its rusk bread and an important stop for travelers coming to or returning from Mashhad.

> The process of bread-making was carried on in the public common by the women of the town. Owing to the large number of caravans, and of pilgrims passing over this highway, there is here a demand for bread which occasions quite a business for the bakeries. These were all in front of the houses, and consist of a bank of earth made smooth and leveled on top, and covered with cement or a pavement of brick. In the pavement were the holes called tanours, or ovens. Two or three women sat on each terrace engaged with this work. As I wanted to see the process of bread-making as carried on in a systematic way, I went to one of the terraces. … One woman mixed the flour and passed it to another, who kneaded it and rolled it with a wooden roller. With a dexterous movement of her hands she took the cake of dough upon the tips of the fingers, causing it to revolve until it became thin as a knife blade. She then passed it to a third woman, who received the cake upon a pad, over which it was stretched to the full size. A fourth woman took up the pad with her right hand, and, kneeling over the side of the fireless though hot oven, with a quick motion dashed the dough against the cemented side, where it was soon done and browned, and whence it was quickly removed.[73]

Public sale of bread

The person who sold the bread was called *dokkandar*, *tarazudar*, or *pachaldar*.[74]

When the bread was baked and ready for sale, and there was no immediate client to buy it hot from the oven, it was put on display for sale. "The bread shops are not recessed, but simply a section of wall, stepped, and on the steps descend the brown blankets of bread, exactly like a drugget laid down a staircase."[75] Bakers also displayed their bread "for sale on raised slabs in long straight strips that look as if they sold it by the yard."[76] These slabs were "sloping boards which reached from floor to floor."[77] At Kuchan (Khorasan) bread was not displayed on such boards, but "exposed for sale on dirty rugs thrown over inclined planes near the ovens."[78] There were also other ways to offer bread for sale. For example, "Directly they are baked sufficiently they drop off and are hung on a big nail or suspended over a horizontal stick in readiness for purchasers. Persians eat quantities of hot bread and carry off the long cakes from the bakery hanging over their arms."[79]

---

70. Sykes 1910, p. 99.
71. Collins 1896, p. 224; De Lorey 1907, p. 226.
72. Hay 1937, p. 82; Collins 1896, p. 224.
73. Bassett 1886, pp. 194-95.
74. Rowghani 1385, p. 214.
75. Sackville-West 1992, p. 96.
76. Bradley-Birt 1910, p. 41.
77. De Lorey 1907, p. 226.
78. Moore 1915, p. 97.
79. Sykes 1910, p. 213.

Fig. 22: Street baker and bakery shop in Shiraz (Weston 1921, pp. 455-56).

Fig. 23: Baker's sale slat and seal (Rowghani 1385, pp. 99, 100).

Urban bakeries served a local customer base, living in the same city quarter as the baker. Therefore, most of his customers were regulars, many of whom bought bread on credit. Because they could not read or write, bakers had developed a simple system (just like retailers in Europe) of marking the quantity of bread bought on the slate by a customer. One method, as in Europe, was an about one meter long stick in which the baker carved teeth (see figure 19) each time that customer so-and-so had bought one unit, usually one *man*, of bread. Another method was that bakers had a seal that was unique to their shop (e.g., two facing animals). Each seal imprint on a piece of paper signified the purchase of one *man* of bread. If the customer had bought half a *man* of bread, only half the seal was printed on the paper.[80]

Because bakeries were often closed, on strike, or the bakers wanted to take a rest, people generally bought bread for more than one day. They dried it and saw to it that it was not exposed to humidity, because then it could be kept for a long time. When they wanted to eat this bread they moistened it and it acquired all the characteristics of fresh bread.[81] Usually, the bread was bought as soon it was ready "and quickly carried away by purchasers on their heads, under their arms, over their shoulders, according to preference as to how you wear your bread!"[82]

Again, there were ambulatory bakers. For example, in the 1970s in Gilan, on the occasion of big events, mostly religious, ambulatory bakers baked bread on the *saj*.[83] There were also bakers who delivered bread to the homes of paying customers. "A Persian baker rolls out his dough into large thin flat cakes, pitches them for a few minutes into a heated oven, or in default of this on a heap of charcoal embers, and then throwing them over his shoulder, as we should a coat or cloak, marches off to distribute them to his customers."[84] In Mashhad in the 1830s it was part of the everyday street scene to see "men, or veiled women, [who] moved through the crowd with baskets of fresh and stale bread, or sat in convenient places to sell it."[85] A modern development was that bread was distributed in a carriage. Hall noted around 1920 that the second carriage was "stacked high with the early-morning production of a small bakery; succulent new-baked bread loaves three feet long."[86]

Because Iranian bread had other forms and shapes than in Europe, a British traveler observed that "The word loaf does not, I presume, exist in the Persian language, unless it is in reference to sugar, for it certainly cannot be applied to the bread of the country."[87] Europeans, therefore, generally referred to Iranian bread as cakes or flap-jacks, because the breads were so large, about a couple of feet long and

---

80. Rowghani 1385, pp. 99-100.
81. Olmer 1906, p. 20.
82. Morton 1940, p. 122; Sackville-West 1992, p. 96 ("you buy the bread by weight, and carry it away thrown over your arm like a travelling-rug."); Bradley-Birt 1910, p. 55 (the charvadar came with "a long roll of bread under his arm.").
83. Bazin and Bromberger 1982, p. 80.
84. Mounsey 1872, p. 109. For a letter ordering a baker to bring bread to a relative's house, see [http://www.qajarwomen.org/archive/detail/61].
85. Conolly 1834, vol. 1, p. 324 (stale bread was sold at a reduce price). In medieval times such wooden baskets or trays were known as *batuk*.
86. Hall 1947, p. 80.
87. Mounsey 1872, p. 109.

Fig. 24: Horse cart transporting bread (Rowghani 1385, p. 72).

a foot wide.[88] Moreover, "The bread thus produced varies in consistency, being sometimes so fleshy it can be folded up like a napkin, at other times thin, crisp, and so light that on one occasion while we sitting at a meal the wind caught it and blew it some distance away."[89] It had also other benefits as Mrs. Rice pointed out: "Another advantage is that much of the cooked food sold in the bazaars is folded up in bread and nothing of its goodness is lost."[90]

---

88. Collins 1896, p. 224; Sykes 1910, p. 213.
89. Collins 1896, p. 253; see also, Mounsey 1872, p. 109 ("Being only half baked, the bread always remains flexible, and, besides being the staff of life, serves the purpose of platter and napkin at a native meal.")
90. Rice 1923, p. 178.

Fig. 25: Various Iranian breads (Mage 1993).

CHAPTER SIX

BREAD TYPES

"You can nearly always get some kind of bread. Persian bread varies in quality and kind, but you may count on it, being brown and flat and of unbolted wheat. ... Sometimes it is thicker, sometimes it is thinner; sometimes it is baked dry and crisp with sugar or grease or a bit of ginger, and you break off hunks as if it were a huge cracker." Amory 1929, pp. 65-66.

Ze khabbaz beshenow hadithi ze man
Listen to what I have to say about the baker

Keh afrukht fekram tanur-e sokhan
For my thoughts have kindled the oven of eloquence

Buvad sangakash anchonan delshekar
His punctured crispbread (*sangak*) is so delicious

Ke delha khurad ab az an chashmeh-sar
That hearts are refreshed by those springs.[1]

In this chapter I discuss the ways and manner the various breads might be classified, and that given the complexity, I opted for a simplified presentation. After a discussion of the variety of breads prior to 1600, about which little is known, I discuss *lavash*, *sangak*, *taftuni*, *barbari* and other breads, including sweetbreads and pastries.

Introduction

It would seem that throughout the ages with few changes the variety of breads available in Iran remained more or less the same. This was mainly due to the baking methods that determined the shape and form as well as the size of the bread. This meant that bread was round or oval, flat and thin or thick, that needed to be eaten immediately or could be kept for a long period. However, because the mixture of flour, the kinds of flour, the amount of leavening, and the preparation methods vary greatly from village to village and city to city all breads varied in form, thickness, color, and texture. Basically, luxury bread was the same as normal bread with the difference that expensive ingredients were added to the dough as well as on top of the bread. In general, the quality of bread was determined by the flour mixture and the baking time. Also, during the month of Ramazan bakers did their best to bake excellent bread that was also baked a bit longer and sprinkled with various seeds.[2]

Sedentary people often used more than one baking method to bake bread or pastries depending on the season and the type of bread or pastry they wanted.[3] Furthermore, over the centuries there was a large variety of bread and pastries and not just the most common ones that most people know. This was due to the kind of ingredients used, size and form of the bread as well as special events or holidays that called for more luxurious variations of bread or pastry.

Another distinction is that bread baked in towns was different from that baked in villages or by migrant groups. For example, "*Noo* or bread in Larestan is almost always made of wheat flour, baked daily fresh in bakery. There are several types of home made breads each with a specific name."[4] In Owrazan (east of Taleqan), villagers made bread from wheat, barley and millet, but not in an oven but on a *saj*.[5] There were also ethnic differences.

The Armenians and the tribespeople also have varieties of their own. In times of scarcity barley

---

1. Keyhani 1982, p. 271.
2. Shahri 1386, vol. 2, p. 392.
3. Binder 1887, p. 351 (*tabun* and *saj* used).
4. Mahmoodian 2007, p. 310.
5. Al-e Ahmad 1333, p. 28.

bread is made, but the ordinary bread is made of wholemeal wheaten flour; it is leavened, and never made in loaves, but always in thin cakes and flaps. Some is as thin as paper, while village bread may be an inch thick. The latter is made in round cakes, from six to nine or ten inches across, while most of the kinds of town bread are made in long flaps, from one to two feet long. Men are often seen carrying the bread for their houses over or under their arms, as they might carry a coat.[6]

Shapes and sizes of bread varied locally, and scores of names were in use.[7] Therefore, it appears possible to classify bread by type, such as: flat vs non-flat, round vs oval, but unfortunately the data are rather limited and lacking in detail. The thick kinds of bread are eaten fresh, many people buying fresh bread for every meal, but the very thin bread is folded up and tied in a cloth and kept for a long time. It is often sprinkled with water and tied up again for a short time before being eaten.[8] To classify breads by geographic area is another possibility, but this has the drawback that for some areas there are good data, while for others there is none.

In short, the problem with the classification of bread types is that there are pros and cons for each one of the criteria listed. I finally decided to take my cue from the 1933 Tehran municipality regulation for bakeries, which listed the following types of bakeries: (i) *lavashi*, (ii) *sangaki*, (iii) *taftuni*, (iv) *khoshkeh-pazi*, (v) *nan-e siyah va safid-pazi*, (vi) *shirmal-pazi*, (vii) *komaj-pazi*, (viii) *mozdi-pazi* etc.[9] As flat bread was the norm in Iran, these represent the most important types of bread that allow subsuming variants to be classed with them. Therefore, I decided to bring order to the long list of the various bread types as follows: first I discuss *lavash*, then *sangak*, *taftun*, *barbari*, modern breads, special breads, sweet breads, and pastries.

Before discussing the characteristics and other information about of *lavash* bread I first present the breads that were consumed in Iran prior to 1600. Because there was a surprising range of breads available during that period, most of which we only know by name, for very little is reported on the composition of their dough, their preparation and other characteristics.

Breads Prior to 1600

Prior to the Moslem conquest of Iraq, its people allegedly had only one type of bread known as "Ispahan."[10] Unnamed dry bread with raisins and other fruits was exported in the tenth century.[11] At that time, Hamadi mentions thin, wide bread, baked in a *tanur* called *awraq al-riqaq* (leaves of flat bread) also just called *riqaq*.[12] In the Ilkhanid period, three types of bread were served with warm meals in the Rashidi hospice in Tabriz, such as the thin *nan-e tunuk*, baked in West-Persian style like the women of the Qazvini slaves make it, that is, very special (*khass*), toasted (*beryani*) and sprinkled with seeds. The *furni* breads were luxury breads, viz., thick round bread, baked in an oven (*furn*) and subsequently made moist with a mixture of fat, sugar and milk. In the Rashidi hospice four loaves weighed about 100 gram. This bread had to be baked by an experienced baker using the best ingredients. The third kind was round bread, like those of the village of Sijan. Another type of bread mentioned is *gerdeh*, which probably is a flat circular pancake like bread, but thicker than *tunuk*, and leavened. This kind of bread was very popular in Tabriz. Also, mentioned is *gerdeh-ye Siyavani* that was not distributed in the hospice, but paid to staff as a ration. It was probably a simpler version

---

6. Rice 1923, p. 177.
7. Koelz 1983, p. 166.
8. Rice 1923, p. 178.
9. Rowghani 1385, p. 59.

10. Ashtor 1968, p. 1019.
11. Spuler 1952, p. 510.
12. Ahsan 1979, p. 89.

of *gerdeh*, be it that it was to be baked like in Sijan.[13] Bread that was half-baked was called *kavazheh*.

Usually there is not much information available about bread beyond its name, which sometimes just indicates its form or some other kind of characteristic. Some breads referred to their place of origin such as *nan-e gorji* and *nan-e lari*.[14] Many types of bread were round or roundish such as *kolcheh*, *lavash* and *gerdeh*, which characteristic is often referred to by many existing poetic terms. These refer to this kind of round bread as having the form of the sun (*nan-e atesh ruy*, *nan-e zarrin*, *nan-e garm charkh*) or moon (*nan-e kharchang*, *nan-e safid falak*, *nan-e simin*).[15] *Jardaq* or *jardhaq* was also round bread (*mohavvar*); it was quite thick and was baked in an oven.[16] Furthermore, certain other types of bread were round such as *bahnaneh*, a type of white bread.[17]

In addition, there were many breads that reflect the variety in baking methods such as the flour used, leavened or not, and other characteristics that I mention here. Bread with a certain amount of bran added to the flour was known as *khoshkar*, very hard bread made of millet was called *nakhjad*, while bread made of the finest flour unmixed with bran was called *meydeh*.[18] There were several kinds of unleavened breads (*khamsuk* or *khamsug*; *kumaj*, *bimus*, *khoshkfa*) of which *budeh-nan* was a special kind as it was dried for 40 days in the sun. Another special type of unleavened bread was known as *az dast paza*, which was baked in thin cakes on lamina of iron or earth, placed in a baking-pan. *Lavash* was not the only thin bread, because *ghafanj* is another example, while *nan-e tang* or in Turkish *yukheh* seems to be the generic term for this type of bread. Also, there was leavened bread (*mayeh-dar*; *nan-e pahn*), bread baked on coals (*angoshtva*; *sokarva* or *sokalu*), bread baked without salt (*samet*), bread baked of barley, beans and millet (*siyar*), a hard bread baked of wheat and barley (*varhamin* or *varhin*), as well as terms to denote hot or warm bread (*garmeh*), one day old bread (*shab-mandeh*; *nan-e talkh*),[19] dry bread, probably baked with dates (*hashf*), dry mouldy bread (*pibas*; *sabz-nan*), white bread (*shamaz*), barley bread (*tarkhaneh*), and unknown types of bread such as *nan-e firuzkhani* that weighed one *man*, *saqi `arus* (a bride's leg), *shatranji*, *gav-dideh*, and *gav-zaban*.[20]

There were sweet breads and other special breads, such as bread baked in oil or fat,[21] of which *gharmasang*, a thin bread (*nan-e tang*), *chalpak*, bread made with thin layers of dough baked in oil, and *beksemat*, bread fried in oil, then dried and cut into squares to be taken as food for travelers, are examples.[22] Other oil related breads include *rowghanineh* and *angoshtu*. The latter, apart from being a kind of bread usually crumbled before being eaten, also referred to a pancake baked in oil. There also was bread soaked in butter (*babar*), with butter or syrup (*bablus*), or made with fine flour, milk, butter and sugar (*sakaru*). *Nazuk* was thin bread baked of fine flour and butter and *sakar* was bread made of the finest flour with butter and sugar, usually given as present on *Nowruz*. Sweetmeats include *gulanj* that was called *la bar la* or

---

13. Hoffmann 2000, p. 221; see also pp. 291-92.
14. Ata`meh 1360, pp. 142, 180.
15. Borhan 1342; At`ameh 1360, pp. 11, 21, 80, 85, 86, 101, 167. Round bread was also simply referred to as *qors-e nan*.
16. Dehkhoda.
17. Asadi Tusi 1336, p. 150; Borhan 1342. It is also described as being baked in ghee and being called *kolicheh* and as *meydeh*.
18. At`ameh 1360, pp. 55, 122; Asadi Tusi 1336, p. 151.

19. Stale bread was sold at a reduced price. Conolly 1834, vol. 1, p. 324. Bread that was left in the evening was called *nan-e bayat* or *nan-e shab mandeh*. Dehkhoda.
20. Borhan 1342; Steingass; At`ameh 1360, pp. 36, 61-62, 65, 67, 72, 92, 158, 167. *Komaj* was a term also used to denote bread baked in ashes.
21. Spuler 1952, p. 508.
22. Asadi Tusi 1336, p. 106; At`ameh 1360, pp. 10, 16, 40, 42, 53-54, 65, 128, 168

layered, and *malkaneh*, a dry sweetmeat made from seven kinds of nuts.[23]

As in later periods, early bread was sprinkled with seeds to enhance its taste, which was referred to as *khali nan* and *nankhvah*, while in some cases seeds such as aniseed (*alsa; nan-khvah*), bishop's weed (*amush*) were put into the dough and baked with it. Bread with seeds in it was known as *anbus*. Bread was not only eaten with meat, cheese and other condiments, but also crumbled, which pieces were generically known as *fatit, eshkeneh*, or *injidan*, but when put in milk or broth they were known as *tarit* or *tarid*.[24]

Breads after 1600

Although strictly speaking some of the breads mentioned here already were known before 1600 I have nevertheless chosen this cut-off point, because it is only after this date that we have particulars available about the various types of bread.

Lavash

The most well-known flat bread is *lavash* which is a flat, paper thin, flaky, crisp, round, oval or rectangular bread, about 2-3 mm (1/8 inch) thick, usually either made into circular sheets 38 cm (15 inches) across in villages or 60-70 cm long and 30-40 cm wide in cities, unleavened or mildly leavened and nowadays made from flour of 82% extraction.[25] Because it dries rapidly it is sprinkled with water or heated before eating when too dry.[26] "It can be kept for several weeks wrapped in a napkin (*sofra*) and placed in a basket (*sabad*) or in a cupboard of dried earth (*nandan*); for that reason it is very common in western Iran, especially in winter, when daily baking is difficult and the bread keeps longer because of the cold."[27] In cities, towns and large villages *lavash* was baked in a *tanur*, but in smaller villages and among migrants groups it was baked either on a *saj* or in a *tabun* and then also generically known as *nan-e dehati* or 'village bread.'[28]

The dough of *lavash* is the same as that of *sangak*. It is placed in a frying-pan that is inserted in an oven heated with thorny bushes. It is more leavened than the other breads and when well baked it is considered to be the best of the breads. It resembles a pancake. In 1906, each loaf weighed about 300 g and cost 0.10 cents. Often on exiting the oven it is sprinkled with nigella seeds.[29]

Lavash bread was already known in the twelfth century, when it is mentioned by the poets Nizari and Mowlavi.[30] It may be the same as or a variant of *nan-e nazok* or 'thin bread' that is also mentioned at that time,[31] the more so because it was called *taftun* or *nazok corek* in the Turkic speaking part of Talesh, albeit in the twentieth century.[32] *Lavash* was certainly around in the seventeenth century when in 1655 the Ottoman traveler Evliya Chelebi mentions that in Qazvin "there is *lavash* bread." He further reports that Tabriz had white bread and

---

23. Asadi Tusi 1336, pp. 18, 151.
24. Sana'i 1380, p. 573 makes a reference to this custom; see also Atma`eh 1360, pp. 42, 43, 53, 73, 81, 126, 134, 136, 177.
25. Wulff 1966, p. 291; Koelz 1983, p. 166; Binning 1857, 2, 66 (*nooni luwashee*); Faridi et al. 1981, p. 428. As to the meaning of the term 'extraction rate,' nowadays, wholemeal bread is baked with 100% extraction flour, i.e. containing the whole of the cereal grain. White bread is made from 72% extraction flour. Brown bread is made with flour of extraction rate intermediate between that of white bread (72%) and wholemeal (100%). In general, as the extraction rate of the flour increases, so do both the protein and the ash content. However, as the extraction rate approaches 100% (whole meal), the protein content drops slightly, while the ash content continues to rise.

26. Bazin and Bromberger 1982, p. 81; Koelz 1983, p. 166.
27. Desmet-Grégoire 1989. In medieval times the wooden chest or earthen vessel in which bread or sweetmeats were kept was called *karsan, karisan* or *kanur*.
28. Polak 1865, vol. 1, p. 110; Bradley-Birt 1910, p. 268.
29. Olmer 1906, p. 19.
30. Dehkhoda, q.v. *lavash*.
31. Hoffmann 2000, p. 203; At`ameh 1360, p. 168. *Lavash* is also described as *nan-e nazok* in various dictionaries, see Dehkhoda, q.v. *lavash. Nan-e nazok* or *tanok* was made from wheat in Sarvestan (Fars). Homayuni 1371, p. 148.
32. Bazin and Bromberger 1982, p. 81. It was also known as *nan-e taftun* and *nan-e tanuri* in other parts of Iran, indicating that it was oven baked. Wulff 1966, p. 291.

Tiflis even a special white bread, which may also have been *lavash* bread or bread like it. Chelebi further mentions that Qazvin had another flat, but wheat-barley bread.³³ Some two decades later, Chardin writes: "They have again another sort of Bread, which they call *Lavach*, which they make round, -stones, to save Wood; these Stones taking and keeping Fire the best, and heating the Dough sooner; but that Bread is more bak'd in some Places than others." He further specifies, "as large as a hollow Plate, and as thin as Parchment, which they bake upon a round Copper Plate."³⁴ Thevenot in 1665 also mentions bread "so thin that it looks like fine Paper, and they are obliged to lay twelve or fifteen of them together, which they fold into two or four pleats, and some of their fashion is very good: But in some places it is but half baked, very brown, and all full of bits of Straw, so that it looks more like brown Paper than bread; if a Stranger were not told it, he might be mistook them for course Napkins."³⁵ In the nineteenth century,

> The unleavened bread, which is best prepared by Armenians and Kurds, is merely a paste of flour and water, rolled to the thinness of a wafer, and of great size. It is baked on a hot plate, and is hung out to air and dry; it is then folded, when not quite dry, into four. It will keep for several months if kept dry, and is dampened prior to using, when it loses its brittleness, and becomes easily rent, but unbreakable. It is a capital bread for the road, and is invariably carried by Persians when marching, being very portable, and as palatable after a couple of months as on the day it was made."³⁶

Indeed travelers such as Floyer report that "the muleteer takes a hurried snack of a very hard dry bread, often six months old.³⁷

Fig. 26: *Lavash* bread (Nader Souri, Mage 2013).

Lavash seems to have been the bread mostly used in villages, small towns and even towns like Kerman and Yazd.³⁸ In fact until the end of the nineteenth century *lavash* was not baked in Tehran, according to Shahri, but like in most other towns brought in from the surrounding villages.³⁹ It was indeed very popular in villages and among migratory groups. One traveler described this bread as follows, so at to stress its rural character. "Lavash is the name of the common bread as baked in the ovens made in the ground. The only difference between this and the former is in the qualities imparted by the different processes of baking."⁴⁰ The common bread in the village of Owrazan (east

---

33. Chelebi 2010, pp. 219. Tabriz also had barley bread, Tiflis a large-grain bread, while Hamadan's bread was somewhat dark, implying that there was barley in the flour mixture. Ibid., pp. 34, 105, 204.
34. Chardin 1927, p. 233.
35. Thevenot 1971, vol. 2, p. 96.
36. Wills 1893, pp. 335-36.

37. Floyer 1882, p. 340; Ballantine 1879, pp. 69 and 85 (thin wafer-bread), 122 and 211 (bread in thin large cakes).
38. Olmer 1906, p. 19.
39. Shahri 1386, vol. 2, p. 393.
40. Bradley-Birt 1910, p. 268.

of Taleqan) was of two types, a thick and a thin type, the latter was called *bali nan*, which was the same as the large, thin *lavash* bread,[41] while in the Boluk-e Zahra villages (Qazvin) it was known as *gerdeh* and in Yush as *gateh nun* or big bread.[42] In Davarabad (Khorasan), e.g., *lavash* bread were large circular sheets often two or more feet wide and as thin as the dough allowed. "They are baked on an indoor hearth, frequently at a 'lavash party,' a communal project among neighbors, kinswomen and friends." The fresh, crisp and crunchy loafs are not consumed but stored. At such a 'party', "scores or even hundreds of loaves may be baked. Each participant takes her share, stacks them neatly, wraps them in cloth and stores them in an umbar or yakdan away from vermin. Here they keep for months." They are sometimes eaten crisp, but usually "sprinkled with water like so much laundry."[43] *Lavash* was very popular bread among migrant groups such as the Baluch.

> A wheat bread even more delicate than *galfach* was the very thin, 3 millimeter (1/8 inch), unleavened lawash, also around 38 centimeters (15 inches) across. *Lawash* too, was cooked on a *tin* and *padink*, but in a different manner. The *tin* sat on the stand, heated up, and the *lawash* dough was dramatically punched into a disk as the baker, rather like a showy pizza crust baker, flipped it in the air and flopped it onto the lightly greased *tin* for 10 seconds on one side, then on the other. It was then ready to eat. *Lawash* was the bread of choice among the Baluch, invariably provided for guests and featured at feasts, and eaten alone, in *hatuk* or with pieces of meat or eggs. *Lawash*

had to be eaten immediately, for in the dry air of the desert, its staleness arrived in minutes rather than hours; and stale *lawash* had a consistency and taste like nothing so much as old cardboard. Both because of the extra work in baking and its poor storage quality, *lawash* was thus rarely made for daily, household consumption.[44]

In the rural areas bread similar to *lavash*, but much thinner, was also eaten. It was unleavened. When fresh it was soft like a fabric, and was much appreciated as such. Exposing it for a few minutes to the sun it becomes dry, and breaks very well.[45] It is probably the same bread that Wulff described as follows: "Bread made from the same dough [as *lavash*], but stretched very thinly is known as *nan-e khunegi*. After baking, it is almost as thin as paper and is also the oldest known bread in the Middle East and Central Asia."[46]

Not only for Iranians, but also for Europeans *lavash* was the staple bread. Binning describes "*nooni luwashee*, a very thin scone or wafer, is baked on an iron girdle, like cakes in Scotland,"[47] while Floyer relates how he had breakfast with "pieces of thin wafer bread about two feet across, which serve as plates."[48] Europeans found it difficult to get accustomed to it, according to Polak in the 1850s. Therefore, at the Legation bread was baked like at home.[49] The same held for some British consuls like the one at Nasratabad (Sistan), whose wife wrote: "The wheat and barley are often sown together in one crop and then reaped together and threshed and ground without being separated. I used to wonder whether it was on this account I so often found that our home-made bread was apt to

---

41. Al-e Ahmad 1333, p. 28; Homayuni 1371, p. 149 (Sarvestan -*lavash*).
42. Al-e Ahmad 1337, p. 63; Tahbaz 1343, p. 44.
43. Alberts 1963, pp. 175-76. Also the staple bread in Owrazan, where *bali nan* is the same as the large, thin *lavash* that was eaten with cheese as a side dish (*qateq*). Al-e Ahmad 1333, p. 29.
44. Salzmann 1994, p. 72.
45. Olmer 1908, p. 20.
46. Wulff 1966, p. 291.
47. Binning 1857, vol. 2, 66-67; vol. 1, pp. 161 (bread baked in large round cakes, thin as paper), 189 (thin bread).
48. Floyer 1882, p. 128.
49. Polak 1865, vol. 1, p. 110.

turn sour the second day after baking. The white bread made from flour imported from Quetta or Delhi kept quite sweet."[50] In 1851, Binning opined that "The best kind of bread is about three quarters of an inch thick, while some of the inferior sort, baked on the girdle, is almost as thin as cartridge paper."[51] The British diplomat Eastwick, who was in Iran in the early 1860s, wrote "while I was in Persia, I had for the most part to put up with the bread of the country, which resembles the Indian chapatti, thin, unleavened, and unpalatable."[52] This dislike was probably due to the fact that when fresh "the Persian flaps are edible, but after a few hours they turn tough, bitter and are hardly enjoyable," while often they were "mostly not well baked and difficult to chew."[53] At Kuchan, "wheat bread-the only kind known in Persia-baked in enormous cakes no thicker than a knife-blade, and full of bulby inequalities, looking rather like huge pancakes much under-cooked."[54] Jackson notes that Nakhjevan bread was so much better than the bread in Iran he later had to subsist on.[55] Nevertheless, he also opined that Iranian bread "is generally moist when served and often a bit soggy; but when allowed to grow dry and crisp, it is excellent to the taste, though sometimes fatal to the digestion."[56] The American journalist Mumford described Iranian bread as having "about the thickness of heavy brown wrapping-paper, and in sheets of about the same size. Enforced subsistence on it for a while led me to believe that the nourishment involved is about the same in amount. And yet millions of Persians are alive, and feed upon nothing else in the way of food."[57]

In the twentieth century, *lavash* remained the preferred bread of Iranian consumers, because it is tasty and when well baked is easily digestible and it is still the most consumed bread despite the increase in the availability of a large variety of breads in the market. *Lavash* was the preferred and most common bread for most Iranians; in Talesh, e.g., it was the daily food in the 1970s.[58] At that time, Gilani bread eaters ate above all *lavash*, but often also *barbari* bread that they bought daily or every other day from a bakery. In the large Gilani towns above all *sangak* was eaten like in Tehran.[59] In Tuyserkan, in the 1940s, both in the town and in its surrounding villages *lavash* bread was the staple, baked at home. There was no bakery apart from a *sangak* one. *Barbari, taftuni, mashhadi*, etc. were not available and not even known to most people in Tuyserkan. Most houses had an oven and baked every day. The bread, if prepared from good wheat, remained good for weeks and only needed to be sprinkled with water to be fresh again. Although there was no bakery in Tuyserkan villagers who baked brought *lavash* for sale to the town; this bread was known as *deseleh-paz*. Townsmen, who could not bake at home bought it in layers and ate it over time.[60]

Due to population growth and migrants, Tehranis who wanted their bread always fresh at each meal unlike other cities, had to stand more and more in line. To avoid this hassle they bought their *lavash* ready-made, which led to the creation of alternatives. Many villagers and migrants bought their bread in the morning from specific bakeries, it was their regular shop or *patuq*, and therefore they paid more. The bakers in view of this growing demand began to adulterate the weight

---

50. Benn 1909, p. 73.
51. Binning 1857, vol. 2, pp. 66-67.
52. Eastwick 1864, vol. 1, p. 254.
53. Polak 1865, vol. 1, p. 110.
54. Moore 1915, p. 97.
55. Jackson 1910, p. 22.
56. Jackson 1910, p. 111.
57. Mumford 1901, p. 10.

---

58. Bradley-Birt 1910, p. 268; Bazin and Bromberger 1982, pp. 80-81.
59. Bazin and Bromberger 1982, pp. 80-81.
60. Gol-Mohammadi vol. 1, p. 297. Also in Sarvestan (Fars), Homayuni 1371, p. 149. *Mashhadi* bread is large flatbread covered with sesame and black cumin seeds.

and composition of the dough, which made the bread look less appetizing. This also gave rise to the appearance of ambulatory bread sellers who kept the bread in nylon bags, a.k.a. *zard chubeh'i* that they sold to car drivers who did not have the time to open the bags.

In the mid-1980s, the *lavash* bakeries changed their baking method by installing ovens that were at ground level. Moreover, all workers performed their duties while sitting (*pokht neshesteh*). This bread was known as *lavash-e zamini* and became popular, because the loaves were bigger and tastier due to the larger ovens. But because the loaves were so big the *shater* had to bow and bend (*do la va rast*) 4 times, and work long days (17 hours), they asked for higher wages. Also it was bad for their health. It was therefore decided to have the *shater* do his work standing and to that end they made a pit in the floor next to the oven. Over time this *lavash-e zamini* suffered from smaller weight and a reduction in taste.

A third type of *lavash* is machine made (*lavash-e mashini*). Because it is so thick its inside (*maghz*) remained unbaked and did not have a good taste. Thus it could not replace *lavash-e tanuri*. Bakers intended to improve the quality of this bread in the future; whether they did so is not known, to me at least.

The fourth kind is also machine-made and seemingly is nevertheless different from its like. It is well baked on both sides, i.e. evenly toasted (*gol andakhteh*) and thus it is tasty. It is sold dry, wrapped in cardboard because of hygienic considerations. It is only sold at its place of production in Tehran-e Now road. The fact that people line up is a sign of its popularity, and each buyer purchases more than one package. People elsewhere in Tehran do not know about this bread and even if they did they all cannot get it.[61]

In addition to *lavash* there were many other very thin flat breads. *Tiri* or *nan-e tiri* may have been the same or similar to it, and with *lavash* it is the thinnest bread in Iran with the same characteristics.[62] The name is probably due to the fact *tiri* is rolled on a wooden board with a roller (*tir*). Among the Lors, this roller is also used to take the bread from the pan.[63] In Larestan (Fars), there are three thin breads. First there is *nun-e dartasheh* also known as *nun-e oshk* or *nun-e hoshk*, a paper thin, 50 cm wide, unleavened bread baked over the *barezeh* or *taveh*, long enough to get dry and crunchy. The second one is *nun-e reshteba* that is the same as *nun-e dartasheh*, but instead of baking, they are placed under the sun to dry; they are used as noodles or as flakes in *restaba polow*. The third one is *nun-e lahm*, a kind of bread, similar to *dartasheh*, but soft and slightly sodden or doughy. Three to five of them are kept stacked together to be served with *mahveh* at breakfast. They remain fresh for two to three weeks; they are also called noon-e nazok, thin bread.[64] In Sarvestan (Fars) they also had a kind of thin breakfast bread called *nan-e tali* that was baked on a *toveh*.[65]

Sangak

Sangak is a bread type that is unique to Iran and nowadays made from flour of 87% extraction. It is a sourdough flat bread, softer than *lavash*, of the thickness of a finger (3-5 mm), some three foot long (90-95 cm) and more than a foot wide (30-40 cm), triangle-shaped and baked on hot stones. It has neither crumbs (*maghz*) nor crust, but is flexible, brown, very little risen, and very little baked. It is also known as *nan-e khamiri*.[66] It was luxury bread, "with the outward semblance of a thick chamois skin" and mostly found in towns.[67]

---

61. Zavosh 1370, pp. 240-43.
62. Koelz 1983, p. 166.
63. Feilberg 1952, p. 95.
64. Mahmoodian 2007, p. 266.
65. Homayuni 1371, p. 149.
66. Wills 1893, p. 334; Olmer 1908, p. 18; Jackson 1911, p. 236; Faridi et al. 1981, p. 428. The figures between brackets indicate the current dimension of the bread.
67. Polak 1865, vol. 1, p. 110; Jackson 1911, p. 236. "This

This is clear, for example, from the situation of the small town of Sarvestan (Fars), where around 1940 *nan-e sangak* was baked in three bakeries, which were mostly eaten by non-natives and government officials, because the staple was *lavash*. Each bakery baked 30-40 *man* of bread each day.[68]

Fig. 27: *Sangak* oven (Rowghani 1385, p. 85).

Like the Iranians, Europeans considered it to be an excellent type of bread. "Thoroughly good bread is the result, crisp, appetizing, and satisfying. Eaten hot with butter, it is the finest of breads after the Russians. Of course it is absolutely pure. The term 'flap-jack' is applied to this form of bread by the Europeans in Persia."[69] Because *sangak* bread was baked in long sheets, it was described as looking "more like the shoemaker's sole leather than anything else."[70] Like other bread, *sangak* was sold by weight, but if a client wants well-baked baked bread they let it stay longer in the oven, called *du atasheh*, and then he is charged per piece.[71]

Nan-e sangak dates from Safavid period at least that is the period from which we have historical evidence of its existence. Allegedly Sheikh Baha'i (1547-1621) discovered the *sangak* baking method.[72] A fact is that the first mention of this type of bread indeed dates from this period. The earliest mention is in the dictionary *Borhan-e Qate`* written in 1651 and by Tavernier,[73] which implies that it must have existed prior to that date. Evliya Chelebi in 1647 reported that in Tabriz pebble bread was baked, while in Qazvin "there is white as cotton pebble-bread."[74] Around 1670, Chardin reported, "another sort which they call *Senguck*, that is to say Flint-bread, because it is bak'ed in Ovens made as ours are, the Bottoms whereof are cover'd with large Flint Stones, as big as a Wall-Nut and two Fingers high. This Bread is not thicker than the ordinary Bread; it is made long-ways, and weighs about a Pound and a half [0.68 kg]. The Bakers bake it upon Flint."[75]

To bake more *sangak* bread a larger oven was required than the *tanur*, viz. the *tanur-e sangaki* or *kureh*. The *sangak* oven probably was an upscaled version of baking bread on stones in the rural areas, and therefore, likely to predate the Safavid period. Sykes made an interesting observation in this regard. "The country barley bread is often made in thick flaps, called *sanjak*, the name implying that it is baked on hot stones, which are placed at the bottom of the oven, and when fresh and crisp it is excellent.[76] Given the sheet-like shape of *sangak* it is likely that it predates the Safavid period, because this type of bread was already common in the tenth century, but its baking method is unknown.[77]

Sangak baking requires many workers and a large oven; in Tehran around 1900 only 100

---

kind of bread is to be had only in large cities where ovens are made for baking it." Bradley-Birt 1910, p. 268

68. Homayuni 1371, p. 153.
69. Wills 1893, p. 335; Binning 1857, vol. 2, pp. 66-67; Buckingham 1829, vol. 1, p. 206.
70. Wishard 1909, p. 116.
71. Olmer 1906, p. 18.

72. Zavosh 1370, p. 244 (He allegedly also developed *beryani* and *khoresht*, which is also unlikely); see also Rowghani 1385, p. 80 who also doubts the 'discovery' by Sheikh Baha'i. *Sangak* is not mentioned at all by the fifteenth century poet Atma`eh 1360, who devoted his entire *divan* to food items, including breads and pastries.
73. Borhan 1356; Tavernier 1930, p. 282.
74. Chelebi 2010, pp. 34.
75. Chardin 1927, p. 233.
76. Sykes 1910, p. 213.
77. Spuler 1952, p. 508.

bakeries were allowed to bake it.[78] Olmer, who made a study around 1900 of the various oven types used, wrote that only in Tehran he saw real ovens to bake *sangak*, but they were all primitive ones.[79] This is understandable as *sangak* bakeries were limited in number. For example, in Tuyserkan, granted a small town, there was only one *sangak* bakery to serve the entire urban population in the 1940s.[80] Wills, around 1880, provided a description of a primitive *sangak* oven.

> A huge arched oven is half filled with small pebbles from the river. Upon these pebbles is placed a pile of brushwood; this is fired and fed until the stones are sufficiently hot; the fire is then pushed into a corner, and the flaps of dough are placed on the heated stones by means of a peel, as many as twenty loaves being put on at a time. Batch after batch are baked in this way, the stones being stirred occasionally when they get too cool to bake well, and the fire is raked forward and fed again, and so on. Or at times the fire is simply sifted from place to place in the oven, the loaves being placed on the stones as they are heated.[81]

Some 20 years later Olmer, who made a study of the various baking ovens, described the *sangak* oven as follows. It has an elliptical archway in brickwork. The back is filled with pebbles [D], which "being washed, are spread upon an iron plate, and then put into the oven."[82] An opening [C] allows the entering and removing of the bread. At [A] is the fuel, wooden twigs, thorn branches, dry herbs, which lick the archway before exiting the straight chimney [E]. The oven remains hot day and night. One bakes 5 to 6 times per day. Output of bread in proportion to flour is 9/8 and because there is no sifting, the yield of wheat in the bread is 9/8 instead of 15/16.[83] The price of bread varied in 1905. One piece weighed about 750 grams or 1 *charak* and costs 0.15 francs. One *batman* cost 1 *qran* to 1 *qran* 4 *shahi*s (0.17 to 0.20 francs/kg)[84]

The dough was made in the same way as that of the other breads, but baked in a different manner. Depending on the kind of wheat used, different quantities of leavening and salt were required. Also, certain types of wheat (*khaldar*, *zang-zadeh*, *talkhehdar*, and *siyabordar*) were not used to bake *sangak*, not even to mix them with other kinds of wheat.[85]

The oven described by Olmer in 1906 employed five workers. The *nandar ar* is responsible for heating the pebbles and keeping them hot, while he also rakes the pebbles so that their surface is even. He further regularly 'soaps' the stones with a flat shovel to prevent the bread from sticking to them. To that end there is an opening in oven, which he also used to sprinkle seeds on the bread, if demanded by a customer. The *boteh gozar* took care of the fuel and the heating the oven. The *atashandaz* took pieces of dough, manually kneaded them for a while and put them on the shovel of the fourth one, called *shater*, who put the bread on the stones. Finally, the *nangir* recovered the bread after 4-5 minutes when it was baked.[86] However, the size of the staff depended on the size of the output. Also, Olmer forgot to mention the dough maker and the baker who sold the bread as well as the jack-of-all trades (*padu*), unless these five workers performed more than one function. According to

---

78. Olmer 1908, p.19.
79. Olmer 1908, p. 17.
80. Gol Mohammadi 1371, vol. 1, p. 297.
81. Wills 1893, p. 335.
82. Bradley-Birt 1910, p. 268.

83. Olmer 1908, p. 18.
84. Olmer 1908, p. 18. The price of fuel for *sangak*: 600 kg per day at a cost of 2 *tumans*. Wages: the *shater*, whose work is hard, 3-4 francs/day; the others 1.50 to 2 francs/day. Ibid.
85. Rowghani 1385, pp. 83-94, who provides details as to the varying quantities of leavening and salt. The preferred types of wheat were: *lo`abdar*, *charb lo`abdar*, *qors-e khoshk*, *saf lo`abdar*, *saf khoshk*, *charand*, and *afatzadeh*.
86. Olmer 1908, p. 18; for a very detailed description of a *sangak* oven and the way the baking process proceeded, see Rowghani 1385, pp. 108-83; Bolukbashi 1347.

Rowghani, himself a *sangak* baker, a 1960s bakery with a daily throughput of 480 kg of flour employed eleven persons as follows:

Table 6.1: No. of persons employed in a large *sangak* bakery

Function	No. of persons	Spefication
Shater	2	*Shater + nangir*
Nandar ar	2	*Atash-andaz + dast beh sikh*
Khamirzan	2	*Khamirgir* or *khalifeh + vardasht*
Boteh gozar	2	*Boteh gozar, padu-ye buteh gozar*
Dokkandar	1	.
Pishkar	1	.
Padu	1	.

Source: Rowghani 1385, p.180. For a description of their tasks, see Ibid., pp.202ff.; Bolukbashi 1347, pp. 36-40.

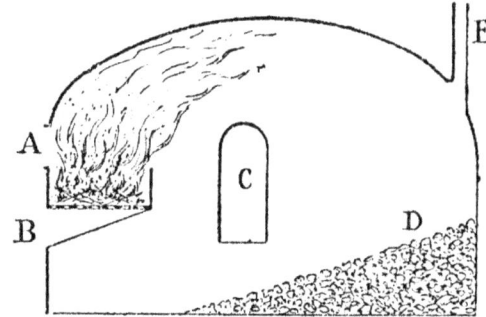

Fig. 2. — Four à cailloux.

A Entrée du combustible.
B Cendrier.
C Ouverture pour le pain.
D Cailloux
E Cheminée.

Fig. 28: Schematic drawing of a *sangak* oven (Olmer 1908, p. 18).

Nowadays the oven and the pebbles are heated by oil or gas. Initially the *motorchi* replaced the *buteh gozar*, but in the 1960s he was replaced by the *padu*. Finally, there was also the *nanforush*, who peddled bread of the first dough in the morning and of the second dough in the afternoon that was left unsold on the counter and/or took bread that had been ordered to the homes of the clients concerned.[87]

Wulff described the typical *sangak* oven of the 1960s as having an inclined, brick-built bank (*sang-kuh*) that is covered with clean river pebbles (*sangak*). In front of the bank there is a fireplace with an iron grill (*sehpayeh*). Fuel and air enter through a hole in the side (*surakh-e zamburak, sulakh-e zamburak*). The oven is covered with a cupola (*taq*) of sun-dried bricks. It has one or two smoke holes (*dud-kash*). When after the firing the pebbles are hot, the fire is either switched to another oven via an iron shutter or the heat is reduced to baking temperature. The dough is the same as with *lavash*, but yoghurt is added instead of leaven. The bakers stand between the trough and a long wooden-handled shovel (*paru*) with a blade of ca. 18 sq. inch and somewhat convex. The end of the blade rests on the ledge in front of the oven and the end of the handle rests in a wooden fork. The baker wets the shovel blade with water (*ab-e khamir*), takes a certain quantity of dough from the trough and stretches it over the shovel blade. He then enters the shovel plus dough covered blade into the oven and puts the dough on the hot pebbles. When he prepares the next bread his assistants watches the baking that takes about 2 minutes. When baked the assistant takes out the bread with a two-pronged fork (*du-shakheh*). The bread weighs

---

87. Bolukbashi 1347, p. 40.

about 1.5 lb (0.68 kg), is soft, and shows the imprint of the pebbles, hence its name.[88]

On demand by the customer, *sangak* bread was sprinkled with sesame, poppy, nigella or coriander seed (*siyah-daneh*) before placing the dough into the oven.[89]

Fig: 29: *Sangak* baking hook (Bolukbashi 1347, p. 33).

Taftun

Taftan, nan-e taftan or *taftun* is a flat, soft, round, somewhat elliptical bread, but thicker than *lavash* made from flour of 84% extraction. It is 40-50 cm in diameter and 5 mm thick and has small holes on its surface. It was and still is a popular type of bread. Because it becomes twisted (*tafteh*) in a hot oven it got its name.[90] Another explanation is that because this bread is thicker than *lavash* it had to stay longer in the oven to become hot or *tafteh*, another meaning of this verb.[91] It was also known as *nan-e komaj*, and was circular in form. It was mostly used to dip in *abgusht* and similar dishes. *Taftun* bread had to be eaten as soon as possible, because after two days it became so hard that is was not edible anymore.[92] It may be this bread that Thevenot described in 1665: "They make large Cakes half a finger thick."[93] Like *sangak*, *taftun* is intermediate in thickness.[94]

The dough for *nan-e taftun* or oven bread is prepared in the same way as that of *sangak*, but it contains less water. Grey flour of bad quality is used and less leavening is used.[95] The oven, which is much larger than the ordinary village *tanur*, is round. In the back the breads are placed on a pile of sand; in a hearth the cheapest fuel is placed, dried horse or camel dung, although since the 1950s mostly low-quality fuel oil was used. This type of fuel produces a lot of smoke and a strong smell that impregnates the bread and does not make it appetizing. In 1900, the dough in Tehran consisted of large balls weighing about 400 g; it was poorly baked and was sold at 7-8 cents. It was the bread of the poor, it was awful, according to Olmer.[96]

A *taftun* bakery in the 1960s employed the following staff: (i) *khalifeh* who makes the dough; (ii) *chunehgir* who makes bread lumps from the risen dough; (iii) *nunavar* who flattens the lumps with a roller; (iv) *shater* who takes the flattened dough and with a *nandan* sticks it to the wall of the oven; (v) *nunvasun* who takes the baked bread from the oven; (vi) *tarazudar* who sells the baked bread; (vii) *kash sab* who pours the dried whey into the water and mixes it; (viii) *pishkar* who looks after the flour, sieves, stores and weighs it for use by the doughmaker; (ix) *padu* or *pakar* or the jack-of-all trades, (x) *vardas* who assists the dough maker, and (xi) *nunforush* who peddles *taftun* bread for sale.[97] Figure 27 provides a plan of the workplace of the various bakery workers as well the various functional parts of the bakery.

---

88. Wullf 1966, pp. 294-95; see also Rowghani 1385 and Shahri 1368, vol. 2, pp. 385-87.
89. Polak 1865, vol. 1, p. 110; Wullf 1966, p. 295.
90. Zavosh 1370, p. 243; Koelz 1983, p. 166; Polak 1865, vol. 1, p. 110; Faridi et al. 1981, p. 428.
91. Bolukbashi 1348, p. 45.
92. Rowghani 1385, p. 37.
93. Thevenot 1971, vol. 2, p. 96.
94. Koelz 1983, p. 166.
95. For a detailed description of the making of dough, see Bolukbashi 1348, p. 48.
96. Olmer 1908, p. 19. Mazut is a heavy, low quality fuel oil.
97. Bolukbashi 1348, pp. 49-50; Shahri 1368, vol. 2, pp. 388-90.

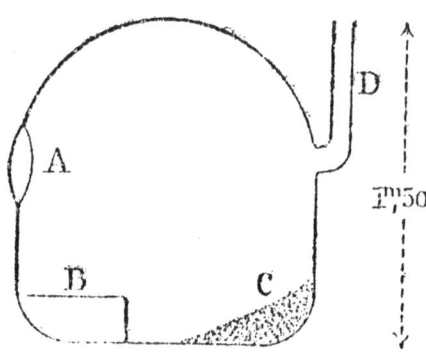

Fig. 30: Schematic drawing of a *taftun* oven (Olmer 1908, p. 20).

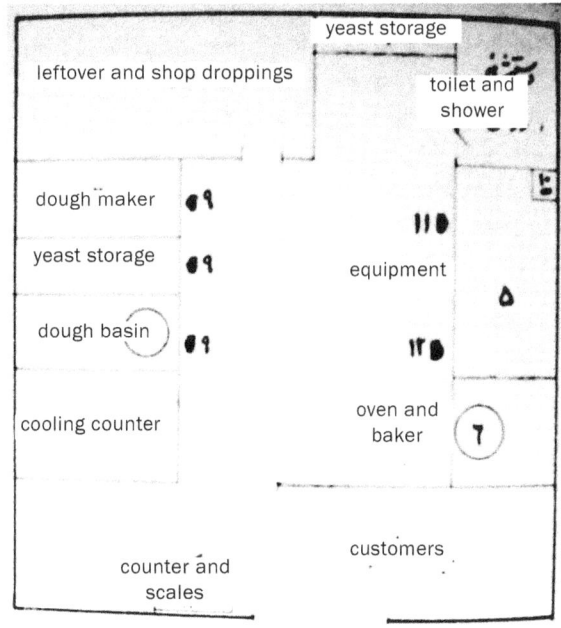

Fig. 31: Schematic view of a bakery (Bolukbashi 1348, p. 47).

In Larestan, *taftun* is a luxury bread made with fine wheat flour with added yeast and butter separated into circular patty and covered with a thick sheet of cloth to make it rise. Then decorative designs are engraved on top using the tine of a specific tiny tong. Then the top surface is smeared with saffron and sprinkled with sesame seeds and finally baked in oven; they are served at breakfast. This type of *taftun* remains fresh for a long time and thus is good to send as a gift to friends and relatives far away.[98] *Taftun* was also baked in villages. In Davarabad (Khorasan),

> Taftoon is a flat circular loaf about three-quarters of an inch thick and a foot across, baked in semi-subterranean ovens in the household hayats. A supply sufficient for the needs of all families in the hayat is made daily by one or more women of the hayat households, for without shortening the bread stales quickly in the dry air. Balls of grayish dough are patted by hand into the flat discs while the oven, more or less a cylindrical cave, is heated with brush and dung. When all is ready the baker extends an arm down into the oven and slaps the loaf onto the clay lining. When it loosens, it is baked; and when baked, it is usually consumed soon afterward. One such loafs weighs about 1 kg [2.2 lbs], the normal portion for one adult per meal.[99]

According to some, *nan-e taftun* in a different form is the same as *barbari*. *Taftun* like *barbari* is baked in a *tanur*. In 1988, some *taftuni* bakers changed their oven to that of the *for-e gardun*, a new Iranian system. This is better from the point of view of health and ergonomics. Because the entire

---

98. Mahmoodian 2007, p. 86.

99. Alberts 1963, p. 175

surface of the bread is exposed to the heat, while the inside is also baked and the surface is smooth. Also, it looks more desirable than the *taftun-e tanuri*, yet consumers have not yet grown accustomed to it.[100]

Like *taftun* other thick breads were also baked in villages and by migratory groups. The common bread in the village of Owrazan was of two types: one *lavash*, the other *jow kelas*, which is a thick, small, round black barley bread. The same held for the village in Boluk-e Zahra (Qazvin), where in addition to *lavash* or *gerdeh*, thick barley bread was consumed that was locally known as *doruzhdeh* or large.[101] In Baluchistan a type of bread was baked known as *galfach*, which:

> like all Baluchi breads, was round and flat, in this case about 38 centimeters (15 inches) across and a bit less than a centimer (3/8 inch) high, relatively light, leavened, made of wheat. The bottom of *galfach* was smooth, while the top was bumpy and also marked with what appeared to be a triangular brand. *Galfach* was baked in a characteristic fashion. After the dough, *hamir*, was prepared, had risen, and was ready to bake, the amount appropriate for one *galfach* was placed on a large, very shallow, concave iron disk, *tin* (pronounced 'teen'), was spread across the disk, and was pressed down and flattened with the fngertips, leaving indentations. Meanwhile, a small hearth fire had been started-in the center of the tent in the winter, toward the end of the tent or outside in warmer or hot weather-and the twigs had been allowed to burn down to hot ashes. On top of the hot ashes was placed a small, iron, triangular stand, *padink*, and on top of this the disk with the dough, the dough facing down, about 4 inches from the hot ashes. After 5 to 20 minutes, the bread,

triangularly seared from the hot iron stand, was removed from the *tin* with a spatula, *nan gwag*, and was ready to eat. *Galfach* was eaten on a daily basis, plain or with clarified butter, *rogani pas*, or with yoghurt, *bastag* (Persian: *mast*), together with other foods such as onion, or in a liquid *hatuk*. *Galfach* was too airy to hold well and was usually eaten fresh.[102]

In the village of Yush, the common bread was *gateh-nun*, i.e. big bread, or as big as contemporary machine bread. It was made from wheat (*gandom-e divak*) and water (*ow mal*).[103]

Barbari

The thickest bread, like a thick pancake, is *barbari* or *Khorasani*, which were its Tehrani names. It is a recent newcomer as it was introduced by Afghan immigrants, who were called *barbaris* by the Iranians. They settled in the south of Tehran in the second half of the nineteenth century and were the exclusive bakers of this kind of bread.[104] Its main baking location was Tehran; in other towns it was less used. Therefore, it is also known as the bread of native Tehranis, although it is made in some towns in E. Iran, whence it came via Tehran. This leavened bread is shaped like *taftun*, but thicker and made from flour of 77% extraction. It is of medium hardness, oval-shaped, 3-4 cm thick, about 70-80 cm long, 40-50 cm wide, and weighing about 900 grams each. This bread comes the closest to European bread; it is more expensive than the other common breads. The original bread is different from what is baked nowadays. The original one was

---

100. Zavosh 1370, pp. 243-44.
101. Al-e Ahmad 1333, p. 28; Ibid., 1337, p. 63.

102. Salzman 1994, p. 72.
103. Tahbaz 1342, p. 44.
104. Mostowfi n.d., vol. 1, 400; Shahri 1386, vol. 2, p. 393. "Barbaris are emigrants from Afghanistan, from Firuzkuh, on the Kashan river, with the administrative centre Qal`a-i-Nau. In European literature they are called the Hezara. By them this name is apparently never used, but is applied to the Iranian tribes Timuris and Jamshidis." Ivanow 1926, p. 155.

like *taftuni* only thicker, higher and its two corners more stretched out; it was baked in a subterranean oven and became popular in Tehran and Mashhad, where many Barbaris were located.¹⁰⁵

Nowadays, the *barbari* oven is about one meter higher above ground and made with bricks and can bake 50-60 loaves at one time. This type of *barbari* is the same as the *sughati* bread of Baku. The latter type of bread baking was learnt by Iranian migrants working in Baku before 1917. This bread brought as gifts (*sughati*) then spread to some towns in Azerbaijan and then to Tehran and other towns. In some towns of Azerbaijan, such as Zanjan, where until 60 years ago *barbari* was called *Baki panjeh kashideh-ye Baku'i*, or 'Baku baked stretched bread.' The reason for this was that the *shater* when flattening the dough did so on a special table in front of the oven and before putting it on the baking shovel - *paru*, he made furrows in it with his finger point so that after the bread was baked it had a special pattern called *panjeh kesh Baku*. Now this is done with a special wooden instrument. In other Azerbaijani towns they called this bread *somy*, in Gilan *pirvoy* after the Russian word, indicating the path of penetration of this type of bread.¹⁰⁶

Barbari was also known as *taptapi*, *nan-e tabrizi*, Baku'i and Afghani,¹⁰⁷ and in general, any kind of thick bread is called *nan-e kopoli*. But sometimes these names are used with different meanings, such as in Larestan, where *taptapi* is a kind of thin circular bread baked on a *taveh* over wood burning fires. It was very popular in Lar where it was made daily and served fresh at breakfast spread with melted butter and drops of *mahva*; it is now baked in an oven.¹⁰⁸

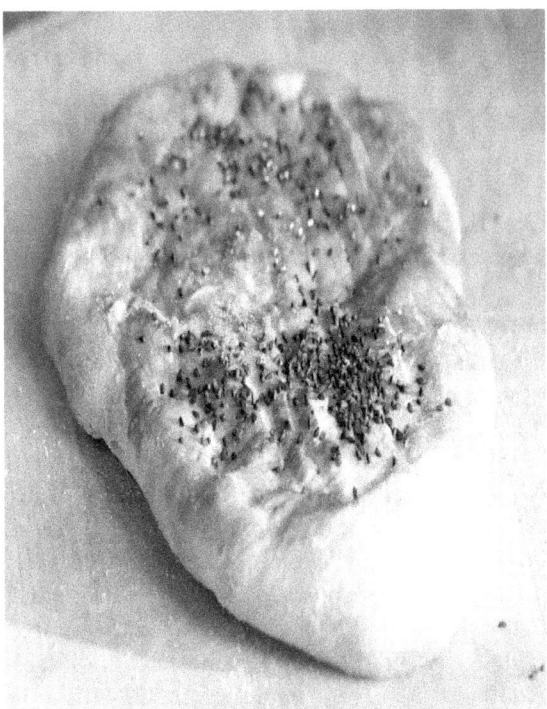

Fig. 32: *Barbari* bread (Mage 2013).

There were quite a few other breads that were thicker than *lavash* and quite similar to *barbari* that were made in villages and certain towns. "The dough, made from flour with high rates of extraction, salt, water, and leaven, is left to stand for a rather long time, or else it rises during baking. A single cook can flatten the pieces of dough by hand and press several at a time against the oven walls with a cushion; baking time is about 30 minutes." Compared to the bread more common in villages or the bread specific to pastoral nomads, it seems to be an intermediate type of bread, which can be baked, for ten minutes, either on a *saj* or in a *tanur*. It keeps for no more than a day or two and thus is usually made every day.¹⁰⁹

---

105. Rowghani 1385, p. 37; Zavosh 1370, p. 246; Faridi et al. 1981, p. 428.
106. Zavosh 1370, pp. 246-47.
107. Koelz 1983, p. 166; *Nan-e tabrizi* cost 3 *shahi*s in Dezful in 1882, suggesting that this was either an early diffusion of *barbari*-type bread or some other kind of bread. Najm al-Molk 1341, p. 22.
108. Mahmoodian 2007, p. 80. *Taptapi vapokh*. A small circular cushion used to spread dough by slapping back and

forth to make it flat and round and then flip it over the *taveh* to bake. Mahmoodian 2007, p. 80-81.
109. Desmet-Grégoire 1980, pp. 271-73; Digard 1973, pp. 190-91.

This type of bread was known under various names. In Talesh it was called *penjekesh*, but east of the Safidrud it as referred to as *kulas* or *kulus* was baked for special occasions, or when little time is available, for example when the women take part in the agricultural activities in summer.[110] Further east, in Kandelus (Mazandaran), this type of bread was again known as *penjikash* (normal bread, long and stretched).[111] In Yush, the name of the bread depended on the shape and form given to the dough. If the balls are pressed in round form against the oven wall this is called *lavash*, if there is hand impressed on it they are called *panjeh-kash*. If they are somewhat elongated they are called *patrazi* (i.e., *pa darazi*). Smaller round breads are called *tetok*, and with a glass they make patterns on the dough.[112] In Owrazan, when there is a party or guests they make *panjeh-kash*, which is long and light and made with wheat and milk and smeared with egg yolk on top, sometimes also molasses. Another type is *gort*, its dough made with milk and mixed and covered with mashed walnuts which becomes crisper (*bereshtehtar*). They also make other breads which are part of a family's skills.[113] *Golaj* is bread similar to *barbari*, but baked to 1.5 inches thickness, which is popular in Gorgan and Mazandaran.[114] In Baluchistan,

> The most hardy wheat bread was the dense, heavy *wari* around 5 centimeters (2 inches) thick and about 38 centimers (15 inches) across, with a tough crust. However, *wari*, unlike *galfach* and especially *lawash*, would hold its moisture and remain edible for quite a few hours, up to a whole day. So *wari* was favored for times when bread had to hold for a period, such as overnight for eating at breakfast, but especially for occasions such as meals during migration, when food preparation had to be kept to a minimum, and as people depended upon ready-to-eat food that had been prepared ahead of time.[115]

Nan-e bulki

Among the new types of bread *nan-e bulki* is one of the most interesting *nan-e fori* that is used to prepare sandwiches. It has been known since 1931. As indicated by its name it is baked in a *fourre*, i.e. in a European oven. The motor of the old *fourres* worked like a primus stove. The modern ovens are fully automated and don't have the problems of the old ones. This type of bread was also brought by Iranian migrants. Nowadays the output of European oven baking is referred to as *nanha-ye fantazi*, and the old method is no longer used. The heat source for the modern oven is electricity and they are simple to operate. They bake all kinds of bread such as: *nan-e sabusdar* (bran) without salt, *shirin, rowghani, sukhari* (rusks), etc. in various forms and shapes, adapted to consumers' wishes, hence the name *fantezi*. As a result, demand for breads such as *rowghani, qandi* and *shirmal* has completely fallen off. *Nan-e furi* uses a special kind of yeast that gives a nice taste and makes it more digestible. This yeast is from a tree flower that grows in N. Iran and is known as *khaml* (dogsbane?). In the past these bakeries prepared the yeast themselves, now it is supplied by the Grain and Bread Organization (*Sazman-e Ghalleh va Nan*). Initially *nan-e furi* was mainly consumed by foreigners, but now Tehranis also eat it as a normal part of their diet.[116] Hajj Ezzat al-Din Shahrivari was the first person to introduce *nan-e bulki*; Shahrivar is a location near Ardabil. Thereafter many people from the same village worked in the same trade and they dominate this trade. Outsiders are rare, but invest

---

110. Bazin and Bromberger 1982, p. 81.
111. Jahangiri 1367, p. 81.
112. Tahbaz 1342, pp. 44 45.
113. Al-e Ahmad 1333, p. 29.
114. Wulff 1966, p. 291.

---

115. Salzmann 1994, pp. 72-73.
116. Zavosh 1370, pp. 247-48.

often with a Shahrivari. A person who owns one-fourth of a bakery received 500,000 *riyal*/month fixed payment in 1990; a high-level government official made 8,500 *tuman*s at that time.[117]

Already in the 1950s, "Numerous varieties of wheat, dark-rye and so-called French bread are widely available in Tehran, thanks to the demands of the foreign colony and Armenian minority, but most villagers have not sampled them, and those who have disliked their flavor and flimsiness and were shocked by their prices."[118] Since around 1970, with the growing expatriate community in Tehran and increased Westernization of the middle-class, rye bread loaves were made and promoted by some non-traditional urban bakeries as well as so-called 'diet' (*rezhimi*) and 'fancy' (*fantezi*) bread. Other types of European bread (*nan-e tost, nan-e mashini*) can also be found in Tehran and other large cities.[119]

Speciality Breads and Pastries

Aside from breads baked for normal consumption, there are special kinds for the holidays and other special occasions. The normal dough is enriched with milk, sugar, honey, eggs, shortening, or yogurt and therefore these breads (*nan-e shiri, fatir, nan-e shirin, nan-e shirmal*) are actually closer to pastry.

Nan-e khoshk

Shahri lists five different bread doughs under the heading of *khoshkeh-pazi*: (i) dough prepared with oil (*rowghan*); (ii) dough prepared with little oil and milk or sugar, during baking shireh is smeared on top of it (*shirmal*); (iii) dough mixed with flour and sugar (*qandi*); (iv) dough mixed with sugar and ginger (*zanjabili*); and (v) dough mixed with milk or milk and water (*shiri*).[120]

Bread like a rusk or biscuit generically known as *nan-e khoshk* (or as *nan-e dunameh*) in modern times has a long history. Already in the tenth century a kind of dry bread or biscuit, was reported known as *kak* or *ka`k*. It was much older as it already mentioned by Strabo ten centuries earlier. The bread may be of Egyptian origin.[121] Later similar kinds of rusks or biscuit type breads were also baked in Iran notably *nan-e rowghani*, *nan-e khoshk*, or *khoshkeh*. It was thicker than *nan-e Semnani* and its dough balls were two and a half times bigger; it is the same as to-day's *nan-e rowghani*. This bread becomes dry two hours after having exited the oven, can be stored, and made fresh again by sprinkling water (*gol nam*) on it.[122] In Tabriz in the 1950s, there were two types of dry bread or *khoshkeh*, there was the European type and a bigger version called *panjareh*, so called because it had holes in it.[123]

Nan-e khoshk is made from unleavened dough, but contains melted sheep's butter or fat, or nowadays sheep milk. In 1900, the dough was kneaded with 4 parts of flour, 2 parts of water, and one part of leaven, or dough of the previous day. After kneading for 5 minutes, one-quarter of a salty solution was added and one-quarter of sheep or cow fat. This was kneaded for one quarter of an hour, which resulted in a very thick and homogeneous dough that is spread out on a marble table with a wooden roller. After some time they cut circles of 80 cm diameter, these circles were placed in a willow form covered with cloths. Then a man takes the bread, moulds them and puts them to the

---

117. Zavosh 1370, vol. 1, pp. 251-52.
118. Alberts 1963, p. 176.
119. Desmet-Grégoire 1989.
120. Shahri 1368, vol. 2, pp. 390-91. In the fifteenth century there was a type of bread called *juvalak*, which was baked

red-hot in ghee. At`ameh 1360, p. 174. For a letter asking a relative to send ginger bread, see [http://www.qajarwomen.org/archive/detail/27].
121. Spuler 1952, p. 508 (*ka`k*); Elahi 2010. This type of bread, made for travelers, was also known as *baksamat*. At`ameh 1360, p. 65, who also mentions *kak* and *nan-e khoshk*. Ibid., pp. 12, 16, 19, 23, 26, 42, 59-60 (*kak*), 107, 127 (*khoshk*), 167 (*nan-e rowghani*).
122. Rowghani 1385, p. 38.
123. Oral communication Hasan Javadi 2011.

wall of the oven. It is seldom that they fall. Thus, one puts 12 breads which stay there for quarter of an hour. During that time the other ovens are heated. Each is used in turns. The ovens number about 12 and are like the *taftun* oven, but the hearth where the fuel is has an air intake, which allows

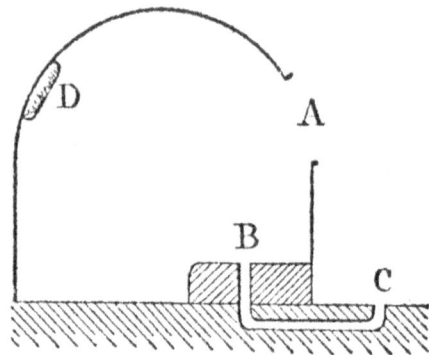

Fig. 4.
Four pour le pain roghani.

A Ouverture.
B Sole pour le combustible.
C Appel d'air.
D Position des pains.

Fig. 33: Schematic drawing of an oven for *nan-e rowghani* (Olmer 1908, p. 21).

it to reach much higher temperature with a less bad odor. The oven is heated by burning ca. 2 kg of horse and camel dung. When all is burnt, a man with a wet broom passes along the entire interior surface to remove the soot that falls in the back. The bread is rather white, dry and good and in 1905 cost 3 *qran*s, 10 *shahi*s per *man* or 0.60 fr/kg.[124]

Rusks, biscuits, and a special form of very dry bread, called 'twice-fired,' are specially made for travelers; and the Armenians prepare a kind of bun, which is made with flour and ghee, slightly sweetened and sprinkled with sesame seeds. Sesame and poppy seeds are often used to ornament and favour the breads, especially the 'tannur' variety.[125] It was also made in the rural areas such as in Kandelus (Mazandaran), where it was called *rah-nun* or 'road bread' (and less so *nan-e rowghani* or *shirini*) which was given as a present when going on journey, hence the name.[126] In the 1950s, *nan-e khoshk* or *rowghani* bread became dry and brittle like biscuits. It was available unsweetened or ordinary (*ma'muli*), often sprinkled with sesame seed (*konjed*) and in a sweet variety (*shirin*) for which grape syrup (*shireh*) or sugar (*shekar*) is added to the dough.[127]

Nan-e Semnani

The so-called *nan-e Semnani* was a totally white wheat bread, just like to-day's *nan-e Osku'i*. Both breads are named after the town where it was made. Osku, a town in the environs of Tabriz, exports its dry bread to Tehran and hence its name. When *nan-e Semnani* came out of the oven it was nice and fresh, but it became totally dry after two hours. This allowed this bread to be stored for a long period and when needed for consumption it sufficed to sprinkle water (*gol nam*) on it to make it fresh again.[128] Semnan, in particular was famous for its so-called "tea-bread (nun-i chai), a kind of rusk or cake for which Semnan enjoys a particular renown." It was also known as *nan-e semnani* or *nan-e khoshk*.[129] Not every one was enamored of

---

124. Olmer 1908, pp. 21-22. Wages as for *sangak*; the job of the man who put the bread in the oven was very hard, as he had to place half his body into the very hot oven; he worked 2 hours and then left. Price of dung: 1 *qran* per 10 *batman* (1.60 fr/kg). Fat: 1 fr/kg. Ibid., p. 22. See also Shahri 1368, vol. 2, pp. 391-92.
125. Wills 1893, p. 336.
126. Jahangiri 1367, p. 81.
127. Wulff 1966, p. 291.
128. Rowghani 1385, p. 38.
129. Jackson 1911, p. 151; Safinezhad 1345, p. 38.

the Semnan rusks. Goldsmid related that in 1872, at Semnan, "we received from the Governor presents of a kind of bread or rusk for which the place is celebrated, but which, as it had been baked the year before, we did not appreciate."[130] In Qom, the British novelist Sackville-West found "the brown native bread, as crisp as a biscuit."[131] In Larestan, there was a similar kind of bread resembling biscuit in taste and structure, which was called *taftu*.[132] There is also *nan-e khoshk- e-shirin*, sweet brittle bread and *nan-e khoshke-tanur*, brittle bread, which both are baked in gentle heat.

Shirmal

Other special, or luxury, varieties includes that of *nan-e shirmal*, which is made like *barbari*, except that milk instead of water is used, in addition to a bit of sugar; it is eaten during breakfast or with tea. It is also called *nan-e dashtari*, a fine bread, more like a cake, eaten on feast days and often sent as a present to friends and relatives.[133] On special occasions fine bread (*nan-e dashtari*) is baked. For the dough of that bread (*nan-e shirmal*) sugar, honey, eggs, milk, and yoghurt are added with flour (*ard-e dashtari*) from which the coarser particles have been sifted. After rolling and stretching many slots are cut in the dough and it is baked in a *tanur*, where the cuts open and appear as lattice work. Often poppy seed, sesame, cardamom, grated roots of nard plant (*sombol-e hendi, nardin, nigella sativa*) are sprinkled over the bread.[134] In Tehran there was a type of bread known as *nan-e tereshti*, which was a tasty, sweet, round, thick bread prepared with milk that came from the village of Teresht, situated at 10 km from Tehran.[135] There is also *shirmal* called *tar kelas*, where instead of walnuts, fresh mountain herbs are mixed in the dough. They also make *shirmal* with honey, such as *valok* and *abeshan*.[136] In the village of Yush, they bake better breads such as bread with *gandom-e shuleh* or *gandom–e `Iraq* and instead of water they make dough with milk, so that it becomes *shir-mal*. They also bake it with a little *rowghan*.[137] The bread preparation is the same as for *nun-e atash*, only the dough is thicker, while one often adds some milk, in which case the bread is called *shir-e kolba* or *shirkulba*.[138] Among the Feyli Lurs, *chezanal* is a wheat bread, of which the dough is mixed with milk.[139] The Turkmen also made "bread with oil or clarified butter."[140]

Nan-e qandi

Sugar bread or *nan-e qandi* or *shekari* is sweet bread like *taftun*, is either eaten at breakfast or with tea. It is similar to *nan-e gisu*, an Armenian sweetbread. These types of bread are not recent innovations, for Clavijo in 1400 reported that after having drunk milk, various rice dishes were brought, as well as "thin cakes of bread sugared over, and some vegetables."[141] Such breads were first baked in oil and then sugar was sprinkled on them.[142] *Nan-e tutak* is a small version of *nan-e qandi*, the size of a hand that is especially made for children.[143]

---

130. Goldsmid 1876, vol. 1, p. 384.
131. Sackville-West 1992, p. 120.
132. Mahmoodian 2007, p. 86.
133. Wulff 1966, p. 291; see, e.g., [http://www.qajarwomen.org/archive/detail/40]. *Shirmal* perhaps is the same as the fifteenth century milk-baked bread (*nan-e shir pokhteh*). Atma`eh 1360, p. 66.
134. Wulff 1966, p. 295.
135. Shahri 1386, vol. 2, p. 393.
136. Al-e Ahmad 1333, p. 29.
137. Tahbaz 1342, p. 44; see also Al-e Ahmad 1337, p. 63.
138. Bazin and Bromberger 1982, p. 82.
139. Feilberg 1952, p. 96.
140. Conolly 1834, vol. 1, p. 164.
141. Le Strange 1928, pp. 247, 267 ("pancakes and sugared bread."). For the nineteenth century, see Lycklama 1873, vol. 1, p. 383 (sugared bread).
142. E`tesam al-Molk 1351, p. 229.
143. Shahri 1386, vol. 2, p. 391, n. 1.

Komaj

According to Olmer, *komaj*, *kumaj* or *nan-e komaj* was a kind of bread that originally seems to have been peculiar to Isfahan. It was more expensive than the other breads, because it was better, more leavened and better baked.[144] However, it seems to have been a popular kind of luxury bread in the fifteenth century.[145] This was certainly the case in the sixteenth century, because recipes for several varieties of *komaj* are given in a contemporary cookbook.[146] In the mid-nineteenth century this bread was described as "The *koomaj*, a small thick cake, is made in a metal shape, and cooked in a *koora* or small oven, like pastry. The best kind of bread is about three quarters of an inch [20 mm] thick, while some of the inferior sort, baked on the girdle, is almost as thin as cartridge paper."[147] Thus, there appears to have been more than one kind of this bread. The deciding factor, of course, is that it had better ingredients and was pastry-like, as is clear from the situation in Kandelus (Mazandaran) where *kemaj* dough was mixed with milk, ghee, *sar-e shir*, etc.[148] Likewise in Tabriz, where *komaj* is a soft brownish croissant type of bread with egg on top- often made for Ramazan.[149] However, the same term also could denote a different type of bread. In Veramin, *nan-e taftun* or *komaj*, was a thick wheat bread, like the circular *barbari* of to-day, but brownish in color; it was mostly used in *ab-gusht* when fresh; but after two days it became very dry and hard and inedible.[150] *Kumaj* or *kemej* bread is most appreciated and its dough is made with milk, or clarified butter, yoghurt, ground nuts and saffron (Deylaman), or eggs and milk (Eshkevar). It is prepared on the occasion of festivities, in particular when family members leave on journey.[151]

Fatir

Apart from being a generic term to denote unleavened dough, *fatir* also referred to a special kind of this bread. It was a thin, circular, unleavened bread of about 20 cm wide. According to Koelz it "is sometimes seen," but in Lar it was bread that was usually served at breakfast.[152]

SWEET BREADS

In the fifteenth century and later, very thin bread, was known as *nan-e mashush*. It was mostly baked during feasts, enriched with grape syrup or *dushab* and egg-white after which it was eaten.[153] In Tabriz, this type of bread was known as *kuka*, of which there were two types (i) normal and (ii) *kuka-ye ichli* (meaning- with filling) on top covered with egg yolk.[154] Elsewhere in Iran, "There is a distinctive bread here called *kiuke*. On round slabs of well raised dough, a foot across, a design is put on with a mold, or even by hand, and the whole smeared with eggwhite and saffron so that it has a glazed golden surface. Its attractiveness is further increased by a crimping of the border."[155] In case grape juice was used the bread was also called *nan-e dushabi*. A variety of this bread was when pieces of bread, not necessarily *khoshkeh*, were thrown into *dushab* and then eaten. According to Reineggs, "dushab with bread is a delicacy to the hungry."[156] *Paplus* was a kind of bread known in the fifteenth century that was soaked in oil and syrup.[157]

---

144. Olmer 1908, p. 20.
145. Atma`eh 1360, pp. 17-18, 32, 50-51, 60, 79, 82-83.
146. Anonymous 1360, pp. 41-49.
147. Binning 1857, vol. 2, pp. 66-67.
148. Jahangiri 1367, p. 81; see also Al-e Ahmad 1337, p. 63 and Anonymous 1360, pp. 41-49.
149. Hasan Javadi oral communication (2014).
150. Safinezhad 1345, p. 38.
151. Bazin and Bromberger 1982, pp. 82-83.
152. Koelz 1983, p. 166; Mahmoodian 2007, p. 179; Jahangiri 1367, p. 81.
153. Atma`eh 1360, pp. 166, 175; Borhan 1342.
154. Hasan Javadi oral communication (2014).
155. Koelz 1983, p. 165.
156. Chodzko 1842, p. 60; Reineggs 1807, p. 121.
157. At`ameh 1360, p. 178.

Shol-sholak is a kind of pancake as it made with watery dough and in this way put on a very hot and flaming *saj*. Because of the liquid nature of the dough it becomes round and very thin, and like a pancake, each side is baked in turn.[158] Probably something like it is *tiri*, a very thin cake rolled on a wooden board with a roller (*tir*). This roller is also used to take the bread from the pan. Feilberg did not know how the dough was made, but said the bread was delicious.[159]

Bardiari is bread made from wheat crushed on the *berdingelow* and thus contains many large pieces of grain.[160] The Lurs also made "*nun-e saki-karr*" that is prepared the same way as normal bread, but the hollow side of the *towa* is washed and sprinkled with water. It is then put on the fire with the wet side is up. When the *towa* is almost dry a big ball of dough is placed on it which is stretched with the hands, the imprint of which is seen on the bread. Later the *towa* is put back again and thus the bread is directly above the fire, which is low at that time. This bread is darker than normal bread.[161]

In Sarvestan (Fars), *nan-e shirini*, is a special kind of sweet bread baked at *Nowruz*; it is unleavened, but mixed with pears, ghee, molasses, sugar, *hel* and cloves. It was not much different from *nan-e nazok*, save that it is finer. When it is on the *saj* and is somewhat crisp (*bereshteh*), they cut it nicely in slices with a knife. Sometimes they do not cut it but bake the two sides and then take it; this is mostly done for themselves not for guests.[162] Also, in Tuyserkan there were several sweet breads baked at home such as *nan-e charb*, *khoshk*, and *kolucheh*.[163]

---

158. Homayuni 1371, p. 153.
159. Feilberg 1952, p. 95.
160. Feilberg 1952, p. 96.
161. Feilberg 1952, p. 95.
162. Homayuni 1371, pp. 150-51.
163. Gol Mohammadi 1371, vol. 1, p. 298. A round sweetbread made with oil and sugar known as *kolucheh* or *kolicheh* was already well-known in the fifteenth century. Atma`eh 1360, pp. 26, 32, 50, 84, 92, 113, 162.

In Larestan (Fars), a flat, circular bread about the size of pita bread, was baked over the *taveh* and hence its name *bala taveh*. It was served at breakfast with honey, and was a rich person's dish. In the same area, *shaliteh* was baked, a kind of soft, thick bread, the size and shape of pita bread. It is

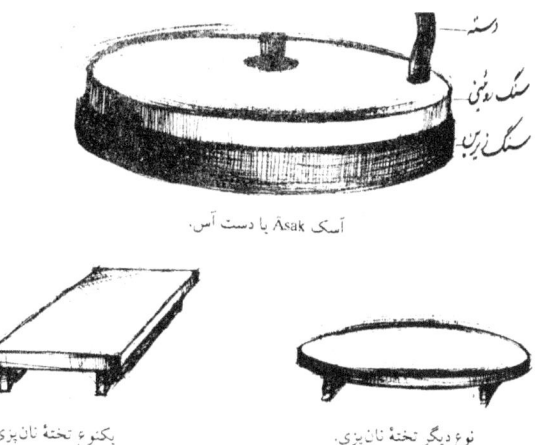

Fig. 34: Rural baking implements (Homayuni 1371, p. 152).

usually smeared with butter and *mahveh* (paste of anchovy fish, mustard, salt) and served at breakfast; it remains soft and fresh for several days.[164] Another bread from Larestan, which apparently is the "best kind of all breads" is *gapok*. It is circular, about 30 cm in diameter, 4 to 6 mm thick and is baked in a *tanur*. When its surface is smeared with *mahva* and butter it is called *gapok-e mahva va rowghani*. It is served by itself at breakfast with tea, otherwise is served with fried eggs, sunny side up or scrambled, jam or honey. *Gapok* remains fresh for several days and when it gets dry it is cut into small pieces to make *talit* to serve at lunch. *Gapok* was baked at home; a variety of it which is called *now* was made daily for sale in bakeries in the larger towns such as Lar and Bandar-e Lengeh. According to Mahmoodian, nowadays this bread is made in modern ovens, but it is not as good as when baked

---

164. Mahmoodian 2007, pp. 42, 174.

in a *tanur*.¹⁶⁵ Yet another Larestani bread is *jaradak*, which is homemade bread, which is covered with melted butter and powder of yellow flower petals; it is popular in Lar and Khur where it is also called *jarazok*. Another variety of this bread is known as *jaradak-e khamir sheri*, which is a kind of *taftun*.¹⁶⁶

The Jews of Kurdistan baked *laxma raqiqa* bread, which was thin and flat, round and dry, and about 50 cm in diameter. It was baked once a month on a convex iron plate (*doqa*). It was made of the same dough as their thick bread, but it was flattened-out to a thin leaf and baked on both sides for a few seconds. This bread could be turned into a sweet cake by folding and filling it with cheese or nuts."¹⁶⁷

If bread was not covered with some condiment, it was also used in dried form to mix with butter, oil, cheese, or honey, which dish is known as *changal*, *changali* or *changal khast* and one that was well-known in Safavid Tabriz in 1647.¹⁶⁸ A similar dish in Tabriz is *duymaj* that consists of dried *lavash* crumbs with butter and cheese.¹⁶⁹

'Roller' bread

This is a special kind of bread that is made from the dough that stuck to the dough roller at the end of the baking activity. In Sarvestan (Fars) the baker scrapes dough from the roller or *tir* with a knife and makes small thick pieces of dough. One piece is heated in a small pan (*toveh*). The dough is placed on the small depressed convex part of the *saj* and when one side is ready it is then turned around. Then the pan is scraped clean and a new piece is put in it to be baked.¹⁷⁰ The bread was also made in Larestan, called *chovali*, when bread was home made. Despite the fact that women used a roller or *choveh* around which a thin sheet of dough was wrapped to prevent sticking there nevertheless were still pieces of dough that stuck to it. With a roller, the dough was flattened over a circular smooth flat stone (*khu*) into a wide, very thin patty to be baked on the top of the *bereza*. *Chovali* was a poor quality bread that was saved for servants. The bread was also mentioned in a Lari proverb: *agar nabashad gapoki agar nabashad chovali*, i.e. if there would be no *gapok* (the finest Lari bread) then there is always *chovali*. This proverb means that you should be content with what you have.¹⁷¹ A similar kind of bread was made in Owrazan (east of Taleqan); it was not thin, but made into solid small buns. It was this kind of bread that they softened in *ash*, milk or *dugh*.¹⁷²

Pizza-like bread

There were breads that were mixed with vegetables such as onions, herbs and asafetida. In the fifteenth century there was *kashkineh*, bread made of barley, millet, beans, and lentils.¹⁷³ In Hamadan and Tuyserkan a kind of luxury bread baked in the villages and some urban households was known as *gerdeh*, which was much like *barbari*. It was produced by making a crust of onions and walnut kernels on it and therefore it was called *gerdeh-ye maghz*. It was like pizza and very tasty.¹⁷⁴ According to Goldsmid, at Burj-i-Alam Khan, near Deshtak some of the bread was excellent, "but another sort was mixed with asafetida in large quantities, which

---

165. "*Gapok bauna*. A round cushion-shaped implement over which the spread dough is placed to slap on the wall of [the] *tonoor* to get baked into *gapok*." Mahmoodian 2007, p. 211.
166. Mahmoodian 2007, p. 96.
167. Shwartz-Be'eri 2000, p. 46.
168. Chelebi 2010, p. 16. It was already well-known in the fifteenth century, see Atma`eh 1360, pp. 12, 30-31, 38, 42, 50, 57-58. *Bushnazheh*, a mixture of flour, date-syrup and bread is variety of *changal*. At`ameh 1360, p. 180.
169. Oral communication by Hasan Javadi (2014).
170. Homayuni 1371, p. 150. A similar kind of bread was made in Baluchistan, Ibid., p. 150, note 1.
171. Mahmoodian 2007, p. 115.
172. Al-e Ahmad 1333, pp. 28-29.
173. At`ameh 1360, p. 172; it also referred to baked wheat soaked in sour milk and dried in the sun, after which raw onions, a purslain stalk are put on it.
174. Desmet-Grégoire 1980, pp. 271-73; Gol-Mohammadi vol. 1, p. 298.

makes it very unpalatable and nauseous, though the natives delight in it."[175] In Jewish villages in Kurdistan, *zudita tanura* bread was baked in an oven as implied by its name. It was a round, thick bread, 20 cm in diameter, eaten fresh. The dough was prepared a day in advance, from flour, salt, water and yeast. The dough was kneaded into balls and spread with a mixture of oil, hot pepper and chopped onion. The balls were then flattened, the lower side moistened, and then placed on the interior wall of the glowing oven, a quilted patchwork cloth protecting the hands.[176] In Sarvestan (Fars) a type of bread called *qopak* was baked, when one side of *lavash* is toasted then some boiled spinach is put on it and it twisted (*pichideh*) in such a way that the spinach is also baked and becomes crisp (*bereshteh*).[177]

Bread enhancements

Bakers early on realized that the attraction of bread is partly in the eye of the beholder. Therefore, in the tenth century bakers used borax (*bawraq al-khubz*) as a glazing for bread, imported from Van. This was not only done to make the bread more attractive, but also to slow down molding thus allowing the bread to be stored longer. A contemporary *hisba* manual discouraged its use on health grounds.[178] Another method to make bread more attractive to customers was to whiten the bread (*kafur dar mahasin kashidan*), because they like white bread. More common and less hazardous to one health was the custom to sprinkle bread with a variety of seeds such sesame, caraway, poppy and others to enhance the taste of the bread.[179] This custom already existed during the Safavid period, if not earlier, as the following quote shows:

> They strew generally upon all the Bread, excepting that which is in Leaf, some sleepy Grain, as the Seed of *Poppies*. Seed of *Sesame*, or *Turkish* Corn, of that which they call the Seed of *Mielle*, which the *Botanists* call *Nard*, or Pepperwort; that inclines them to Sleep, which is what they would have it do in the *East*, where they generally lie down after their Meal, as well in the Morning as at Night. Ancient Histories inform us, that they always us'd after their Meals in the *East*, the white Poppy-seed, roasted for the same end. Others strew Anis-seed, or Fennel-seed in the Room of it.[180]

The seeds were usually sprinkled on the bread before it is baked. Around the turn of the twentieth century, "poppy seed, a sort of caraway, and another small round seed are much used for this purpose."[181] Bread sprinkled with such seeds was known in Safavid times and earlier as *nan-e tokhme-ru*, or bread with sweet-smelling seeds on them.

Sweetmeats, confections and pastries

Bakers also made a large variety of sweetmeats, confections and pastries. Before the Safavid period many of these sweet morsels are mentioned, but usually we don't know much about their confection. Apart from various kinds of *halva*, a term that denotes any kind of sweet cake or pastry made with flour, there were *halqachi*, a pastry in the form of a ring, *samuseh* or *sanbuseh*, a small pastry of minced meat of triangular form, *farusheh*, any kind of pastry made with almonds, *qata'i*, a pastry of triangular shape of filled with meat, almonds, pistachios, and *lut*, a mouth-filling pastry. Furthermore, *shab-e gharib* a pastry or sweetmeat distributed at the grave on the first night after the internment

---

175. Goldsmid 1876, p. 278.
176. Shwartz-Be'eri 2000, p. 46.
177. Homayuni 1371, p. 149.
178. Mez 1922, p. 438; Ahsan 1979, p. 88, n. 84; Schwarz 1993, vol. 8, p. 1507.
179. Hay 1937, pp. 103, 270; Von Freygang 1823, p. 326 (poppy seed over bread, "which they consider in Persia as very salutary after meals."); Tavernier 1930, p. 282; Thevenot 1971, vol. 2, p. 96; Rice 1923, pp. 177-78. *Zinyan* was a kind of caraway seed sprinkled on bread, it is also called *nan khvah*, *nankheh*, and *nan javani*. Borhan 1342.
180. Chardin 1927, p. 233.
181. Rice 1923, pp. 177-78.

and *golshekar* or *golqand*, a kind of *halva* prepared with conserve of roses and honey.[182] There also were many sweetmeats such as *abdandan, abarmadaran, ard-e rowghan, angosht-e `arus, batasheh, barfi, barkanj, balbalani, pareh, panid, parghul, parmavard, poghzul, pashmak, tark, to bar to, halqehchin, qatayef, golaj, la bar la*, and *luzineh*, a diamond-shaped almond cake, about which pastries little is known.[183] According to a sixteenth century cookbook, other sweetmeats were also made such as several varieties of baklava.[184] In 1647, Evliyeh Chelebi mentions the baking of buttered rings, puffy three-cornered pastry, fancy Yazd bread, flaky pastry filled with thin layers of chicken in Tabriz. In 1654, he mentions among the delicacies of Qazvin: Hamadani biscuits and Turaj[185] pastry with fillings.[186] *Nan-e kolaj* is another seventeenth century sweetmeat, which is very thin bread made from starch and eggs. It was dipped in sugary syrup and then eaten.[187] In the nineteenth century, E`tesam al-Molk mentions *nan-e qalebi* and *zaban-e mirza* as sweetmeats,[188] while a cookbook from that period lists 42 sugar-based sweetmeats (*shiriniha*) in addition to 18 others some of which included grains as part of the dough such as *nan-e kolach-e berenj, nan-e kolach-e shir, nan-e komaj ard-e berenk, nan-e nakhudchi*, and *nan-e berenj*.[189]

Sweetmeats and pastries were not only made by professional bakers, but also by women in towns, villages and nomad camps. In the village of Yush, for example, various kinds of sweetmeats were made such as *tutak, gushfil, bishdizik, reshteh beh reshteh*, and *mamo jing jing*. The dough for *tutak* is the same as for bread, but they put sugar and walnuts on them, and it is small. The dough of *gushfil* is made with flour and eggs and it is made red in ghee (*rowghan*). *Bishdizik* is honey or molasses that is poured into hot oil and on top of which candy sugar pellets are sprinkled. *Reshteh beh reshteh* is made with rice mucilage (*lo`ab-e berenj*) placed on a hot plate, it is heated and on top candy sugar pellets are sprinkled. *Mamo jing jing* is cooked mixed honey and *berenjak*. These are made for festivals, marriages, but also for evening party, when *shab-chera* has to be eaten, and sometimes, nuts, raisins and fruit.[190] Not only sugar was used as the basic ingredient for the preparation of rural sweetmeats, but also dates, which was a substitute for sugar in the rural areas in the South. In Baluchistan, for example, peasants made *ranginak* a kind of cake made with dates, pistachios, flour and fat. *Kolombeh* was a cake filled with dates; *kumatsh khorma* was date-bread baked in oil, and *chagmal* was a popular food item that consisted of bread, dates, and fat.[191]

On special occasions certain breads are made that may be considered sweetmeats, and are also called *nan*. A special kind of these sweetmeats is those that use rice flour to make pastries such as *nan-e berenji*. In Gilan small quantities of rice flour were made with small hand mills (see fig. 31) to bake cakes and other delicacies. For this purpose so-called broken rice grain (*eshkor*) was used. In the nineteenth and early twentieth century, with this flour, a large variety of pastries and sweetmeats

---

182. At`ameh 1360, pp. 10, 12, 16, 25, 35, 38, 39, 40, 41, 44, 51, 62, 72-73, 75, 83, 100, 126, 167; Steingass. The latter gives three different readings for *qata'i*, viz. *qatabi, qatafi* and *qatani*.
183. Steingass; At`ameh 1360, pp. 12, 18, 35, 37, 49, 50-53, 75, 76, 87. *Qatayef* is a cake made of fine flour, honey, sesame-oil and almonds; *golaj* is a thick piece of well mixed rice starch that is then baked with sugar, almonds or hazelnuts; it was also called *la bar la*.
184. Anonymous 1360, pp. 181-84, At`ameh 1360, p. 142.
185. Turaj sometimes means Turan or Turkey or Turkish, which perhaps is meant here.
186. Chelebi 2010, pp. 34 (Tabriz), 219 (Qazvin).
187. Borhan 1342.
188. E`tesam al-Molk 1351, pp. 239, 241.
189. Anonymous 1389, pp. 3-18, 48-53, 62.

190. Tahbaz 1342, pp. 45-46; see also above under *nan-e berenji*.
191. Gabriel 1940, p. 129. For sugar-based sweetmeats, see Floor 2003 b, pp. 360-75.

were baked such as *khekareh-derijd, kaka, paludeh, ferini, mushtakeh,* and *nan-e berenji*.[192]

In the plains of Gilan, rice bread (*nan-e berenji, bejenan* or *nan-e gandomi*) is made with flour that is a mixture of rice and wheat. The dough

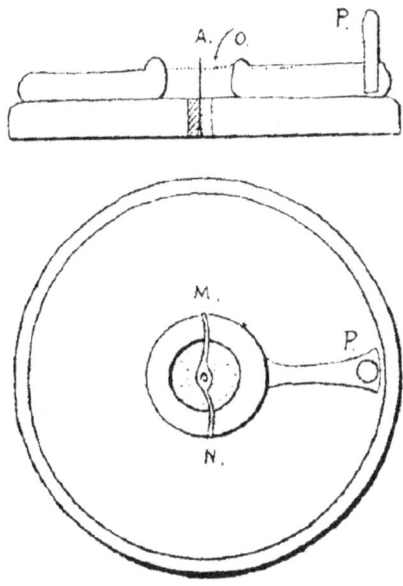

Fig. 35: Mill to make rice flour P, handle; A, fixed axis; M.N iron guide traversed by the axis; O, orifice to insert the rice. (Rabino-Lafont 1911, p. 32).

is heated a little and some wheat flour is added, because rice flour has no gluten and thus cannot be made into bread. After rising, dough is formed into lumps which are rolled into thin cakes. They are either baked on the back of an inverted pottery bowl (*gemej*) or on a *saj*. There are varietes of rice bread such as *kholpanun* or *kholfanun* in particular, whose taste is enhanced by trigonelle (*kholpa, shambelileh*), or the rice flour is baked in oil and mixed with eggs or milk. Bread eaters consume it with cottage cheese, ghee, or yoghurt. The *kalan, kelen* contains milk or eggs, or milk and cream; in the Rudbar area often *pâte au lait* (*shir-e kulva*) is mixed with olive oil.[193] In Gilan and in many other places (Shiraz, Kermanshah, Qazvin, etc.) rice cookies (*laku*) are made. In Tabriz such rice cookies are known as *duyi churayi* or *nan-e berenji*.

---

192. Rabino-Lafont 1911, p. 32, which also has recipes for the preparation of each.

193. Bazin and Bromberger 1982, pp. 82-83. For a letter asking a relative to send rice bread, see [http://www.qajarwomen.org/archive/detail/27].

Fig. 36: Sangak bread with a wedding blessing written on it on a ceremonial setting (Batmanglij 1986, p. 216).

CHAPTER SEVEN

SPIRITUAL ASPECTS OF BREAD

When Iranian tribes moved into the lands that later bore their eponymous name, they probably did not yet know how to make bread. As Harmatta argued, the fact that there is no common word for bread in proto-Iranian, and that in Middle Persian three different words were used to denote 'bread', indicates that the early Iranians were not familiar with bread making. The Iranians entered into an area where bread making with its set of beliefs was already more than three millennia old.

Bread, food fit for gods

Although we lack data on the beliefs of the peoples inhabiting Iran probably they were not much different from that of their neighbors and their initial overlords such as the Sumerians, Elamites and Babylonians. In Sumeria and Babylonia eating bread and drinking beer were considered to be the blessings of civilization, as Endiku is told in Gilgamesh. Nomads were despised, because "they know no barley."[1] This attitude and apparent fact confirms that the Iranian tribes under Babylonian sway indeed did not know how to make bread. Likewise, one millennium later nomadic Turkic peoples in Central Asia were unfamiliar with the making of bread, which was a delicacy among them. Traveling Arabs, therefore, presented Oghuz chiefs among other things with sheets of bread as gift.[2] This situation persisted also in later centuries, when bread making had spread into Transoxiania. Clavijo noted around 1400 that Tatars could do without bread on the march, and made do with meat and milk of their flocks.[3] In the 1740s, this still held for the Kirgiz and other Tatars living around Lake Baikal, who "have no grain, nor any kind of bread."[4]

Bread, therefore, was not just a mere food item; it was not just a sign of civilization either, but it was literally food fit for the gods. As a result, bread was offered to the gods as a sign of worship. A standard text concerning offerings to the gods is: "the bread looks nice and the beer tastes good," indicating that the gods had been present in the temple and appreciated the offerings.[5] This same ritual of offering food to the god or gods, in particular bread, was also adopted by the Iranian tribes. The Soghdians had a religious rite where each year a table with meat, a beaker of wine and bread were offered to Faris and nobody was allowed to touch it.[6] Even as late as the mid-nineteenth century, the Ossetes sacrificed bread and flesh upon altars in sacred groves.[7]

The making of ritual offerings to divine beings was in particular practiced by those that adopted the Zoroastrian religion. This ritual was known as *drōn*, meaning the "sacred portion." In later Zoroastrian tradition *dron* denotes only the flat, round unleavened wheat bread that constitutes the regular offering. According to stipulations preserved in *Nerangestan* (1.8.A-C), *dron* must be prepared from dry, ritually clean, unleavened wheat flour moistened with pure water and kneaded only by priests or their wives. During preparation each *dron* is marked on one side with nine shallow incisions, arranged three by three,

---

1. Bienkowski-Millard 2000, p. 59. The Massagetae also did not know bread. Polo 1993, vol. 1, p. 256, n. 4.
2. Ibn Fazlan 2005, pp. 37-41; Benjamin of Tudela 1907, p. 80 (the Ghuzz or "the Kofar-al-Torak, who worship the wind and live in the wilderness, and who do not eat bread, nor drink wine, but live on raw uncooked meat.").
3. Le Strange 1966, p. 191. The Bedouin tribes of Arabia also were unfamiliar with bread eating. Pellat.
4. Hanway 1753, vol. 1, p. 348.
5. Potts 1997, p. 189.
6. Spuler 1952, p. 510.
7. Von Haxthausen 1854, pp. 395-96.

while the words *humata*, *hukhta*, and *hvarshta* are recited thrice each. *Frasast*, unmarked wheat bread of the same type, is also made and consecrated with the *dron* by the *zot* "officiating priest". Nowadays, Zoroastrians in Persia make *dron* from leavened dough.[8]

Already, this ritual existed under the Achaemenids, when bread was put on top of the sacrificial offerings to the gods.[9] Sasanian kings also practiced the ritual. Shapur I (r. 240-70 CE) ordered that one lamb, one *griw* and five *hofan* of bread, and four *pas* of wine should be sacrificed daily at the fire temples for his own soul, the souls of the close family, and the members of his court. Bread was also given to the souls of the righteous to eat in paradise. Part of the funeral ritual was the scattering of morsels of bread around the corpse.[10] This may also explain the expression of bread morsels or *nan rizeh* used by Rumi (see below). A similar custom existed among the Rus, who "brought bread, meat, and onion, and strewed them before" the dead chief.[11]

BREAD, A SACRED MATTER

The holy nature of bread and its use as an offering to the divinities continued under later religions practiced in Iran such as Christianity. Kremer even went so far as to suggest that the breaking of the bread in the early Christian community, from which the rite of Holy Communion developed, clearly was inspired by the *dron* ceremony.[12] However, there existed a N. European custom where bread was eaten as substitute for the meat of the ritual animals.[13] Not only Zoroastrians were afraid to eat the devil's bread so were Christians. Therefore, Armenians baked white unleavened bread once a year and marked it with the sign of the cross.[14]

The religion of Islam also ascribes a hallowed nature to bread. According to Abu Said Al-Khudri, the Prophet said: "The (planet of) earth will be a bread on the Day of Resurrection, and The resistible (Allah) will topple turn it with His Hand like anyone of you topple turns a bread with his hands while (preparing the bread) for a journey, and that bread will be the entertainment for the people of Paradise."[15] The relationship between bread (food) and the divine is most clear when realizing that one of the 100 names of the Islamic god is *al-Razzaq* or The Provider of daily bread. Therefore, bread in Islamic beliefs is of great religious significance.

> The honor due to bread is great, for souls live by Islam, but phantoms- that is, bodies- live by bread. Therefore the Prophet said, "O God, bestow on me Islam, bread, and food, for without food I could not perform the prayer, the fast, and the pilgrimage." The prophet said, 'God created barley and wheat from His own splendor, that is, from His light. When, in city and countryside, these are treated without respect, they complain to God, saying, 'Lord, we are shown no respect, but have been abased.' Then God causes famine and need to appear among men.[16]

---

8. Choksy 1995.
9. Briant 2002, p. 243.
10. Back 1978, pp. 337, 344, 367; Jackson 1910, p. 389.
11. Ibn Fazlan 2005, p. 68.
12. Von Kremer 1890, p. 9. See also Moosa 1988, pp. 118, 126-27, 135-36, 236-38 on the role of bread in similar ceremonies among the Qezelbash and other heterodox Shi`ite sects.
13. Frazer 1907, vol. 2, pp. 289, 321, 366.
14. Reineggs 1807, p. 118. The Qezelbash women around Marsovan (Turkey) "mark every loaf of bread with the sign of the cross." Moosa 1988, p. 423.
15. Bukhari, vol. 8, book 76, number 527. Bread was a piece of divine light, according to the Ahl-e Haqq, a heterodox Shi`ite sect, a belief that was of Mithraic origin. In Ahl-e Haqq cosmogony, God created the Saj-e Nar, the fiery baking plate, on which he caused water to foam out of which he created the world and mankind. Moosa 1988, pp. 202-06
16. Meysami 1991, p. 88. The term *qasim al-arzaq* or distributor of daily bread is also used. Among heterodox

Clearly bread was a substance that was impregnated with the sphere of the holy, and thus acquired itself a holy and hallowed nature; indeed it was considered a blessing from God. In fact, a classical Persian word such as *jan-jan*, not only denotes "the Great Spirit, God," but also bread.[17] This reverence not only held for urban dwellers, but also for nomadic groups such as the Qashqa'is who "treated bread, the staple food, with care, for they believed it contained God's blessing."[18] Bread, therefore, must be respected. In the *Arda Wiraz-namag* a ninth-century Pahlavi text it is said that those who throw bread to dogs will themselves be torn by devils looking like dogs.[19] In Davarabad, "its waste is a cardinal sin."[20] From Khorasan it is further reported that if someone sees a piece of bread lying on the ground he has to pick it up and put it in a hole or fissure of a wall so that the bread cannot be trodden upon.[21] This is not only an Iranian belief, but it was also practiced in Austria as late as the nineteenth century[22] and the same attitude was found among Transylvanian Rumanians, who in particular considered throwing bread crumbs into the fire as taboo, because that might cause disaster.[23] It is perhaps this custom that Mowlavi refers to when he wrote:

Chun nan pokhteh z tab tu sorkhru budam
Chun nan rizeh kanunam ze khak rah bar chin

چون نان پخته ز تاب سرخ رو بودم
چون نان ریزه کنونم ز خاک ره بر چین

Like baked bread I was redfaced because of your heat
Now pick me up from the road like a piece of bread.[24]

BREAD DISTRIBUTION, A RELIGIOUS DUTY

Religious festivals were an occasion to share god's bounty and feed the poor, especially during the month of Moharram. Public representations of the passion plays (*ta'ziyeh*) were staged, at which, according to Wills:

> The crowd are often regaled with sherbets by the personage at whose cost the tazzia is given, also pipes, and even coffee; and the amount expended in pipes, coffee, tea, etc. to the numerous guests is very considerable indeed.[25]

Also, a Moslem who has not observed the obligatory fast during Ramazan has to give so-called *eftariyeh* to the poor, which gift has to be at least equal to the amount of bread that he has consumed during the month of fasting. But even outside religious holidays, families make periodical gifts of bread, nut, sweets, etc. to the poor on Thursday night. This is also done on the anniversary of a death. During those visits a small quantity of "a peculiar kind of bread" is eaten, and "what remains is given to the poor."[26] Bread offerings had a preventive sacrificial value. In many villages, once a year each family provided a village feast, a goat or sheep was killed and roasted.

Shii`te sects Ali is considered to be th Provider of daily bread. Moosa 1988, pp. 140-41
17. Zavosh 1370, p. 218; Dehkhoda.
18. Beck 1991, p. 43.
19. Gignoux 1994, pp. 94, 188.
20. Alberts 1963, p. 174.
21. Shakurzadeh 1346, p. 285.
22. Von Kremer 1890, p. 1. For other customs and beliefs in Europe and in the Middle Eeast concerning bread, see Ibid., pp. 2-7.
23. Frazer 1900, vol. 3, 1900, pp. 465-46.

24. Mobasheri 1389, p. 363.
25. Wills 1886, p. 283. At *ta`ziyeh*s "food is provided for the crowd by the patron of the Takeeah. The provision consists of large quantities of boiled rice." Bassett 1887, p. 306.
26. Morton 1940, p. 108; Wills 1886, p. 249.

Pieces of it are put into dough made of ground wheat and water and recooked. What would have made bread for the family for many weeks in cheerfully used up in a day, for the villagers are convinced that these feasts appease evil spirits and keep illness away.[27]

In Baluchistan to bring about good fortune or to prevent the opposite, or to express thanks for either of them, Sarhad nomads organized a *patir* or *sisir*, a food distribution event to ask god for assistance or to propitiate his wrath by distributing bread, dates, and candy among the members of the camp community. This was further expressed by the custom of *topak*, social solidarity, through the sharing food, either by the rich to the poor or by sharing in a camp member's loss of an animal by buying part of its meat.[28]

The same kind of ritual was performed in case of illness. Gonbad-e Kheshti in Mashhad is the tomb of Ebrahim, brother of Imam Reza. Needy women come there to beg for his intercession to grant their need or wish, in which case they promised to distribute one *man* of bread and 30 *sir* of yoghurt among the needy.[29] Sick women in Kerman leave gifts on a mountain, among which bread, in the hope that the queen of the fairies takes pity of them.[30] In Lurestan, the Eelyats keep up some very superstitious customs. A traveler was surprised to see a number of pieces of bread soaked in oil, laid upon a rock near one of their encampments. His companion, who knew what was meant by this, said, "You may tell how many sick are lying within those dark tents." Each piece of bread was an offering made by a sick person to a holy man who had been long dead. They thought the saints would be pleased with their little gifts, and would send them health."[31] In Azerbaijan, among the Nestorians, when a boy fell and broke his arm, "the household decided to bake bread and give it as a sacrifice to the poor."[32] In Ardalan territory (Kurdistan), "when any of the neighbouring tribes are unwell, a piece of bread, steeped in oil or butter, placed upon one of the stones, to propitiate the saint, and induce him to help recover the patient, which they conceive he seldom fails to do."[33] In the Ormiyeh area, "For a person who has no appetite they will prescribe a few loaves of bread under his pillow at bedtime."[34]

Bread offerings had a preventive sacrificial value. Once a year each family provides a village feast, a goat or sheep is killed and roasted. "Pieces of it are put into dough made of ground wheat and water and recooked. What would have made bread for the family for many weeks in cheerfully used up in a day, for the villagers are convinced that these feasts appease evil spirits and keep illness away."[35] If mishap had nevertheless struck the community, e.g., no rains had come; then a rain ceremony was organized like among the Bakhtiyaris. Part of that ceremony was the preparation of dough to which seven pebbles were added. The thick bread was then baked on a flat pan over a fire – people then found the pebbles.[36] Similarly, to ensure that a newborn and his mother would thrive and prosper, the child has to be put in the cradle after 6 days, "and they place bread and cheese, sweetmeats and other food near the mother and the child, so that when she eats it nothing unpleasant will befall the child. … In putting the infant into the cradle they tie a little bread and a sweet cake in a handkerchief, and

---

27. Morton 1940, p. 56.
28. Salzman 1994, pp. 81-82, 334. Among the Ahl-e Haqq sacrificial gifts are offered to a sayyed, who is believed to be sinless. Moosa 1988, pp. 228-29. Moslems do the same when visiting a holy shrine.
29. Shakurzadeh 1346, pp. 59-60.
30. Sykes 1901, p. 96.
31. Anonymous 1846, p. 44.
32. Adams 1900, p. 18.
33. Kinneir 1973, p. 146; see also Moosa 1988, p. 151.
34. Adams 1900, p. 209.
35. Morton 1940, p. 56.
36. Beck 1991, p. 162.

fasten it round the child, which they call *tosha*, or provisions for a journey."[37] The same custom existed among the Nestorian Christians, among who "as protection against the genii, a piece of bread is placed on the breast of the baby."[38]

Bread, more than just a word

The role of bread in religious ritual in Iran, whether Islamic or folk-religion, persists until this day for more than one obvious reason. Bread is the staff of life. It figures in innumerable proverbs and maxims, in which sufficient bread epitomizes individual well-being and family security. Making one's livelihood is 'to make one's bread'. To be dependent is to 'receive one's bread from another.' To victimize someone through economic pressure is 'to take his bread way.'[39] "A familiar curse is to wish that a man may have to 'catch his bread from the horn of a gazelle,' thus condemning him to starvation."[40] Malcolm recorded the maxim, "never give orders in another man's house; and accustom yourself to eat your bread at your own table."[41] In modern parlance bread continues to play a powerful metaphor to highlight wrongs and wrong actions. In Keshavarzian's book about the bazaar he gives a number of relevant examples. "Forbidden [*haram*] bread is delicious" cries one veteran in Makhmalbaf's movie, giving voice to the feeling that bazaaris are fakes, not really religious, and use it as a cover for their immoral behavior towards society." Furthermore, he noted that a member of the guild association said that all the ministries, societies, etc. were just "ways to provide jobs and 'to lend each other bread.'"[42] *Nan*, meaning bread or food, also is a signifier for those unfortunate enough not to have bread and thus having to beg for it. In Safavid times and the preceding period, a *nan juy* or 'a seeker of bread' is a beggar as is a *nankhvah* or 'he who wants bread,' which also means 'seed sprinkled on dough.' Finding it impossible to find bread was ironically referred to as *nan shirin budan* or 'bread is sweet.'[43]

Bread dos and don'ts

Bread also played a role in various popular superstitions. Ibn Isfandiyar relates that ca. 700, Yazid b. al-Muhallab (d. 720), provincial governor of Khorasan, had sworn to shed enough blood in Gorgan to turn a mill. However, after having killed many men, he was able to escape from his oath by mixing his blood with the mill-stream and eating bread baked from the flour it had ground.[44] In the Ormiyeh area, Moslems believed that "You must not eat bread with girls for if you do no beard will ever grow on your face." Furthermore, after a Moslem burial, "they give to each one present a piece of bread and sometimes a handful of raisins also."[45] Another belief was that "you should never say that the bread was bad, but you should ask for another one, in an ironic fashion (while grimacing): May God make it increase (*khoda ziyad konad*)."[46] In Khorasan, it was believed that a baker should not sell flour or dough in the evening, lest his shop's leaven diminish.[47] According to O'Donovan, "the inhabitants of Astarabad hold the peculiar belief that the bread made in the town exercises an intoxicating influence upon strangers."[48] Nana Kolthum held the belief that "On Fridays neither bread nor wood should be received for consumption."[49] Furthermore, some say that bread should be [*vajeb*] on the table on the night of *Nowruz* and during

---

37. Atkinson 1832, p. 51; Moosa 1988, p. 146.
38. Mirza 1920, p. 39.
39. Alberts 1963, p. 174.
40. Sykes 1910, p. 278.
41. Anonymous 1828, vol. 1, p. 271.
42. Keshavarzian 2007, pp. 55, 159.
43. Borhan 1342.
44. Ibn Isfandiyar 1905, p.108.
45. Knanishu 1899, pp. 185, 194.
46. Massé 1938, vol. 2, p. 320.
47. Shakurzadeh 1346, p. 285.
48. O'Donovan 1882, vol. 1, p. 186.
49. Atkinson 1832, p. 67.

Ramazan, while other say it is *sunnat*.[50] If you throw bread into the road the cost-of-living will go up. If you chew off the ends of the bread (round or flat) you will grow poor. "If a man should eat the loaf of bread that was baked first, his wife will die."[51]

Bread, don't leave home without it

In Davarabad (Khorasan), "So important is bread that no meal is eaten without it, it is carried in suitcases on journeys."[52] This was not only the case in Davarabad, but throughout Iran. Bread was like the credit card in the well-known Amercan Express slogan, viz. 'don't leave home without it.' When traveling, even for a short distance, people always had bread with them. In the fourteenth century, in the district of Kuran (beyond Siraf), "When a man here is about to go out as a highwayman he will take threshed corn, with some dry bread crumbled, in a wallet."[53] Peasants have a cloth "round their waist, holding bread, tobacco and money."[54] Floyer related that a haji he met near Meybud "was a most generous fellow, and had always his capacious pockets full of bread, sweetmeats, and small coin for anyone who wanted them on the road."[55] According to Polak, when traveling, whether a villager or urbanite, people took a kind of rusk (*nan-e khoshk*), which are rather tasty.[56] Coan met a woman in Kurdistan who "had eggs, honey and small cakes of bread in the folds of her turban."[57]

Bread and marriage

Bread played a role in the marriage ceremony. In ancient Iran the bride having tasted the wine would then sit next to her groom, who would embrace and kiss her; the newlyweds ate from the same loaf of bread, sliced with a sword into two parts.[58] According to Quintus Curtius Rufius, the bread cutting ceremony was a Macedonian custom.[59] Nevertheless, bread continued to play a significant part in the marriage ceremonies of Moslems and other religious groups. For example, part of the Yezidi marriage ceremony consists of "bridegroom and bride dividing a piece of bread between them."[60] Among Moslems, when the mullah married the bride and groom and declared this marriage legal and binding, "a piece of bread was held over the bride's head, sweets were sprinkled over her, which the women quickly picked up and ate, as a 'bride's sweetmeat' brings good luck." … "On a large tray, besides the sweets and bread, there was a saucer with some butter or fat, signifying the hope that life might be free from friction; also a plate of grain, signifying fruitfulness, while the bread was an expression of the hope that they might enjoy plentifulness and prosperity."[61] This type of bread may have been same as what the fifteenth century poet Atma`eh called 'new bride's bread' or *now `arus nan*.[62]

In the Ormiyeh area, among the Assyrian Christians there, "soon after the betrothal the boy's mother will send a breakfast to her intended daughter-in-law consisting of several loaves or cakes of bread called 'kada.'"[63] But it did not end there, because as part of the wedding, "the parents of the boy give to each of their neighbor ladies several pounds of wheat flour to bake bread for the wedding. In Persia they bake very soft bread. Each loaf is about two feet long and one foot wide and

---

50. Atkinson 1832, p. 66.
51. Adams 1900, p. 446.
52. Alberts 1963, p. 174.
53. Ibn Balkhi 1912, p. 49.
54. Sykes 1901, pp. 25; Stark 2001, p. 116 (my escort had stowed away a folded piece of bread in their waist-bands).
55. Floyer 1882, p. 361.
56. Polak 1865, vol. 1, p. 111.
57. Coan 1939, p. 194.

58. Dandamaev and Lukonin 2000, p. 121.
59. Quintus Curtius Rufius 1883, p. 187 - VIII, 16 (Hoc erat apud Macedones sanctissimum coeuntium pignus).
60. Jackson 1910, p. 13.
61. Rice 1923, pp. 143-44.
62. Atma`eh 1360, pp. 41, 47, 56, 57.
63. Knanishu 1899, p. 23.

almost as thin as blotting paper. When the mother of the boy bakes bread for the wedding she takes the first loaf she bakes and carefully wraps it up and hides it."[64] As if that is not enough, after the wedding, when an animal has been slaughtered, the mother of the groom takes the bloody knife and the loaf of bread that she put aside and puts them "under the pillow of the newly-married couple," to ward off evil.[65] To make sure, "Sometimes as soon as the bride has entered the house, they take bread and crumble it over her head as symbols of blessings,"[66] while she does not bake bread "for a whole year after her marriage."[67] Even thereafter, there were bread related rules that the husband had to honor, for "If a man should eat the loaf of bread that was baked first, his wife will die."[68]

Moslems had similar customs. Among the Qashqa'is, before consummation of the marriage, to lower tension, "the bride fed the groom bread she had brought from her mother's hearth,"[69] while newly married women had neatly folded sheets of bread from their hearth with them.[70] Also, amongst the Jews in Iran there were several rituals and beliefs related to bread. On the Sabbath Jews made a special blessing over the bread. "The custom of a special bread or portion (*halla*) known in Yemen, Kurdistan and most Ashkenazic and Sfardic communities, is unknown in Shiraz."[71] In Kurdish Jewish villages, before starting to bake, a traditional religious custom was enacted known as *hafrashat-hala* (Heb.) consisting of throwing a small piece of the dough into the fire, while reciting a blessing.[72] Iranian Jews further believed that to prevent a child from being harmed when no one is with it, one must place a Tora or piece of bread (both symbols of life and sustenance)."[73]

Bread is to be shared

It was considered the pinnacle of bad manners if not barbarism to refuse to share one's food, and many stories exhort royalty to do so. "It says in a tradition that providing abundant bread and food for the creatures of God increases the duration of a king's life, his reign and good fortune."[74] To show that, although a bandit he was not a barbarian, the bandit Kuruglu stated, "I am liberal, always ready to give bread away."[75] Religious advice, therefore, was, "Etiquette consists in eating bread with someone and not alone, for eating alone is not proper."[76] A person who refused to share was known as *nan-e kur*, as well as his bread, meaning both 'unlawful bread' and 'miser'.[77] The same attitude is metaphorically referred to such as when prior to the 1979 revolution, bazaaris who had patronage used that to advance their own position rather than that of the trade or bazaar community. "'They had their bread and were not going to share it,' groaned one wholesaler."[78]

However, proper ethical behavior is not limited to royalty and the power elite, but holds for all of god's creatures. Thus a Christian missionary observed that in Kurdistan, "Even the poor peasant munching his simple meal of bread and cheese, or bread and fruit, asks you to be his guest."[79] Again, this was a characteristic among the Sarhad Baluch, where hospitality was the guiding value for the relationship with those with whom one was at

---

64. Knanishu 1899, p. 28.
65. Knanishu 1899, p. 30.
66. Knanishu 1899, p. 50.
67. Knanishu 1899, p. 59.
68. Adams 1900, p. 446.
69. Beck 1991, p. 362.
70. Beck 1991, p. 394.
71. Loeb 1977, p. 178.
72. Shwartz-Be'eri 2000, p. 46.

---

73. Loeb 1977, p. 219.
74. Nezam al-Molk 1960, 128.
75. Chodzko 1842, pp. 89, 159 (another said: "I grudge my bread to no one.")
76. Meysami 1991, p. 156.
77. Borhan 1342.
78. Keshavarzian 2007, p. 102.
79. Coan 1939, p. 23.

peace. Being a host, known as *nandeh* or 'bread giver', was thus not only a social must it was also an honor, because a guest by honoring the host's tent with his presence acknowledged the latter's substance and standing. It helped that for being hospitable, the host added to his *thavab* or good deeds that god rewarded.[80] This attitude was not peculiar to Moslems, because Nestorian mountaineers in Ormiyeh province "will share their last piece of bread with a stranger or an enemy."[81]

The ethics of not sharing your bread with others made you a non-person. This belief was poetically highlighted by the poet Rumi in one of his poems.[82]

خشک نانه خواست یا ترنانه‌ای
گفت صاحب‌خانه: نان اینجا کجاست؟
خیره‌ای، کی این دکان نان واست؟
گفت: باری، اندکی پیهم بیاب
گفت: آخر نیست دکان قصاب
گفت: پاره‌ی آرد ده ای کدخدا
گفت پنداری که هست این آسیا؟
گفت: باری آب ده از مَکرعه
گفت: آخر نیست جو یا مشرعه
هر چه او درخواست از نان یا سبوس
چربکی می‌گفت و می‌کردش فسوس
آن گدا در رفت و دامن بر کشید
اندر آن خانه به حسبت خواست رید
گفت: هی هی! گفت: تن زن ای دژم
تا درین ویرانه خود فارغ کنم
چون درینجا نیست وجه زیستن
بر چنین خانه بباید ریستن
چون نه‌ای بازی که گیری تو شکار
دست آموز شکار شهریار،
نیستی طاوس با صد نقش بند
که به نقشت چشمها روشن کنند،
هم نه‌ای طوطی که چون قندت دهند

---

80. Salzman 1994, pp. 83-85 (with details about the food and other details of hosting), 337 (re *thavab*); see also de Lorey 1910, p. 38 ("no Bakhtiyari has ever stopped to the shame of 'selling bread'").
81. Perkins 1843, p. 18.
82. Rumi, 4th daftar ??

A dervish knocked at a house
 to ask for a piece of dry bread,
or moist, it didn't matter.
This is not a bakery," said the owner.
Might you have a bit of gristle then?"
Does this look like a butcher shop?"
A little flour?"
Do you hear a grinding stone?
Some water?"
This is not a well."

Whatever the dervish asked for,
the man made some tired joke
and refused to give him anything.
Finally the dervish ran in the house,
lifted his robe, and squatted
as though to take a shit.
 "Hey, hey!"
"Quiet, you sad man. A deserted place
is a fine spot to relieve oneself,
and since there's no living thing here,
or means of living, it needs fertilizing."

BREAD AND SALT

In many cultures the eating and sharing of bread and salt was considered to be a holy binding act.[83] Guests were offered bread and salt on arrival and departure.[84] Hence the wish expressed by Evliya Chelebi's host that "May my bread be lawful to you!" I have eaten your bread; I have broken bread with you,"[85] signifying that there was a bond of trust and security between host and guest. Even kings were bound by this ritual. Nizam al-Molk relates that Bahram Gur said: "I ate your bread and salt,"[86] indicating that he felt that he was bound by the laws of guest-right. When a usurper urged soldiers to kill Mohammad Zeyd ruler of Tabaristan, who claimed his brother's throne in 884, "they refused to kill him, having eaten his bread and salt, but deserted him, and returned to Gurgan."[87] Several nineteen century travelers mention that they felt safe among otherwise thieving nomads once they had eaten their bread and salt. According to Layard, an Arab had shared bread and now it was his sacred duty to protect those with whom he had eaten.[88] Mounsey generalized this by stating that "once you have eaten a nomad's bread you're safe as long as you're amongst them."[89] Similarly, Ella Sykes recounted that one of her brother's servants told her: "If he 'ate the bread' of any one, he felt he must do his utmost to serve that man, and indeed he carried out his principles in practice with us, being most loyal to our interests."[90] Likewise, the bandit Kuruglu felt that once he had eaten somebody's salt and bread he would never betray him.[91] Therefore, the same tale offers the wisdom that "it is better to refuse the salt and bread of a villain than to eat it."[92] But the Zoroastrians believe that although you had eaten the bread of Ohrmaz, it did not prevent people from committing evil and thus siding with Ahriman.[93] The same held true for Moslems who believe that only through correct behavior the bread you eat is *nan-e halal*, or bread honestly earned by the sweat of one's brow.[94]

Not everybody felt that you could put unconditional trust in the bread and salt pact. Fraser, who had traveled for many years throughout Iran submitted that "Toorkomans do sometimes keep the oath of bread and salt'"[95] Likewise, the

---

83. Von Kremer 1890, pp. 18-34.
84. Sheil 1973, pp. 44, 364; De Bode 1845, vol. 1, p. 287.
85. Chelebi 2010, p. 158. Like in English in Persian the term used is also 'to break bread' or *nan shekastan*. Bread broken in pieces was called *kondak* in medieval times.
86. Nezam al-Molk 1960, p. 31.

---

87. B. Isfandiyar 1905, p. 188.
88. Layard 1971, p. 28; de Lorey 1910, p. 38.
89. Mounsey 1872, p. 258.
90. Sykes 1901, p. 33.
91. Chodzko 1842, p. 245, see also p. 280.
92. Chodzko 1842, p. 275.
93. Gignoux 1984, pp. 136, 214.
94. Borhan 1342.
95. Fraser 1973, vol. 2, p. 255.

missionary Coan spoke from experience when he reported that "Malik Yosip replied that he would trust the man who had eaten his bread," but he was mistaken.[96] Breaking one's bread and salt oath was referred to as *nan va namakdan shekastan* or to be engaged in unlawful and bad behavior.[97]

Bread eating etiquette

Given the importance of bread there were, of course, certain rules to be respected when eating. According to a Tradition narrated by Anas bin Malik,

> The Prophet never took his meals at a dining table, nor in small plates, and he never ate thin well-baked bread. (The sub-narrator asked Qatada, "Over what did they use to take their meals?" Qatada said, "On leather dining sheets.[98]

Given the importance of the behavior (*sunnah*) of the Prophet for Moslems, it is not surprising that olama stipulated that "One must eat bread at a sufra, as is the custom of the Sufis reminding them that these travelers are journeying towards the Hereafter."[99] Indeed, Iranians did not eat from a table, but from a *sofreh*, as Clavijo the Castilian ambassador to the court of Timur noted in 1400. "Next they would produce a leather mat for a tablecloth, and this with them is known as Sofra, and on this they would place bread. On the leather mat aforesaid they would place meat in plenty, also bowls of milk and clotted cream with eggs and honey."[100] The *sofreh* was not necessarily a leather mat, but instead people simply spread a cloth upon the ground.[101] According to Gmelin, in 1773,

The place of the table cloth is taken by the Oriental thinly baked bread (see my Journey, 2nd volume) or *tschurek*,[102] which is spread out in long and broad pieces on the serving plates so that you can partake of it without much ado and who wants to drink always sees servants with water jars in front of him. Persians speak little or not at all during the meal. They eat very fast and the meal lasts at most one hour. After the meal once again water to wash is passed around. Coffee, tea and the water pipe are handed out. High-class Persians usually eat only twice per day, in the afternoon and in the evening. During the afternoon meal one is wont to be quiet and well-behaved. At dinner their musicians and singers appear, there one also sacrifices to Bacchus with full cups for as long as one cannot sacrifice anymore. After all it is night, and while it is night, you can do what you like. Lower class people are also wont to breakfast and eat in the afternoon.[103]

It seems to have also been customary that food was served on trays, baskets or bowls, which were called *chashdan* or *chobbin*. According to Chardin, "The People of mean Condition are serv'd in the Morning with one of these Loaves, in a wooden Bason, Painted and varnish'd."[104] However, his statement is at odds with observations of European travelers both before and after the seventeenth century that also persons of quality were served in the same manner. In 1400, Clavijo the Castilian ambassador to Timur noted that "Upon each bowl, as also under it, on every tray they placed a thin cake of bread."[105] In the first decade of the

---

96. Coan 1939, p. 187.
97. Borhan 1342.
98. Bukhari, Volume 7, Book 65, Number 326.
99. Meysami 1991, p. 155.
100. Le Strange 1928, pp. 121-22.
101. Kanishu 1899, pp. 162-63.

102. *Churak*, the Turkish word for bread; Persian speakers use the word *nan*. For those unable to read Gmelin's description in his second volume, Wulff 1966, pp. 291-95 provides an excellent description and pictures of bread making.
103. Gmelin 2007, p. 90.
104. Chardin 1927, p. 233.
105. Le Strange 1928, p. 124.

nineteenth century Tancoigne observed about Iranian eating habits that "At eleven o'clock his breakfast is served up, and consists of bread, cheese, raw herbs or fruits, all on a tray of tinned copper."[106] According to Perkins, it was "a wooden tray, or rather a waiter, from three to five feet long, and two and a half feet wide. This article is thin and light, with sloping edges, three or four inches broad, sometimes tastefully carved, and if it is kept clean, it renders a meal, in appearance, not uninviting. The lighter parts of the meal are brought in upon the waiter, but the more substantial and less portable ones-particularly soups- are placed on it afterward. A row of the thin cakes of bread is spread around the border."[107] Food being served on a tray seems to have been the custom in the Ormiyeh area. In a large family, the patriarch and married sons, "when they eat they will either put bread and food in a wooden tray which is made like a sink and is about three to four feet long by a foot and a half wide, or in a copper one about three feet in circumference, or else they will simply spread a table cloth on the floor which serves them as a table to place the food upon."[108]

At the beginning of a meal, the host broke the bread and gave a piece to each of the guests while saying Bismallah.[109] Then one had to wait one's turn. Williams narrates that at a meal "one of the women took a piece of bread before her turn and was turned out of the room by the host."[110] Among the Turkmen, "a stranger who happened to be present, but not inclined to eat, would break of a morsel and put it on his bosom, not to slight the invitation."[111] It is necessary to stress that Iranians in the 1740s considered it an abomination to cut their bread, according to Hanway.[112] They still did in the 1930s, according to Koelz, who wrote: "Persians break bread and put the pieces in their mouth. Cutting it is *haram*. Our method of tearing it up with our teeth may look queer to them, as does the individuality of our eating habits. The Moslem finds it friendlier and warmer to eat out of the same platter and drink out of the same bowl."[113] It is therefore odd to read that Moore reported that "next they cut the flat Persian bread into strips, which they laid along the edges of the table; after this they brought in enough dinner for a regiment."[114] Although the cutting of bread was in harmony with the Prophet's habits, of whom it is reported in a Tradition that "The Prophet started cutting the bread (into pieces) and put the cooked meat over it."[115]

Bread is used for other purposes by Persians than just for eating. It serves as a spoon to spoon ragout or *khoresh*; in a soup so much bread is chunked that it may easily be eaten by hand; a dish, because the portions are put on bread; the napkin, one uses it to wipe fat fingers or the mouth during eating; yes even as packing paper, because roasts or other fat foods taken on travel are wrapped in it. It is clear why they think that European bread is inconvenient or counterproductive.[116] This practice to use a piece of bread as a wrapper was already customary under the Achaemenids. Aelian wrote that Artaxerxes III (ca. 425-338 BCE) picked up the largest piece of bread and, put some meat on it, cut it up,

---

106. Tancoigne 1820, p. 175.
107. Perkins 1843, pp. 228-29.
108. Knanishu 1899, p. 102.
109. Anderson 1880, p. 81; Conolly 1834, vol. 1, p. 164. In Talebabad, the head of the family said *bism allah al-rahman va rahim* at the beginning and the end of each meal. Talebabad 1345, p. 256.
110. Williams 1907, p. 316.
111. Conolly 1834, vol. 1, p. 164

112. Hanway 1753, vol. 1, p. 224 ("Bread is always broken, not cut."); Rice 1923, p. 178; Knanishu 1899, p. 104.
113. Koelz 1983, p. 200.
114. Moore 1915, p. 135.
115. Bukhari, Volume 5, Book 59, Number 427.
116. Polak 1865, vol. 1, p. 111; Gol Mohammadi 1371, vol. 1, p. 295; Rice 1923, p. 178; Bélanger 1838, vol. 1, p. 159; Jackson 1910, p. 111. The term *nan-e khoresh* does not refer to this custom. As used in medieval times it referred to as a sourish kind of tonic to stimulate the appetite or digestion. It also referred to meat or fish eaten along with bread. Hofmann 2000, p. 227; Atma`eh 1360, pp. 62, 108.

and ate greedily. Thus flat bread was then already in use to serve as an edible 'trencher' plate as well as a convenient scoop as it still until to-day.[117] People, indeed broke bread and put it, for example, into the soup.[118] "When they have soups, they put bread in it to make it thick like hash, then by dipping a portion of thin bread, held by the thumb and the two fingers of the right hand, they lift small quantities and eat it without soiling their fingers."[119] However, that was not always the case. Mme von Freygang critically observed that "he wipes his disgustingly greasy hand upon his napkin, that is to say, upon the bread which covers his table; and finishes his meal by eating his napkin."[120] Although this seems to have been a common practice, according to the olama, "He should not lick the bowl nor wipe his hand on the bread."[121]

---

117. Aelian 1997, p. 41 (ll. 1.7).
118. Knanishu 1899, p. 104 ("cheese is eaten with small morsels of bread."); de Lorey 1910, p. 233.
119. Mirza 1920, p. 124.
120. Von Freygang 1823, p. 165.
121. Meysami 1991, p. 156.

CHAPTER EIGHT

DAILY BREAD OR A MATTER OF RIZQ[1]

تا تو نانی به کف آری و به غفلت نخوری

سعدی

"The main part of every meal is bread."

Knanishu 1899, p. 103.

There was little change in the diet of Iranians until recent times. At least one type of flat bread was always part of every meal. For bread was the major staple, accompanied by vegetables, fruits, cheese, yoghurt and various condiments. Meat was a luxury few could afford and the Islamic ban on the eating of certain meats (e.g., pork, hare, oyster, crab) limited dietary choice and variety. There were, of course, regional differences in diet (e.g. rice and fish mainly were consumed in the Caspian Sea and Persian Gulf provinces). There were also differences between urban and rural consumers as well as between rich and poor. The variety in the diet was further limited by the seasonal availability of certain products due to limited methods of preservation. Caloric intake was less during winter, and was at its lowest level by early summer. Nevertheless, in normal years, on average, the diet provided enough calories for the majority of the population.

---

1. The origin of the Arabic word of *rizq*, 'God's sustenance, provision to mankind,' lies, according to Jeffery 2007, pp. 142-43, in Middle Persian *rozig* 'daily bread' < *roch* 'day', New Persian *ruz*, borrowed into Arabic at an early date, since it occurs frequently in ancient poetry, via Syriac *rozika*.

URBAN DIETS

IMPERIAL PERIOD

It is of interest to note that 'to eat food, have a meal' in both Middle and New Persian is *nan khvurdan*. In Middle Persian it is found in the inscription at Persepolis from the reign of Shapur II, in Manichean texts, and in Pahlavi.[2] Even to-day, in for example Baluchistan, "The conventional phrase for inviting someone to a meal is, *Be-all, nan bur*, 'come and eat bread.'"[3] In Larestan, *noo dada* (i.e. *nun dadeh*) means 'to give food or means of support.'[4] As is made clear hereunder, the fact that *nan* means 'bread' as well as 'food' is not a coincidence, for Iranians were and are first and foremost bread eaters. It did not make a difference whether you were rich or poor, your diet included much bread, the more so if you were poor.

It is therefore of no surprise that both wheat and barley bread was eaten at the Achaemenid king's table,[5] given that it was also good enough to sacrifice to the gods, as discussed in the previous chapter. It was good enough when the king passed in front of their houses that the Iranians presented him with a bull, sheep, bread, wine, dates, fruits, etc., according to custom and means.[6] Like in later times, important Achaemenid imperial officials were given a fief (*dorea*) that had to provide its holders with various kinds of food including bread.[7] Servants and guards ate the remnants of their master's meal: meat and bread, as they did in Islamic times.[8] It is therefore predictable that

---

2. De Smet-Grégoire 1989; Back 1978, p. 493; Sundermann 1984, p. 497.
3. Salzmann 1994, p. 73.
4. Mahmoodian 2007, p. 310.
5. Briant 2002, pp. 286, 289 (soldiers ate meat and bread and so did the king), 291 (bread major item at the table).
6. Dandamaev-Lukonin 1989 p. 179.
7. Briant 2002, p. 419; Dandamayev-Lukonin 1989, pp. 136, 318-19.
8. Briant 2002, p. 315; Dandamayev-Lukonin 1989, p. 145.

scholars studying this period concluded that "The daily nourishment [of the Persians] ... consists of bread, barley-cake [maza], cardamum [a kind of cress], grains of salt and roast or boiled meat; with it they drink water."[9] Those who did not have bread or did not cultivate wheat or barley could substitute it with dates as the date palm argues in the Middle-Persian poem *Draxt asorig* (the Babylonian tree), and many in southern Iran did, as discussed in chapter two.[10] The above also held for the Sasanian period. Later authors report that when an incognito traveling Bahram Gur was invited to eat at a tent, he was offered bread.[11] An old woman had a small piece of land that provided her with four loaves of bread per day; she ate one loaf of bread for breakfast and one for supper.[12]

Medieval Period

Bread continued to play a dominant role in the diet of royalty during the Islamic period as well. The founder of the Saffarid dynasty, Ya`qub b. Leyth said: "my victual used to be barley-bread, fish, onions and leeks."[13] Bread was also taken as a snack during royal wine drinking parties.[14] Like in the imperial period, important officials were given fiefs that were known as *nan-pareh* or 'a piece of bread.'[15] The bread or more in general the food providing nature of such fiefs was clear to the ruler as well as the recipient. The king of India wrote to Alptigin, "you have come from Khurasan through lack of bread, let me give you grants of land."[16] In the tenth century when Abdollah Fazlavey al-Sarvi came to Ispahbad Pazushan of Tabaristan the latter gave him 'bread-money.'[17]

In Abbasid Baghdad, several types of breads were eaten with meat dishes, cheese or olive oil such as *khushnanaj, mutbaq, akras mukallal, khubz al-abazir* and *jardhaq*.[18] Likewise in Iran proper, *beryani*, a meat dish known at least from the tenth century, was usually wrapped in bread.[19] However, generally meat was absent from meals of the not well-to-do. Ibn Battuta reported that in Isfahan, sometimes they will invite a friend and say: "'Come along with me for a meal of *nan* and *mas*' – that is bread and curdled milk in their language."[20] The diet was richer at well-endowed hospices, according to the same author. In Shushtar at the convent of the tomb of an *imamzadeh*, "there was put before each man enough to supply four persons: pilaf of rice flavoured with pepper and cooked in ghee, fried chickens, bread, meat and sweetmeats."[21] In Kazerun, at the convent, they served every visitor, "*harisa* made from flesh, wheat and ghee, and eaten with them breadcakes."[22] In a hospice at Tabriz, all wayfarers received, "bread, meat, rice cooked in ghee, and sweetmeats."[23] However, elsewhere the fare was more austere. In Lar, members of the hospice of the ascetic Sheikh Abu Dulaf Mohammad made a round of the houses every day, and "at each house they are given one or two loaves, and from these they provide food for wayfarers."[24] The Rashidi foundation in Tabriz had a fixed daily ration or *rezq* for a Koran reciter that was 3 *man* (2.4 kg), for others 2 *man* (1.6 kg), in addition to an annual cash amount.[25] According to

---

9. Wieshöfer 2001, p. 75; Briant 2002, p. 328.
10. Desmet-Grégoire 1989; Boyce 1968, p. 55.
11. Nezam al-Molk 1960, p. 25.
12. Nezam al-Molk 1960, pp. 36, 39.
13. Nezam al-Molk 1960, p. 18.
14. Beyhaqi 1324, pp. 99, 147, 188, 281, 471; Manuchehri 1326, pp. 73, 131, 173, 179; B. Isfahan 1905, p. 155; Mobasheri 1389, p. 361.
15. Ebrahim 1343, pp. 7, 127, 149, 172.
16. Nezam al-Molk 1960, p. 119.

17. Ibn Isfandiyar 1905, p. 46.
18. Ahsan 1979, p. 89.
19. Bazargan 1989.
20. Ibn Battutta 1958, vol. 2, p. 295; At`ameh 1360, pp. 69 (with *dugh*), 79, 152.
21. Ibn Batutta 1958, vol. 2, p. 286.
22. Ibn Batutta 1958, vol. 2, p.320.
23. Ibn Batutta 1958, vol. 2, p.344.
24. Ibn Batutta 1958, vol. 2, p.406
25. Hoffmann 2000, pp. 261, 293-94.

Ashtor, Orientals ate wheat bread while Westerners ate barley bread mostly in the middle ages.[26] That may have been true for the well-to-do, but in Abbasid times, barley bread was eaten by the poor, dervishes, as well as in time of war and insufficient supply.[27] This is echoed by Nezam al-Molk who wrote that "a pauper eats barley bread."[28] The hospices may have given some a varied and protein-rich diet, but the Rashidi hospice in Tabriz stipulated that the poor be given *ash* or *bolghur* with 2 loaves that together weighed 0.5 *man* (ca. 400 g) of the lower-quality bread.[29]

Bread was an important part of the elite's diet as well. Clavijo, the Castillian ambassador to Timur's court, wrote that when the embassy arrived at a place it was the custom to bring refreshments immediately, "namely bread and sour milk, followed by a soup that they are wont to prepare with rice and dumplings of dough."[30] This also held for arrival in the prince's camp, where the embassy received immediately "bread and flour together with several live sheep for slaughter."[31] Likewise, rations supplied to the embassy by the governor of Arzinjan consisted of "many dishes of cooked food, with fruit in plenty and wine and bread."[32] Bread continued to be a major item in the food made available to ambassadors also in later centuries such as during the Safavid and Qajar period.[33]

SAFAVID-QAJAR PERIOD

Bread was also the staple in Safavid times, often eaten with milk products and fruit as in later times.[34] The poor in the Caucasus during the Zand period "mostly live on milk, cheese and bread. Bread is unleavened wheat and barley and baked daily, partly in large flat pancakes, partly in thick disks. They bake cakes with quinces, apples, eggs, butter and wheat flour."[35] This also held for Qajar Iran, where the poorer urban classes throughout Iran ate wheat bread mixed with barley or sorghum.[36] In 1870, the British consul Jenner summarized the diet of the urban poor as follows: "The winter diet of the workman consists almost entirely of bread, rice and bad cheese, with a small quantity of tea in the form of a concoction, and the summer diet of bread and 'sayfi', or summer produce, i.e. melons, cucumbers, vegetable-marrows, egg-plants, and various forms of edible gourds."[37] By confining themselves to the above diet, the workmen in this country can just manage to keep body and soul together, Jenner concluded.[38] It was not uncommon that common workers were partly paid in kind, this was cheaper for the employer and had the advantage that the workers's subsistence was ensured. In Tabriz, "In some trades an additional allowance, generally in bread, is given according to the quantity of work executed."[39] Likewise, soldiers' pay consisted of a monthly cash payment and one and a half pounds (0.68 kg) of bread daily.[40]

---

26. Ashtor 1970, p. 3.
27. Ahsan 1979, p. 89.
28. Nezam al-Molk 1960, p. 190; see also At`ameh 1360, p. 14.
29. Hoffmann 2000, pp. 227, 233.
30. Le Strange 1928, p. 156.
31. Le Strange 1928, p. 168.
32. Le Strange 1928, p. 122.
33. Speelman 1907, pp. 47, 88, 142; Thevenot 1971, vol. 2, p. 108 (Russian ambassador); Ouseley 1823, vol. 1, p. 259; Soltykoff 1851, pp. 59 (at Miyaneh, the *mehmandar* organized milk, tea, bread, raisins, grenadine, water melons and some wine), 63 (governor of Zenjan gave order to serve me coffee, tea, pelow, and *churek-murek*, i.e. bread) , 126.

---

34. Tavernier 1930, pp. 280, 282; Thevenot 1971, vol. 2, p. 96; Chardin 1927, pp. 223, 228, 233-34.
35. Gmelin 2007, p. 310.
36. Polak 1865, vol. 1, p. 110.
37. Jenner 1870, p. 397; De Panisse 1867, p. 102; Schwartz 1942, p. 35 ("from the beginning of July to the end of December fruit forms three-fourths of the food of the poorer classes.').
38. Jenner 1870, p. 397.
39. Smith 1871, p. 402; Jones 1870, p. 418.
40. Bird 1891, vol. 1, p. 111.

The dietary situation did not improve in the following years. Around 1880, "Bread, eggs, 'mast' (curds), and cheese form the staple food of the labouring classes in Persia; occasional onions, eaten in chunks as a boy eats an apple with us, render the *menu* tasty, and the eater insupportable."[41] In 1909, Wishard an American medical missionary wrote after 20 years of service in Iran that "the poor are compelled to subsist on dry bread, cheese, and a little tea. Sometimes they are able to prepare for themselves a little soup from the heads of sheep, for which they pay the butcher a few pennies. In the summer time, lettuce, cucumbers, and fruit may be added to the bill of fare. In the larger towns, men may find in the bazaar native restaurants, where for a few pennies a large bowl of soup with rice may be purchased." These were important for the migrant workers.[42] The rich did not eat much bread, they ate rice,[43] but Naser al-Din Shah, for example, had "a light breakfast, consisting of some tea and bread, with a little cheese."[44]

In 1887, Tehran had a population of 150,000 that consumed the following quantity of bread monthly.

Table 8.1: Monthly bread consumption in Tehran in 1887

Sangak flour	594,460 man (each man = 3 kg)
Sangak bread baked	891,690 man
Consumption of lavash flour	936,000 man
Lavash bread baked	140,000 man
Total flour consumption	688,060 man [sic; 1,530,460]
Total bread baked	1,032,090 man [sic; 1,031,690]

Source: Baladiyeh-ye Tehran 1312, p. 11.

Thus, the average per capita consumption was 6 *man* and 30 *sir* (20.6 kg) per month or 688 gram per day. Bread was indeed the life staff of the urban poor, because it was eaten in large quantities. People usually ate bread as their staple, with some cheese and some herbs. A porter ate about 2 *charak* per day or 1.5 kg of bread.[45] A typical meal for a day laborer in Bushehr was "a lump of dates before going to work, some bread (unleavened) and salt fish for dinner [sic; i.e., lunch], and some boiled rice for supper."[46] In the beginning of the twentieth century, "A large proportion of bread is eaten compared with other food, the average allowance being twenty-eight ounces [0.8 kg] a head a day."[47] Europeans were amazed at the quantity of food that Iranians could consume.

> The appetite of some of the lower orders for bread is very extraordinary. I have often been surprised to have a servant ask for an increase of wages, *because* he had a large appetite. Persian invariably pay their servants so much in cash, so much (by weight) of bread, two suits a year, and what is left at meals divided among them. This the European does not do; he gives it all in coin. I have seen a boy eat fourteen pounds [6.3 kg] of new bread and, as a sauce to the bread, a dozen hard-boiled eggs. I *saw* this, and I left him- *still* eating.[48]

TWENTIETH CENTURY

Some men were famous for their devouring capacity. Browne mentioned the case of "Mahdi Hammal ('The Porter') who was well known in Tihran as a man of immense height, bulk and strength, and or voracious appetite. He would eat 1½ or 2 maunds of bread and cheese, and could carry the weight of a *kharwar* [300 kg] on his

---

41. Wills 1893, p. 336.
42. Wishard 1909, p. 188, see also pp. 141, 144.
43. Olmer 1908, p. 20.
44. Wishard 1909, p. 284.
45. Olmer 1908, p. 20.
46. Smith 1871, p. 402.
47. Rice 1923, p. 178.
48. Wills 1893, p. 336 (italics in original).

shoulders. His voracity has become proverbial."⁴⁹ No wonder that among the lower class bread is still called *qovvat-e ghaleb* (the prevailing or winning power).⁵⁰

Despite the political changes that took place in Iran after the constitutional Revolution of 1906 the poor didn't eat better than before. At that time, according to the French diplomat de Lorey, the meals of Iranian servants, who were much better off than common workers were:

> Very simple, and consisted chiefly of bread and cheese, varied now and then with *pilaw*. They drank water and tea. The Persian wil take tea all day along; It does not cost him much more than a farthing a cup. ... Between eleven and twelve his lunch (*nahar*) is brought to him, a solid meal consisting of pilaws and chilaws-baked rice served with meat or vegetables and moistened with butter, sauces, or gravy, or left dry. With this he drinks sherbets and eats fruit. The working classes naturally lead a simpler life: it depends on their means. For them lunch is often only of bread and cheese flavoured with mint-leaves.⁵¹

Meals were not much different in, e.g., Bushehr be it that some items were different. Breakfast consisted of bread and tea, while lunch, before noon, consisted of bread, dates, onions and three vegetables, viz. "kakoll, mangack, and tooleh. These vegetables are found in the fields in winter and spring." Dinner was one hour after sunset: bread, onions, cheese, sometimes soup; rice was eaten twice per week.⁵²

Unfortunately household food consumption data are lacking. Although household food consumption surveys were made in 1937, these were restricted to middle-income families in cities with a population above 50,000. The majority of the urban population did not fall within this range, so the results of that survey cannot help to highlight the situation of low-income groups. According to this survey, middle-class families spent 56% of the income on food, which was made up of the following six categories:

Table 8.2: Urban middle-class household expenditures on food items 1936 (in %)

Category	Sub-groups	Percentage of total expenditures	Subtotal
I. Bread and grain	Bread	29.3	
	Flour	9.9	
	Rice	7.0	
			37.2
II. Meat and fish	Mutton	13.3	
	Fowl	0.7	
			14.0
III. Milk and dairy products	Milk	13.3	
	Butter milk	0.7	
	Butter	8.4	
	Cheese	1.7	
	Eggs	1.3	
			11.3
IV. Vegetables and fruit	Vegetables	1.9	
	Fruit	4.2	
	Dates	0.6	
			6.7
V. Various articles	Spices	3.7	

---

49. Browne 1914, p. 108, 144 n.
50. Zavosh 1370, p. 220.
51. De Lorey 1907, pp. 29, 75. For how wealthy Iranians ate, see Ibid., p. 82.
52. Norden 1928, p. 122.

Category	Sub-groups	Percentage of total expenditures	Subtotal
	Sugar	14.5	
	Tea	5.2	
			23.4
VI. Beverages, tobacco, and opium	Tobacco	5.4	
	Opium	0.8	
	Beverages	0.8	
			7.0
Total			100.0

Table 8.2 shows that of the 56% of income spent on food category I (bread and cereals) represents the most important expenditure (37.2%), in which bread is the main item. Only 14% was spent on meat, mainly mutton, while expenditures of dairy (mostly butter) were only 11%. Households spent little on vegetables and fruit (6.7%), but relatively much on various food items (23.4%), of which sugar represented more than two-thirds. Expenditures on beverages and tobacco were minor (7%) and were mostly for tobacco.[53]

A contemporary impressionistic report reveals the data shown in Table 8.3. According to the same source these were the minimum requirements of a family of four, viz. two *qran*s and eleven *shahi*s (51 *shahi*s). A normal wage rate for an unskilled laborer would be three *qran*s per day, so that the family could save nine *shahi*s. However, most workers could not even afford these expenses. They hardly ever had meat; their daily diet consisted mainly of bread and dates. Cheese was a luxury. So it would look as it the minimum requirements were a wish rather than a reality.

Table 8.3: Prices of necessities of life consumed by the lower classes in Isfahan [54]

Wheat	2 riyals per kg.,	Tea per packet	45.00 /kg
Bread	2	Barley	1.15
Rice	4.15	Straw	0.35
Sugar, moist	26.70	Kerosene	1.50
Sugar, loaf	26.70	Firewood	0.35
Mutton	4.30	Charcoal	1.00
Ghee	21.65	Milk	1.70
Fowls each	10.00	Eggs each	0.25

Using the Isfahan data for 1941 (Table 8.3) as a yard-stick, together with a list of prices referring to the situation in October 1941 we may calculate the level of purchasing power. Since we have no idea what the dietary pattern was in Isfahan at that time, I have used the data of a typically dietary pattern in urban southern Iran (Fars province) for the years 1962-68 which was the closest reliable data available on this subject.[55] From Table 8.4 we see that a few necessities such as fuel and tea are not included. Furthermore, we notice that, among the list of goods of 1941, pulses, fruits, and vegetables are missing. We may safely assume that all these omitted goods, from one or another Table, were used by the working class in Isfahan at that time. The five goods for which we have been able to calculate the expenditure per person per day result in a minimum requirement per family of four persons of 5.68 riyals excluding fuel, tea, fruit, vegetables and pulses, goods for which it is impossible to do without. In only three out of nine textile mills did the men earn a minimum wage sufficient to afford this expenditure. Unless they earned more, they had to starve. A similar situation existed in Azarbaijan in 1936.

---

53. ILO 1937, pp. 881-84.

54. FO 371/40222, f. 37
55. Based on Sen Gupta 1968. Column I refer to the data of Azarbaijan, II to that of Isfahan, and III of Fars.

Table 8.3: Typical Dietary Pattern in Urban Iran Province 1962-68.

Food group	Price 1941	*Possible diets in			Expenditure	
per kg. per diem	grams per caput					
		I	II	III	Expenditures of II	
Bread	2 riyals	400	462	391	0.782 riyals	
Sugar	26.70	57	84	37	0.320	
Mutton	4.30	40	48	32	0.137	
Ghee	21.65	11	17	4	0.086	
Milk	1.70	34	154	55	0.093	
Potatoes	-		46	34	12	
Pulses	-		27	25	6	
Vegetables	-		66	103	39	
Fruits	-		115	17	90	
Total kilocalories	2 210	2 200	1 796		1.4201 riyals	
% of requirement	96	96	78			

*Possible diets made up of different amounts (grams, per caput, per diem) of comestibles listed in the table are represented by columns I, II & III.

Table 8.4: Prices of articles of prime necessity in Tabriz in 1935-36. [56]

Group	Unit	Prices in riyals	
		Dec. 1935	Dec. 1936
Charcoal	batman	2.40	2.40
Wood	kharvar	70.00	95.00
Rice (Resht)	batman	9.00	1200
Rice (local)	do.	4.00	5.60
Bread	do.	2.00	240
Ghee	do.	32.00	44.00
Split peas	do.	7.00	4.60
Cheese (local)	do.	11.00	14.00
Beans	do.	3.40	4.00
Yarma (millet)	do.	3.00	3.00
Cotton cloth	meter	2.40	
Woolen cloth	do.	30.00	
Shoes	pair	40.00	
Soap	batman	16.00	
Sugar	do.	15.00	
Tea	girvanka	10.00	
Eggs	each	0.15	
Chickens	do.	3.00	
Meat	batman	10.40	

Batman = 3 kg; *kharvar* = 300 kg; *girvanka* = 409.5 grams

Another alternative was not to marry, or if married, to leave one's family in the village, or if in town, to have wife and children work as well.[57]

The bleak picture offered by these data tallies with a report by the American Legation on living conditions of workers in August 1941.

> Wages are certainly for more than bare existence, amounting for the common laborer to four to ten rials a day. It may be said that it will purchase a loaf of white bread or that a worker must pay from three to seven rials a day for his food. Thus it will be seen that the wage is insufficient even for food for a family and most workers

---

56. FO 371/20830, f.206.

57. Chaqueri 1978, p. 36.

have a starvation diet consisting of tea, (not white) bread, cheese and onions, with occasional greens and grapes and infrequent rice and cheap meat. It is not possible to buy adequate clothing or even to dream of luxuries such as education of the children. Sometimes the workers' one or more wives and the children work to bring in additional skilled income to make possible a slightly higher standard of workers living.[58]

In the 1950s, bread was still the most important food consumed together with vegetables, fruit and sometimes meat, which represented only 2% of low-income diets. This inadequate diet, i.e. one deficient in proteins and certain vitamins nevertheless provided the majority of the population with sufficient calories. The average daily caloric intake per person was 2,100 kilocalories, of which 60% was from cereals. In good harvest years it rose to 2,200 kcal, which was lower than in Iran's neighboring countries, while in winter 10% fewer calories were consumed. The difference between the diet of the rich and the poor was significant. "The landowning class spends approximately 38 percent of its total budget on food; agricultural laborers, 68 percent; and urban wage earner, 74 percent."[59] Almost two decades later it was noted that the daily caloric intake had dropped to 1,620 kilocalories in 1968, although the earlier higher figures may have been over-estimations. This inadequate and insufficient diet lowered people's resistance to disease and in 1969 a survey in major urban hospitals found that 35 percent of infants under twelve treated in those hospitals suffered from malnutrition. It was further found that "Girls generally get less food than boys, and that the oldest and youngest children in the family are given preferential treatment at meals,

whereas those in the middle ranges receive much smaller portions."[60] In 1940, babies after a few weeks were freely given bread, cucumber, and carrots. When the child was weaned, milk is no longer part of its diet. "Among the poor, children subsist on dry bread and boiled tea."[61]

Bread remained the dietary staple food for the population in the 1950-60s and accounted, on average, for 70% of the daily caloric intake. Several studies conducted in rural and urban environments showed variations in the proportion of proteins supplied by bread, from 60% among farmers to 34% among landowners.[62] In 1961, the US Department of Agriculture in 1961 concluded that "it is doubtful that the Iranian calorie level ever rises much above the 2,350 kilocalories average per capita for all West Asian countries."[63] A group of squatters (*hashiyeh-neshinan*) in Tehran in 1971 had a sufficient daily caloric intake (2,600-3,080 kcal), but most of this came from bread. For those working in the brick kilns this was 980 g/day and those living in make-shift huts (*alvank-neshinan*) 620 g/day, or resp. 78% and 59% of calories were supplied by bread. Protein intake of kiln workers was 108 g/day, and those living in make-shift huts 81 g/day, and most of that also came from bread (resp. 78% and 67%). Animal protein was little consumed, viz. 12 g/day for kiln workers and 10 g/day for those living in make-shift huts, or about 11% of the total, although for about half of the families it was below 10%. FAO at that time proposed that animal protein intake in the Middle East should be 20g/day. Calcium intake is 730 mg (kilns) and 580 mg/day (make-shift huts), mostly from bread (75% for kilns and 55% for those living in make-shift huts). Although in summer fruits are abundant and cheap vitamin A intake was still insufficient. It was 2,300 units lower for kilns and 3,800 units lower for those living in

---

58. Ladjevardi 1981, p. 103 quoting Harold B. Minor, 12 August 1941 (891.00/1816) US National Archives.
59. US Department of Agriculture 1961 a, p. 2; Ibid. b, p. 6; U.S. Army 1963, pp. 142-43; CENTO 1968, p. 107; Mehrbani 1343, p. 360.
60. US Government 1971, p. 152.
61. Morton 1940, pp. 317-18.
62. Desmet-Grégoire 1989.
63. US Department of Agriculture 1961 b, p. 6.

make-shift huts than the international WHO norm. If it was that bad in summer it must have been worse in winter when fruits are not abundant and expensive. It was also insufficient for other inputs (thiamine, riboflavin, niacin, vitamin C). In short, these migrant-squatters lived on bread, and their inadequate nutrition was due to poverty not due to tradition. This is clear from the fact that the workers living in make-shift huts were from the Caspian region, where people normally eat rice, and little bread. Their income varied between 53-80 *tumans*/month, and if they earned more they ate more protein, be it that this was mostly from bread. Animal protein intake remained more or less the same. The reality was more negative, for the researchers observed that these figures were on the optimistic side.[64]

This situation was not atypical for non-migrant urban families either. Poor Jewish families in Shiraz families had "meat only twice per week and in small quantities. By eating less rice and more bread and by using more vegetables, the food budget may be cut by about one-third."[65] This unhealthy dietary situation for poor urban dwellers existed despite the fact that, for example, squatters in Bandar Abbas spent 70% of their income on food.[66] A study carried out in 1972-73 by Hossein Azimi found that 44% of the population was undernourished and 23% consumed less than 90% of the WHO daily caloric intake. In particular 21% mostly in urban areas were undernourished, 20% also mostly in towns were severely undernourished, and 3% (mostly in villages) were dangerously undernourished.[67]

After the Islamic revolution of 1979, the average diet had more than 2,400 kilocalories/day, but fell to 2,200 kilocalories per day in 1986-87 during the worst war years to increase thereafter, while increased access to health care had a positive impact on health indicators.[68] In 2005, the daily caloric intake was 3,425 kcal (vegetable products 91%; animal products 9%) or 185% of the FAO recommended minimum.[69] Of this wheat still represents about 50% or about 600 g/per day.[70]

Rural Diets

Introduction

Food intake in rural areas did not substantially differ much from that in urban areas. As a consequence, the rural diet likewise was usually sufficiently nutritious, but deficient in proteins and vitamins. There was a high incidence of iron-deficiency anemia, for example, among villagers in Fars, which was probably due to high concentrations of phytate in the high extraction flours used and the absence of leaven and fermentation. About half of their caloric intake was bread.[71]

It would seem that from early times onwards the dietary pattern was similar what it was until recent times. Greg Johnson has suggested that, if in Khuzestan the same ration system that was used in neighboring Uruk, existed, the likely daily ration assigned in the Khuzestan settlements may have been 539 g of barley (representing the content of the most common bevel rim bowls) in 2000 BCE. This amount of barley, when baked as bread, represents a caloric value of 1400 kilocalories per day. As this was insufficient he suggests that like in Uruk,

---

64. Dowlat et al. 1352, pp. 8-14.
65. Loeb 1977, p. 80.
66. Nirumand and Ahsan 1351, p. 49.
67. Katouzian 1981, pp. 270-72 quoting from Hossein Azimi, "Aspects of Poverty and Income Distribution in Iran." Unpublished thesis Oxford 1979.

68. United Nations 2001, p. 84.
69. Encyclopaedia Britannica 2009, p. 355.
70. Preedy et al. 2011, p. 266.
71. Reinhold 1972. Phytic acid, or phytate when in salt form, is a form of stored phosporus in plant tissues, mainly bran and seeds; humans cannot digest it.

in Khuzestan the people must have had access to additional food sources.⁷²

The Iranian peasants were hard workers and led frugal lives, and were almost vegetarians. How well they ate depended on how good the harvest was, how good the landlord was, the season's yield (herbs, vegetables, fruits) and their own relative economic situation. In general, peasants consumed unleavened barley, sorghum or millet bread or a combination thereof, while often their landlord got the wheat. The usual kind of bread eaten is often described as coarse, hard or in case of Talesh as "brown, thick, heavy and difficult to digest."⁷³ In Berjand (eastern Iran) the food "is about the worst I have ever seen; strong and greasy: so fond do they seem of highly-seasoned food, that even the bread is thickly covered with shreds of onions and aromatic herbs."⁷⁴ The meal was often accompanied by curds, sour milk (*dugh*), yoghurt (*mast*), cheese, whey (*kashk*), or boiled buttermilk (*shalansh* or *krut*), the product of their own animals. In summer, they further ate lots of fruit, in particular cucumbers and melons, which were usually eaten prior to the meal.⁷⁵ One way to eat fruit was to make grape syrup in which they dipped bread and hence the bread was called *nan-e dushab*, but this was a luxury reserved for festivals and other important events, such as at harvest time, when having guests, or at a marriage feast. The same held for the consumption of rice.⁷⁶ According to Fowler, in the 1830s, when peasants were not oppressed they had an abundant breakfast. "They have 'moss,' or sour milk, which they are very fond of; an abundance of flat bread, which is soft and unleavened; with butter, cheese, honey, fruits in the season, eggs and fowls, rice and tobacco."⁷⁷ Around 1850, in the village of Savand (near Shiraz), according to Binning, "During the year, the family of four will consume about 100 *mann*s of wheat; 100 *mann*s of barley; 100 mans of *dhorrat* (Indian corn); 5 *mann*s of rice; and 3 *mann*s of pulse. These he grows himself, and milk and butter his cattle provides. Fowls provide some eggs."⁷⁸ According to Sykes, in Khorasan people needed some 50 lbs. (22.7 kg) of wheat per month per person. Moreover, "his bread he eats as a rule with curds and mint."⁷⁹

Ramazan amad va dar sofreh-ye zare` nan nist
Dar tan-e dokhter-e u pirahan va tonban nist
Jegari nist keh khunin z gham-e dehqan nist
`ellat anast keh ensaf dar in veyran nist

رمضان آمد و در سفرهٔ زارع نان نیست
در تن دختر او پیرهن و تنبان نیست

---

72. Johnson 1973, pp. 137-39.
73. De Morgan 1895, vol. 1, p. 251.
74. Forbes 1844, p. 163.
75. "With Nestorians a waiter of fruit is immediately set before us, with bread, cheese, butter, honey, sweetmeats, etc." Perkins 1843, p. 429; Knanishu 1899, pp. 103-04; Mirza 1920, pp. 122-23 (breakfast: bread with butter, honey or syrup; noon: meat, potatoes, rice, sherbet; evening: meat, potatoes, rice, cabbage, sometimes kidney beans. He adds that "many never used any butter with their meals."), 179 (Kurdish diet: bread, buttermilk, cheese); Sykes 1969, vol. 2, p. 391 ("curds, cheese, eggs, beetroot, turnips, onions, garlic and various herbs.")
76. Anonymous 1828, vol. 1, pp. 256-57 (the villagers in the plains eat more wheaten bread); Reineggs 1807, pp. 207, 242, 336; Boré 1840, vol. 2, p. 242; Mignan 1839, vol. 1, pp. 246, 306; Fowler 1841, vol. 1, pp. 138 (eggs, honey), 145; Forbes 1844, p. 154 (only barley-bread, mulberries and turnips to eat."); Perkins 1843, p. 133, 156, 170, 280; Polak 1862, p. 130; Wilson 1895, p. 129; Forbes-Leith 1927, pp. 39-40; Sykes 1910, pp. 210, 212-213; Wishard 1909, p. 141 (hard bread with raisins); Fraser 1840, vol. 1, p. 128, 131; Binder 1887, p. 352; Aitchison 1890, pp. 35-36, 76, 134-135; de Morgan 1894, vol. 1, p. 251; Merritt-Hawkes 1935, p. 17; Rice 1923, pp. 60, 89; Morton 1940, p. 55; Ivanow 1931, p. 39 (Walnuts and onions form an important item in the food of local peasants); Al-e Ahmad 1333, p. 27; Tahbaz 1342, p. 44; Lindberg 1955, pp. 172-73; Borhanian 1960. p. 93; E`tesam al-Molk 1371, p. 314 (Qa'en); Fesharaki 2537, p. 45 (Lut area); Salzmann 1994, p. 73; De Windt 1891, p. 140 (Baluchistan).
77. Fowler 1841, vol. 1, p. 145. Although there is no doubt that the population of well managed villages ate well, Fowler idealized the situation Persian villages, however. "I do love the vagabondising about in the Persian villages, which I have done for months at a time; and so fascinated was I with this rustic life, that I had a notion of becoming a Ketkodeh myself." He decided not to when confronted with the less idyllic side of village life. Ibid., vol. 1, p. 179.
78. Binning 1857, vol. 2, p. 47.
79. Sykes 1969, vol. 2, p. 391

جگری نیست که خونین ز غم دهقان نیست

علت آنست که انصاف در این ویران نیست

Ramazan has come but there is no bread on the peasant's table,
And no shirt or skirt on his daughter's body.
There is no heart which does not bleed with sorrow for the peasant;
The reason is that there is no justice in this desolated place.[80]

Twentieth century

Water and some tea were drunk at all three meals. When the men work on a far field they took bread and tea with them for lunch, and also some dates, an egg, or gherkin. Even the well-to-do did not eat well. Only when there was a festival, a party, or there were guests one eats well. Men eat first at guest meals, women and children eat what remains.[81] In the village of Talebabad, near Tehran, the consumption of bread per family was 2.4 kg/day in the 1960s, but in addition they also consumed some *sangak* bread that was bought from Firuzabad, so that daily bread consumption per person was 0.5 kg.[82] In Hamidieh (Khuzestan) bread and onions was the staple. In 1954, bread represented one-third of food expenses of a farmer's family. Per capita consumption of bread was 0.76 kg.[83]

In some areas, such as in the mountain villages of Meymand district, bread was not eaten throughout the year, because they did not have barley, which they exchanged in the nearby towns for firewood, herbs and gums. Here peasants ate oleaster flour (*senjed*), which they stored in leather bags (*mashk*), mixed with dried whey (*kashk*), instead of bread during winter.[84] A special dish for the poor in Azerbaijan was the making of cracked wheat, which was boiled and dried in small cakes.[85] From this flour they also prepare a kind of grits (*belghur*), which especially the Turkish-speaking population liked and which took the place of rice for them.[86] In many parts of eastern Iran, the fruit of the wild pear (*Pyrus sp.*), as well as that of the *taghun*, *tokhm* (*Celtis caucasia*), a common indigenous tree in Khorasan, and of dried mulberries, were all converted into flour and mixed with ordinary flour to make into bread; so also were the seeds of luffa and some other of the *Cucurbitaceae*. The fruit of the ungrafted mulberry trees was not considered worth eating in a fresh state, but it was collected in immense quantities to be dried. The dried fruit, *tut-e-maghz*, was found in every household, for eating as a relish with their ordinary bread diet, or it was made into flour, *talkhan*, to be mixed with corn-flour and baked into bread.[87] The diet could also be very simple during hard times such as around 1740, when the common food of the soldiery, and of the bulk of the people, was bread and salt.[88]

Meat was a luxury and, except on special occasions, such as feast days and weddings, was only eaten by the more affluent. Moreover, meat could not be stored and if slaughtered has to be eaten the same day. Although chickens, sheep, and goats were kept in every household, the majority regarded these animals as producers of income, rather than as meat alone.[89] Armenian peasants in

---

80. From the poem *Zare`* (Cultivator) from Ashraf Gilani, reproduced in Ricks 1984, p. 191.
81. Planck 1962, p. 54; de Morgan 1894, vol. 1, p. 251. In the 19th century, when tea became a popular drink, most peasants could not afford it. Sykes 1969, vol. 2, p. 391.
82. Safinezhad 1345, pp. 456-57.
83. Borhanian 1960. p. 93.

84. Vaziri 1346, p. 163; Hanway 1753, vol. 1, p. 124.
85. Knanishu 1899, p. 109.
86. Polak 1865, vol. 1, p. 111; Adams 1900, p. 202.
87. Aitchison 1890, pp. 35-36, 76, 134-135.
88. Hanway 1753, vol. 1, p. 124.
89. Polak 1862, p. 130; Forbes-Leith 1927, pp. 39-40; Sykes 1910, pp. 210, 212-213; Perkins 1843, p. 170; Fraser 1840, vol. 1, p. 128, 131; Sykes 1969, vol. 2, p. 391; Binder 1887, p. 352; Merritt-Hawkes 1935, p. 17; Rice 1923, pp. 60, 89; Al-e Ahmad 1333, p. 27; Tahbaz 1342, p. 44; Planck 1962, p. 53. However, Watson 1976, pp. 27-28 writes: "As a general rule Persian peasants eat meat three or four times a week, if they cannot afford to eat it every day. In autumn

Qaradagh rarely ate meat, "except when an animal is diseased or injured and must be killed, or when a sacrifice is offered, In the course of one month we had meat only two or three times. This is interrupted by frequent fasts which exclude all animal products."[90] Goat-meat was mainly eaten by the poorer classes, and was considered to be unwholesome. Only in northern Iran was pheasant an article of food and excellently prepared.[91] In Khisht, Binning shared a breakfast of *halim*, "a pottage of wheat and chopped meat; with hard-boiled eggs and dates."[92] In Kurdistan, some among the rural population ate hares, foxes and hogs, a behavior similar to that of the Shaufi tribe near Tehran, who ate porcupines, hedgehogs and lizards, which generally were looked upon as unclean.[93]

In many villages soups (*ash*), stews (*abgusht*), or pottages (*halim*) were eaten, which sometimes contained meat and/or fat. In the villages of Owrazan and Yush the people ate practically every day *ash*, boiled water with vegetables such as lentils or rice and potatoes, or carrots, and *reshteh* (a kind of macaroni); they even ate it at lunch (*chasht*). There were many kinds of *ash* (*kashk-e ash*, (*dugh*) *ash*, *tesh ash*, *mast ash*, *narm ash*), which were all without meat and named after one of the main ingredients such as whey, buttermilk, or yoghurt. To that end there was a bucket of butter milk (*dugh*) to mix with the *ash*, or sometimes *kashk*. Bread, cheese and ash were eaten with a very large wooden spoon.[94] Others ate *abgusht* (litt. meat water), which as the name suggest contains some meat and/or fat in addition to herbs. Another pottage is that of *halim*, porridge of wheat groat and meat. In Sistan, in addition to mostly bread, "ragouts of mutton flavoured with assafoetida as a vegetable, or curds,

they salt mutton for the winter consumption." Given that both his contemporaries as well as twentieth century nutrition studies disagree, one may conclude that Watson was seriously mistaken.

90. Wilson 1895 p. 129.
91. Schindler 1898, pp. 34, 45.
92. Binning 1857, vol.1, p. 173.
93. Fraser 1840, vol. 1, p. 187-88; Aitchison 1890, p. 189.
94. Al-e Ahmad 1333, p. 27; Tahbaz 1342, p. 44.

and in the proper season melons. The wealthy live differently according to taste and means."[95]

To give more depth and relief to the description of the average diet that was consumed by most peasants in Iran, I reproduce two tables that show the weekly menu per day of peasant families in the 1960s. One is of the rural town of Ahar (Azerbaijan) and the other of a village in Fars. It would seem that families in Ahar were slightly better off than those in Fars, because the latter rarely ate rice and dairy products. In both communities peasants mostly ate what they produced, but in the case of the Fars village fruit and vegetables had to come from outside. Their diet was little varied and consisted mostly of bread made from wheat and barley flour, baked daily. In both locations bread was baked at home, but in Ahar there was a professional bakery, which mostly served those who lived in Tehran or had no family. Large families and permanent inhabitants maintained that the bakery bread was not filling, i.e. its quality was not good. It was made with wheat, with additions and villagers, therefore, prefered to make their own bread.

Table 8.5: Weekly menu of a middle-class farmer's family of 10 persons in Ahar

Morning	Noon	Evening
Saturday		
Bread, cheese, tea	Abgusht (0.25 kg meat, bones, fat-soup with potatoes, onions, beans, peas, tomatoes), yoghurt, bread	Rice with lentils, dates, yoghurt
Sunday		
Bread, cheese, tea	Abgusht, bread, yoghurt	Bread, butter, sweetmeat, tea, yoghurt
Monday		

95. Bellew 1873, p. 159.

Morning	Noon	Evening
Bread, cheese, tea	Abgusht, bread, yoghurt	Gheyme-polo (sheep stew with rice, peas and fried onion) yoghurt
Tuesday		
Bread, cheese, tea	Kallehpacheh (soup with stomach, feet, and lungs of sheep)	Leftovers of noon, fried eggs, yoghurt
Wednesday		
Bread, cheese, tea	Abgusht, bread, yoghurt	Bread, rowghan, grapes, yoghurt
Thursday		
Bread, cheese, tea	Abgusht, bread, yoghurt	Fesenjan (walnut-based stew), goulash, rice, yoghurt
Friday		
Bread, cheese, tea	Abgusht, bread, yoghurt	Bread, fried eggs, fried tomatoes, onions, meat leftovers, sugar melons, yoghurt

Source: Djirsara 1970, p. 45.

Meat was seldom eaten. A more wealthy family eats the same, only more often and more meat as well as more grapes and melons. Lower class families, depending on their situation, eat less often and less meat and rice, and mainly on Sundays. Also, because they do not have their own animals they eat less animal products and thus suffer from a protein deficit. Plant fats were hardly eaten; mostly animal fat, in particular ghee (*rowghan*), but because of its high price used in small quantities only. For months there was no milk, while too few eggs were produced. Both quantitatively and qualitatively this was an insufficient diet, which impacted on the susceptibility to illness and the lack of stamina.[96] Consequently, there was a high incidence of malnutrition.[97]

The same pattern that occurred in Ahar and Fars was found in the villages of Qom province, where bread was the basis of all three daily meals in the 1960s. The staple was *nan-e taftun*, round and flat, which is baked in each house in a *tanur*. In the morning people only ate bread, with or without a bit of cheese, and some tea; at noon the meal consisted of a meat ragout, grilled meat, giblets or eggs, and in the evening *abgusht* or *ash* with bread in it, eaten with a spoon. Rice was eaten only on special occasions. In summer a bowl of yoghurt with cucumber was eaten, while with the meal water or *dugh* was served in a single glass that was passed around. Fruits were eaten in between meals. The caloric value of the meals was adequate (2,500-3,000 kilocalories), but unbalanced. Between 37-55% of food intake was bread, people ate relatively little protein, while the amount of vegetables was also inadequate, because farmers prefered to sell these.[98]

Table 8.6: Daily dietary pattern in villages in the Marvdasht plain (Fars) in the 1960s

family	Day	Breakfast	Lunch	Dinner
Well-off	Sat.	Bread, tea, roasted entrails	Bread, tea, liver and kidneys baked in fat	Bread, tea, mutton with potatoes, tomatoes, lemons
Poor		Bread, tea	Bread, tea, fried eggplants	Bread, tea

96. Djirsara 1970, pp. 45-47; Planck 1962, pp. 53-54. See also, Borhanian 1960, p. 93; Al-e Ahmad 1337, p. 26; Tahbaz 1342, pp. 44-45. "The poorer peasant and even those of the middle class seldom taste meat and rarely can afford to eat rice." FO 60/327 (1870).

97. Planck 1962, pp. 56-60.

98. Bazin 1970, pp. 84-85.

family	Day	Breakfast	Lunch	Dinner
Well-off	Sun.	Bread, tea, yoghurt	Mutton with eggplant, melons; – guest in Gondashlu	bread, tea, soup with meat, potatoes and beans
Poor		Bread, tea	bread, tea, grapes	Bread, tea, fried eggplants and tomatoes
Well-off	Mon.	Bread, tea	Mutton stew with potatoes, tomatoes, onions, melons – guest in Zarqan	Bread, tea, stew as at lunch
Poor		Bread, tea	bread, tea, beef meatballs with lentils, grapes	Bread, tea, leftovers from lunch as soup
Well-off	Tues.	Bread, tea	bread, tea, mutton with potatoes, tomatoes, onions fried in rowghan	Bread, tea, soup with meat, turnips, beans, tomatoes and onions
Poor		Bread, tea	Bread, tea, melons	bread, tea, pomegranates
Well-off	Wed.	Bread, tea	Bread, tea, eggplant and tomatoes fried in fat	Bread, tea, rice
Poor		Bread, tea	Bread, tea, soup with potatoes, tomatoes, onions	Like lunch
Well-off	Thur.	Bread, tea	Bread, tea, raw gherkins, 1 egg (the father only)	Bread, tea, rice, melons
Poor		Bread, tea	Bread, tea, half a sugar melon	Bread, tea, dates
Well-off	Fri.	Bread, tea	Bread, tea, mutton stew with tomatoes, potatoes, onions, melons	Bread, tea, soup with met, tomatoes, beans, peas, onions
Poor		Bread, tea	Bread, tea, beef with eggplants fried in oil	Bread, tea, rice with peas, potatoes and mutton – guest in Gondashlu

Source: Planck 1962, p. 55

The diet of the peasants was, of course, really bad after a poor harvest or some other mishap. For example, after locusts had damaged their crops, peasants "had to live on half-rations throughout the winter, and must continue to do so until the grain was ripe." The landowner usually supplied these rations.[99] In 1912, when cereals were twice as expensive as normal, the peasants in Yazd subsisted on millet, cotton seed, turnips, beetroot, etc.[100] "Many families, for weeks together, have no bread in their houses." Especially in the period before harvest time, their suffering was great.[101]

This frugal diet was practically universal in Iran. Although adequate in terms of caloric intake it lacked in variety, certain vitamins and sufficient

---

99. Sykes 1910, pp. 210, 212.
100. *DCR* 5048, p. 51.
101. Anonymous 1859, p. 82.

proteins. Coan, a missionary who had lived most of his life in Iran, therefore, opined in 1939, "In a land where the people depend almost entirely on wheat and are great bread eaters, anything that will take its place is an incalculable blessing." He in particular referred to the positive impact that the introduction of potatoes, tomatoes, sweet corn and other vegetables might have on people's health.[102]

There were two regions where the dietary pattern was not dominated by bread, but by rice (Gilan, Mazandaran) or dates (littoral of the Persian Gulf). These were also two regions where fish was eaten and much more so than in the rest of Iran. Sunflower seeds were also used as food on the Caspian coast.[103]

In the provinces of the Caspian littoral, the diet was considerably different from that of the rest of the country, if only because the staple was rice.[104] People did not eat bread, which was only to be found in the large towns and the households of the grandees.[105] In the 1820s, according to Fraser, the diet was as follows:

> Rice and mass, or sour milk; sometimes rice boiled down with a little milk to a thick gelatinous substance, with mass, and a sort of poor cheese; butter milk, and much of an acid which is made of sour oranges, and wild pomegranates; such, and the like, for the principal fare of most orders in Mazunderan. Those who can afford it, mix a little butter with their rice, and season it with salt, or dried fish, or meat, according to their means; but bread is little used. They do not like it, and say that their stomachs cannot digest it, and that it makes them ill; but wheat is little cultivated, and of inferior quality in Mazunderan; so that those who eat bread, use the wheat which is imported from other provinces.[106]

It was only in the mountainous areas, where wheat and barley were grown, that bread and dairy products were the staple, but rice was eaten at lunch. The consumption of bread in the lowlands only dates from the 1940s, where it has become normal to have breakfast with tea, or butter and honey, or jam. In the towns people buy bread at the nearest bakery; mostly *lavash* or *barbari*. *Sangak* was only sold in Fuman and Sowma'eh Sara in the 1970s. Outside the towns people baked bread at home, either on a *saj* or in an oven. It is a *lavash*-type bread, or a domestic version of *barbari*, the so-called *panjeh-kesh*, meaning that the dough is grabbed 'with five finger'. Nevertheless, people still eat more rice (40-65%) than bread (0-25%) according to diet surveys.[107]

As to the quantities of rice consumed in the 1870s the daily food intake was as follows: "At their meals the adults get through 10 oz. [283 g] of rice for breakfast, 22 oz. [622 g] for the midday meal, and at supper they consume about 22 oz.; actual dry rice is about 27 oz [ca. 2,900 kcal]. In the spring the food is varied by wheaten bread, and during the summer the women take to the men in the fields a delectable compound of rice, spinage, and whey, seasoned with a handful of powdered garlic."[108] One hundred years later not much has changed, apart from the fact that bread has become a regular food item in Gilani and Mazandari households. In the Qorveh and neighboring districts bread and dairy was the staple, but very little meat was consumed. If there was meat it was mostly used for the preparation of *abgusht* (with potatoes, onions, beans, peas, rice, etc). Breakfast consisted of bread and tea, yoghurt, milk or cream; at noon mostly *ash-e dugh*

---

102. Coan 1939, p. 230.
103. Adams 1900, p. 129.
104. Jaubert 1821, p. 425.
105. Jaubert 1821, pp. 337, 425; Fraser 1826, p. 216 (bread in Resht).

106. Fraser 1826, p. 88
107. Bazin 1980, vol. 1, p. 57; de Morgan 1894, vol. 1, p. 251 (rice is a luxury in the mountains).
108. Government of Great Britain 1882, p. 1071 (or in total 1.5 kg rice/day). See, however, Afzal al-Molk 1373, p. 63, according to whom the food in Mazandaran was very bad compared with that of central Iran.

was eaten, and if possible *abgusht*. If the noon meal was warm then dinner was cold. *Dugh* (buttermilk) and yoghurt (*mast*) were regularly consumed, but rarely butter and eggs. During the work season, working outside their own area, farmers ate bread and buttermilk (*dugh*) that they took with them.[109]

PERSIAN GULF LITTORAL DIETS

In the Persian Gulf littoral, the staple food was dates and fish and very little bread was consumed.[110] According to Harrison, in the 1930s in Baluchistan, "The standard of living is lower than in other parts of Iran and sugar and tea are rarities. After Nu Ruz (New Year's Day, March 21) feast which we gave our men, the Bashakirdis reported that they had drunk more tea in one day than during the previous course of their lives. Inland they live principally on dates with which they drink copious draughts of water, eking this out with a little dried fish, bread, meat, or berries of the *pish-*palm as rather infrequent luxuries."[111] Likewise in Hormuz and Moghistan, where in the fourteenth century "their food is fish and dried dates. They say in their tongue *Khurma wamahi luti padishahi*, which means 'Dates and fish are a royal dish.'"[112] Marco Polo reported that "The people [of Hormuz] never eat meat and wheaten bread except when they are ill, and if they take such food when they are in health it makes them ill." Their normal food consisted of dates, salt-fish, and onions.[113] On the Makran coast, dates and fish are eaten.[114]

This dates and fish diet was enriched with grains as well as fruits and vegetables. The poor had to do with the most inferior qualities of those common food items as well as with those that only the poor ate, such as the red, sour fruit of the *lul* tree.[115] In addition to fish, other forms of protein were also consumed. In Choghadak (near Bushehr), for example, poor families ate the jerboa (the size of a large rat, sits upright on its hind legs, and feeds itself with its fore-paws like a squirrel, and can make large leaps), although it was believed to be unclean food for Moslems.[116] Inland from Bushehr the diet started to change. The village diet in the port's hinterland did not include dates and fish. Dinner in one village consisted of rice, lentils, peas and a herbs mixture "with bread, a white curd cheese and immense quantities of a very hard and tough lettuce, and also radishes, leaves. Meat is not for every day, but, unless the people are very poor, it is Friday (the Islamic Sunday) treat. All the people who are lucky enough to have a milk-giving animal eat mast [yoghurt]."[117]

DIET OF NOMADIC GROUPS

A stated above the diet of nomadic groups was similar to that of the sedentary rural population, be it that they were somewhat poorer than their village brethren. After all, it was mostly nomadic groups who consumed acorn bread for part of the year (see ch. 2). Some Bakhtiyari sections "scarcely raise sufficient corn for their own wants, and are frequently exposed to much misery from absolute famine."[118]

Bread was also the staple among nomadic groups. The Lur nomads lived on a diet of barley bread, yogurt and butter-milk, and very little meat, "for a dead ewe no longer produces milk nor a ram wool."[119] A man easily ate one loaf, women and children each a half one or less. "Since it takes one kilo of flour to make three or four of these nans, an average family of four or five persons would

---

109. Mahmudi 1352, pp. 75-77.
110. Flandin 1851, vol. 2, p. 284.
111. Harrison 1941, p. 4.
112. Ibn Battutah 1958, vol. 2, p. 400.
113. Polo 1993, vol. 1, pp. 107-08.
114. Harrison 1941 p. 3; Ouseley 1819, vol. 1, p. 228; Kempthorne 1835, p. 282.

115. Faramarzi 1379, p. 646.
116. Binning 1857, vol.1, p. 156.
117. Merritt-Hawkes 1935, p. 17.
118. Layard 1846, p. 18.
119. Merritt-Hawkes 1935, p. 226.

need at least 3 kg of flour every day."[120] Among the Kurds in the 1880s, the men ate >700 g of bread per day, which is similar to what sedentary households consumed.[121] "In a family with three children and three adults, about 22-24 loaves of bread were baked each day."[122] Therefore, it was quite normal that tribal employers paid their servants only in bread. For example, each individual *sovar* in the service of the Bakhtiyari Ilkhans "receives four pounds of this a day."[123]

The Bakhtiyaris had a similar diet as the Lurs. "The ordinary food of these hardy wanderers [Bakhtiyaris] is mas, or dry curds, goats' flesh, goat's milk, and acorns."[124] In modern times, Bakhtiyaris, who usually baked their own bread, but bought bread in towns when they visited urban locations.[125] All migrant groups in the Zagros range ate acorn bread part of the year due to poverty (see above). The Turkmen in the 1870s also mainly ate bread. Breakfast consisted of freshly baked bread, which was "has an intensely clayey taste and odour," and this was "washed down by weak green tea, usually sugarless," because sugar was a great luxury.[126] As better food, the Turkmen ate "rice or yarma (bruised wheat), and sour milk; and on a great occasion a sheep is killed, and soup or pilau is made."[127] Dinner consisted in leathery bread with fowl, mast or coagulated milk, and boiled rice.[128] In short, the diet of migrants was a meager one. Harrison relates the diet of his Lur camp servants in the 1940s "Their staple diet of bread with a mouthful of tea and sugar during most of my time cost them fourpence daily, which left something over for a little fat and meat."[129]

As in the case of the village population I reproduce two weekly diets by a group of Feili Lurs and of Afshar tribesmen in Kerman (3 days only) to give depth to the above summarized description of the typical average diet of migrant groups. The dietary pattern was very much similar to that of sedentary rural dwellers. Bread is the main food product. One adult needs 7-8 *man* (21-24 kg) flour per month. Bread is eaten with all meals, sometimes without anything else, sometimes with grape syrup, walnuts, cheese, yoghurt or milk, once, and with well-to-do families twice; a warm meal is eaten with the bread, while pulses, fried potatoes, and carrots are also consumed. Some fruit or fresh vegetables are only eaten during harvest time. Poor families hardly ever eat rice, the wealthy a few days per week, but without condiments and only with bread. Normally, Lurs eat much rice, *mast*, *dugh* and bread. Table 8.8 does not entirely reflect a normal daily Lur diet as Feilberg, the author of the table, was a guest and his hosts went out of their way to serve him the best they could offer.

Table 8.7: Dietary pattern among Feili Lurs in 1935

28 May 1935	Morning	Flap bread, mast, tea
	Noon	Halva, bread, buttermilk (dugh)
	Evening	Bread, tea, rice, buttermilk
29 May	Morning	Mast, bread; later fresh butter and buttermilk
	Noon	Salted rice, cup of cold buttermilk, tea (at farmer's household)
	Evening	Rice, may something else
30 May	Morning	Buttermilk, yoghurt (mast), bread. Yoghurt with maize bread morsels in it

---

120. Mortesen 1993, p. 245. A quantity of 700 g of bread is 2,300 kcal.
121. Binder 1887, p. 352.
122. Frederiksen 1996, p. 116.
123. Cooper 1925, p. 52.
124. Stocqueler 1832, vol. 1. p. 119; Najm ol-Molk 1342, p. 158.
125. Beck 1991, p. 207.
126. O'Donovan 1882, vol. 1, pp. 149, 212.
127. Conolly 1834, vol. 1, p. 164.
128. O'Donovan 1882, vol. 1, p. 370.

129. Harrison 1946, p. 57.

28 May 1935	Morning	Flap bread, mast, tea
	Noon	Bread, butter, buttermilk. Rice cooked in buttermilk
	Evening	Kebab; later rice. Rice and meat in a pomegranate sauce
31 May	Morning	Probably bread, kebab and buttermilk
	Noon	Bread and butter; grilled minced meat, bread, buttermilk
	Evening	Rice and boiled mutton
10 June	Noon	Thin cake (tiri), tea, cold butetrmilk. Eggs friend in ghee
	Evening	Rice
29 June	Noon	Bread, butter, buttermilk with *fiyaleh*
30 June	Morning	n.a.
	Noon	Bread, fresh butter, eggs fried in aromatic herbs [102]
1 July	Morning	Yoghurt, bread
	Noon	Kebab
	Evening	Kebab, tea, rice, and boiled meat
2 July	Morning	Bread, yoghurt, kebab, tea
	Noon	Bread, halva, browned minced meat in balls, buttermilk with *fiyaleh*
3 July 1935	Morning	Yoghurt, bread, tea

Source: Feilberg 1952, p. 102.

Among the nomadic Afshar of Kerman the living standard varied considerably; the wealthier a family, the more they consumed goods that have been bought in the market.[130] Those who have large herds eat better than others; the khans eat 1-2 times per week meat (goat, lamb). If there are many visitors a sheep is killed. Cultivators eat little meat.[131] Poor Afshar ate very little animal protein. Meat was seldom eaten, only at emergency slaughters, feasts and similar occasions. Eggs were also rarely consumed. Their supply was also limited as the chickens of one family only laid 1-2 eggs/day, or 1-2 eggs/per person/ week. In 1975, the diet of a well-to-do family, having 100 animals and some land, and a poorer family with 40 animals and a little land as shown in Table 8.9.

Table 8.8: Three days of diet of a group of Afshar (Kerman) ca. 1970

Meal times	Well-to-do family	Poorer family
Morning	Bread, walnuts, cheese	Bread, walnuts
Noon	Bread, rice, eggplants	Bread, walnuts, cheese
Evening	Bread, cheese, eggplants	Bread, lentils
Morning	Bread, cheese, walnuts	Bread, walnuts
Noon	Bread, lentil soup	Bread, fried potatoes
Evening	Bread, whey (kashk), dates	Bread, whey (kashk), cheese
Morning	Bread, walnuts, cheese	Bread, walnuts
Noon	Bread, rice, eggs	Bread, eggs, cheese
Evening	Bread, carrots, cheese	Bread, walnuts, cheese

Source: Stöber 1978, p. 105.

This was the diet in the fall, when there were no fresh milk products, and therefore walnuts and the like were eaten. At the meals water was drunk, but before, and in between tea was drunk. The poorer family hardly bought anything, while the richer family bought rice and fruit and vegetables not self grown.[132]

In short, it would appear that the majority of Iranians were quasi-vegetarians, not by choice, but because they could not afford to buy meat, most of the time. As a result, they had a diet that in normal years was adequate in terms of calories, but deficient in proteins and vitamins.

---

130. Stöber 1978, p. 105.
131. Feilberg 1952, p. 102.

132. Stöber 1978, pp. 105-06.

CHAPTER NINE

BREAD, A RIZQ ANALYSIS

"In Persia cheap and plentiful bread is the test by which administrations and Cabinets stand or fall."

—Shushtar 1912, p. 170.

"Any scheme that will reduce the price of bread, and keep the people well fed, will go a long way toward solving many of Persia's present problems."

—Wishard 1909, p. 339.

Introduction

Agricultural production considered from an economic point of view has two important functions: first, to provide prime necessities for those inside and outside the agricultural sector, and second, to enable the financing of imports. In preindustrial countries like Iran, where more than 85 percent of the population was engaged in the agricultural sector, the economic basis of the country was land and its products.

Agricultural production was characterized by a low level of technical specialization and labor division. Landlords showed no great interest in improving agricultural production as indicated by a low level of investment in this sector, while the peasants were not encouraged by their masters to work for increased productivity.

Landlords were only interested in extracting the agricultural surplus, i.e., the agricultural production minus the consumption of the agricultural sector, or, in other words, that part of the production that would end up outside the agricultural sector. In industrialized countries the flow of goods from the agricultural sector is countered by a return flow of commodities that are needed or appreciated by those working in that sector. Thus, an exchange relationship exists. In preindustrial society no exchange relationship existed. Therefore, the flow to the city, or agricultural surplus, was obtained by politico-legal compulsion.

One can say that redistribution of production takes place, sharing out the agricultural production to the various classes of society, but in unequal proportions. The largest individual share belonged to the shah and his court, then smaller shares went to the provincial and national elite (*teyul*, *vaqf* and *molk* holders) and lastly were the peasants who took the remainder, which was, of course, the smallest share per individual.[1]

The central government had a fair amount of control over the supply and distribution process by virtue of owning large tracts of land, taxation, and granting fiefs to meritorious members of the elite, or taking it back from them when disgraced. Purchase or requisition of grain, the latter of which euphemistically was designed as a form of taxation (*sader*), as well as the storage of government grain in state granaries completed the instruments for state control of the redistribution of the agricultural surplus.[2]

The grain market proper was small, i.e. there was no national market, because the trade in grain was mainly urban and local in nature. Like the shah, all members of the urban based elite had grain brought from their estates to their homes in the cities. This grain was used for their households, which not only consisted of their own extended families, but also of their retainers, followers and other dependents. They sold the remainder in the market, which they tried to manipulate to their own advantage. The shah, although not adverse to such practices, often held grain in state warehouses to be used when

---

1. See Lambton 1953; Floor 1999, chapter one; Ibid., 2003 a.
2. Floor 1999; Ibid 2003 a; Issawi 1971, chapter eight.

social or political occasions arose. If necessary he had recourse to distributing his grain in the market, in particular in time of famine. Provincial governors acted in a smilar manner.

Thus, members of the elite, the middle class as well as anybody with sufficient means, acquired grain from their village[s] or in the market after harvest time and stored a year's supply. The same was done with regard to flour, beans, oil, and other products. Foodstuffs like butter, cheese, fruit, vegetables, and meat were usually bought daily in the market. Wheat, more often than not, was ground in private homes by simple hand mills.[3]

It was only the urban lower classes, who represented more than 60 percent of the urban population and whose numbers increased towards the end of the nineteenth century, that had to have daily recourse to the market not only for fruit, vegetables and dairy and other products, but also for their bread, the most important part of their diet. This they bought from the public bakeries, which bought their flour from wholesale dealers.[4]

The local nature of the market implied a limit to the exploitation of the productive classes of society, who in this case were the peasants, because redistribution did not aim at maximization of profits. One can say that there was satiety in consumption. The condition of the relative stability of the redistribution of agricultural surplus in Qajar Iran came to an end when the growth of foreign trade also stimulated domestic trade, urban growth, and a monetized economy. Growing imports had to be paid for out of agricultural surplus since it was the economic basis of the country.[5]

The Qajar economy in the second half of the nineteenth century was geared more to money than to barter. This change had important implications for the objective of production. The economy of consumption was slowly being replaced by a system of production for profit. This different production ethos meant that the volume of output became a matter of concern to landlords, who consequently demand greater production or a greater share in output. This could either be achieved by introducing new techniques and crops, by increasing the size of arable land or by increased exploitation of peasants. The option of new techniques was not feasible for various reasons. The land tenure system provided no incentives for peasants to increase production. The capital outlay needed to provide the necessary irrigation works to increase production was considerable, so that from lack of money, no investments of importance were made. Issawi remarks that "in Iran expenditure on – or even interest in – irrigation schemes seems to have been negligible."[6] Therefore, the increase in the size of arable land was mostly in the form of rain-fed agriculture. Finally, landlords had themselves no idea how to improve production and produce more efficiently. They, therefore, had to fall back on introducing new crops or by raising the labor rents (the agricultural surplus), which easily could result in overexploitation. This development aggravated existing tensions within the peasant communities created by their oppressed position, and led to internal migration, some of which was to the cities. This was partly offset by the increase in the cultivation of crops such as opium and cotton.[7] In addition to increased exploitation, the composition of the surplus started to change. To raise their revenues

---

3. Amir Khizi 1339, p. 320; Polak 1865, vol. 1, p. 111; Wilbraham 1838, pp. 42-43 ("The greater portion of the higher classes possess villages, within a day or two's journey of the capital, and draw from thence their supplies of wheat and barley and straw: they keep their fifteen or twenty mules; and, when they do not themselves require them, they either let them out, or send them to the provinces bordering upon the Caspian to fetch rice or fuel- a part of which they can sell for sufficient to cover all expense of that which they retain for their own use.") See also [http://www.qajarwomen.org/archive/detail/28].
4. Issawi 1971, chapter two; Kasravi 1319, vol. 1, p. 196.
5. Floor 2003 a, chapter one.
6. Issawi 1971, p. 206.
7. Floor 2003 a; Anonymous 1910, pp. 616-25.

landlords started to produce cash crops (e.g., opium), while after 1873 merchants organized the production of carpets on a scale never seen before. The ever-growing need for money also led to the demand for payment in cash instead of in kind.[8]

To understand how the bread situation could be influenced, either negatively or positively, I discuss the most important factors that affected the operation of the grain distribution system. The importance of the provisioning the Iranian urban population and its political and socio-economic implications has been aptly formulated by Millspaugh as follows:

> Bread was the staff of life of the Persian masses. Grains and bread therefore bore a vital relationship to the economics of the country; and in addition the question of food had obvious social implications. Furthermore, conditions had compelled the government for many generations to control the collection and in varying measures and different ways, the distribution of flour and bread. Thus, the question of food was always more or less political; it might create or kill cabinets.[9]

Since ancient times it was part of the task of the government secure the supply of food to the cities as well as to fix prices of products like bread, meat, wood and fodder.[10] Failure to do so led to social unrest, which could be very embarrassing or damaging to the authorities concerned. Unfortunately, subsequent governments in Iran, whether or not Islamic, were not very successful in doing so. As in Europe, food scarcity or worse, famine, was a recurring evil. For example, in 569 AH/1173-74, there was a drought in Kerman, when there was nothing to eat but date stones which were ground into flour. When the date stones ran out the hungry 'roasted' and boiled old leather tablecloths (nat`ha) and buckets that were eaten. Every day a few children disappeared in the city, who were slaughtered, there were even people who ate their own children. In the whole the city and its environs not one cat remained, while day and night dogs and hungry people were fighting in the streets, if the dog won it ate the human being, and if the human being won he ate the dog.[11] Fortunately, food scarcity and famine was local in nature and when Kerman suffered the other provinces need not have suffered the same problem. It was rare that there was a nationwide famine, although these sometimes occurred.

Part of the supply of wheat was controlled by the government while the remainder had to be bought in the market. More often than not, the problem was not that there was no food, but that interested parties (the ruler, his officials, and wealthy private individuals) regarded the urban food supply as a source of income. Moreover, it was one that if properly manipulated could yield very high profits, be it at the cost of starvation of a portion of the population. To make greater profits in the wheat trade, government officials (from the governor to the private grain owners) would form a wheat-corner and create an artificial bread shortage. One of the principal participants was invariably the *nanva-bashi* or head of the bakers' guild.[12] There were, of course, governors who did not allow such shenanigans.[13]

---

8. Floor 2003 a.
9. Millspaugh 1945, p. 99.
10. Aubin 1908, p. 37; Polak 1865, vol. 1, 135.
11. Ebrahim 1343, p. 131.
12. For the nineteenth century, see, e.g., Shuster 1912, p. 171; Mostowfi n.d., vol. 2, p. 394; Algar 1969, p. 50; Adib al-Molk 1349, pp. 7, 94-95 ; Hajj Sayyah 1346, pp. 482, 507, 510; Meshkat al-Soltan 1376, pp. 17-18 ; `Eyn al-Saltaneh 1376, vol. 1, pp. 323, 390-91, 416, 464, 488, 562, 603, 892, 958; Fragner 1979, pp. 148-67; Martin 2005, pp. 91, n. 20, 100-04.
13. See e.g., Tavernier 1930, p. 258; Ehtesham al-Saltaneh 1366, pp. 448-55 (bread corner in Kurdestan broken ca. 1898).

To avoid such a situation governments, since Achaemenid times appointed a market overseer, called *mohtaseb* in Islamic times, whose task it was to ensure that government-fixed prices, weights and measures were respected. To that end, at least since Safavid times, he, in consultation with the *kalantar*, held a meeting each month with the heads of the bakers', butchers', grocers', forage sellers' and coal sellers' guilds to fix the maximum price of products sold by their members. The monthly price list drawn up by them, called *tas`ir-e ajnas*, was announced by *jarchi*s or public criers.[14] Low prices were not only important to the local urban population, but also to visitors. According to Conolly, "The stay of many of the poorest pilgrims is regulated according to the price of bread at Meshed."[15] The bakers had the custom of lighting lamps when bread was cheap.[16] Beginning in 1852 the monthly price list was published in the government gazette in Tehran.[17] However, this official, even when he was not corrupt, had to deal with the reality that the cause of high prices usually was well-connected and powerful people against whom he could do little.

Only after some people had died and the mood among the population became highly explosive, i.e., when the situation in the city had become really desperate, would the government step in. For example, in February 1715 harem eunuchs had cornered the grain market of Isfahan and caused the price to rise steeply so that people started to riot. Although a new "supervisor of life necessities" was appointed, this had only a temporary downward effect on prices, for he was bribed by grain merchants and bakers. A new official was appointed, which made no difference in the situation and on 16 June 1715, a group of demonstrators forced Shah Soltan Hoseyn to remain in Isfahan.

When he wanted to leave to go to his pleasure garden outside the city, women and children threw dirt at him and he was forced to return to the palace.[18] In Kerman, in the early years of the twentieth century when bread scarcity was severe, a group of shopkeepers and sayyeds came to the British missionary house and announced that if they were given cheap bread they would become Christians. They refused money to buy bread when that was offered to them. As a result the British consul went to see the governor and "got him to promise that bread should be lowered to a more or less normal price by gradual reductions spread over a period of ten days." This is exactly what the would-be 'Christians' had hoped for and they did not return for their conversion.[19]

The members of the wheat-corner, forewarned by the government, would sell their grain to the retail dealers who then bore the brunt of an outraged public opinion. The government ordered the prices to be lowered on penalty of the bastinado or worse. The bakers then protested that they had bought expensive wheat and could not sell their bread any cheaper, for they would then lose money. If the bakers (or butchers) refused to give in, they were flogged, had their tongues cut, or had their ears cut off or nailed to the door of their shop; sometimes a few of them were baked in their own ovens.[20] Nezam al-Molk mentions a chief of the bakers in the eleventh century was trampled to death by elephants, because the bakers in Ghazna

---

14. Floor 1985; Aubin 1908, p. 37; Polak 1865, vol. 1, p. 135; Binning 1857, vol. 1, p. 337.
15. Conolly 1834, vol. 1, p. 239.
16. Kosogovski 1344, p. 47; de Rochechouart 1867, p. 181.
17. Mostowfi n.d., vol. 2, p. 18.

18. Floor 1998, p. 27.
19. Malcom 1905, pp. 235-36. A similar thing happened in Tabriz in August 1896, where after a bread riot, "a great many Persians had gone to the British Consulate-General to ask for relief from the famine, and protection from the local authorities." Bigham 1897, p. 103.
20. Stack 1882, vol. 1, pp. 216-17 (governor cut off ears and plucked out the beard of a baker); Wills 1886, p. 38; Polak 1865, vol. 2, p. 74; Sykes 1902, p. 56 (baking bakers alive in 1073); Jackson 1910, p. 273 (3 bakers at Shiraz had their tongues cut out for selling their bread at too high a price); De Lorey 1907, p. 226 (baker baked in oven).

wanted to fix higher prices for bread.[21] When in 465 AH/1072-73 bread prices rose very high in Bardsir, while the flour was further adulterated with *ard-e siyah* and rubbish (*tobah*), the Seljuq Soltan ordered some of the leaders of the bakers (*ma`aref-e khabbazan*) to be thrown into their ovens.[22] This kind of punishment was applied until the beginning of the nineteenth century, despite the fact in 1850, Amir Kabir, the great reforming prime-minister, had ordered abolishing of such barbaric practices.[23]

Main problems of bread supply

Notwithstanding the importance of this problem, the government was never able to deal with it, and, until recent times, bread scarcity and even famine was one of the structural problems facing Iranian consumers. The broad issue was aggravated by several factors, which I discuss in the following paragraphs. Although I focus on and adduce material from the situation during the Qajar period, these remarks also apply to earlier periods.

First, there was the factor of difficult and costly transportation, which accounted for at least half of the problem.[24] The roads connecting the cities with the production areas were either bad or non-existent. This constituted one of the biggest challenges to the Iranian government. It explains why Iran normally a wheat exporting country, was subject to deficits in certain areas, while in other districts grain was unsalable. The large urban centers that consumed far more than they produced were almost completely dependent on their hinterland for food, and suffered from this anomalous situation. This situation was graphically described by Fateh as follows: "Persia is like a hungry person who has plenty of food in another part of the house but is unable to partake of it because of his physical inability to walk."[25] The difficulties in transportation resulting from the inadequate road system were further aggravated towards the end of the nineteenth century by the growing un-safety of the roads. This was the result of the waning power of the central government, which led to the resurgence of banditism.

In addition to unsafe, bad or non-existent roads, the scarcity and lack of organization of transport at times made the conveyance of food impossible. Transportation of any kind of goods depended entirely on the availability of pack animals, mainly mules and camels. As the muleteers and camel drivers did not operate on a tight schedule they were not always available when they were needed. Merchandise often had to wait for months for the arrival of transportation. Even during transport, goods were subject to long delays, because of the whims of the muleteers.[26] Wilson, however, believes that the lack of transportation facilities had a beneficial effect on the local food situation.[27] Although there is no denying that this was occasionally true, he is wrong to generalize. As is clear from the discussion below, the fact that there was plenty of grain in storage did not necessarily mean that there was plenty of bread in the bakeries. The contrary was often the case.

The disorganization of the transport system was aggravated by the fact that after years of food scarcity or famine, the number of pack animals had dwindled. This was normal, because the animals were eaten; the owners could not fed them the barley and they ate them instead of letting them

---

21. Nizam al-Molk 1960, p. 48.
22. Ebrahim 1343, p. 13.
23. FO 60/196, (letter 18/02/1854).
24. Millspaugh 1945, p. 99.
25. Fateh 1926, p. 44; see also Molkara 1325, p. 56; Curzon 1892, vol. 1, p. 638.
26. Issawi 1971, chapter 4; DCR 1662, p. 22.
27. Wilson 1932, p. 54 ("Thanks in part to the lack of transportation facilities there is generally at least twelve months' supply of grain for the whole country in storage at the larger centres of population, in government granaries and in the hands of merchants, and serious scarcity is not general unless two very bad years occur in succession.")

die.²⁸ Moreover, officials were in the habit of appropriating the muleteers' animals whenever a governor went on a journey. This custom was known as *mal begiri* and the merest hint of it sent the muleteers into the hills with their animals.²⁹ Needless to say, this custom was detrimental to an already disturbed transportation system, especially since the appropriations would occur a few times per year. Even when better roads and the introduction of motorized transport reduced the cost of transportation significantly, this did not mean that the situation of food distribution was improved, let alone solved.

The second factor that adversely affected the bread issue was the system of government, which may best be described as a spoils system and presented an additional obstacle in the way of the development of a sound food policy. The Qajar government provided only the minimum of social services and left the organization of the economy to the free play of the market. The government rewarded its supporters by giving them the right to enrich themselves at the expense of the inhabitants of a district or a province. During their tenure the governors practically fleeced their subjects. The central government interfered only when the population rioted and then only out of fear that the balance of power would be disturbed rather than out of compassion for the population's condition. Abrahamian rightly remarked that "It seems that state intervention in the economy was not so much a reflection of its power but of its weakness in coping with public disturbances."³⁰

Likewise the consequent corruption, which pervaded all layers of society, offered the best opportunities to the elite. In 1912, for example, "The Governor and great men of Tehran combined to form a corn ring, and not all the miseries of the population from the famine price of bread could make them forgo a single kran of their ill-gotten gains."³¹ There were religious leaders who abstained from these nefarious practices, but their number dwindled towards the end of the nineteenth century. Although religious leaders continued to play an important role in the political affairs of the country, the discontent and distrust of the population was also directed against them.³² Rich religious professionals were in league with other wealthy landowners, especially government officials and merchants, who like them had invested heavily in land, to speculate with the price of bread or meat in the cities.³³ There were some religious leaders who assisted the hungry during times of scarcity. Haji Mohammad Baqer, the leading *mojtahed* of Isfahan, during the 1840s allegedly distributed the unlikely high sum of about 240,000 *tuman*s, during a period when he tried to acquire total political control over Isfahan.³⁴ Eastwick reported that Haji Mullah Rafi` distributed 2 *tuman*s "to each individual of several thousand people in 1861 during the famine. He did not, however, tell me that this was money collected at his instance from the rich, and that he himself only gave his influence."³⁵

Mirza Javad Aqa, the *mojtahed* of Tabriz, who was not only rich, but also greedy, persisted in pursuing his private interests.³⁶ In 1895, when the Russian road from Rasht to Tehran was planned, he publicly agitated against it. According to Gordon, "He saw that the new road was likely to draw away some of the Tabriz traffic, he set himself the task of stirring up the Moullas of Resht to resent, on religious grounds, the extended intrusion of Europeans into their town. The pretence of zeal in the cause was poor, because the Resht Moullas are

---

28. Bleibtreu 1894, p. 95; DCR 3748, p. 4.
29. DCR 1662, p. 4; DCR 1953, p. 4.
30. Abrahamian 1974, p. 13; Amin al-Dowleh 1341, pp. 225-26.
31. Moore 1914, p. 147.
32. Algar 1969, p. 255; Gordon 1896, p. 24; Nateq 1362.
33. Polak 1865, vol. 1, pp. 325-26; Greenfield 1904, pp. 130-31; Kosogovski 1344, p. 239.
34. Denis 1843, p. 140; Tonkabuni 1364, p. 109.
35. Eastwick 1864, vol. 1, p. 333.
36. E`temad al-Saltaneh 1345, p. 1001. Religious leaders were also called upon to mediate in case of high bread prices, see e.g. [http://www.qajarwomen.org/archive/detail/91].

themselves interested in local prosperity, and the agitation failed."[37]

A particularly well known case was the bread ring organized by one of the leading religious professionals in Tabriz, the well-known and very wealthy *mojtahed* Nezam al-Olama during the terrible famine in Azerbayjan. Amir-e Nezam, the *pishkar* or governor of the province asked permission to open the granaries of the biggest hoarders by force. Mozaffar al-Din Shah replied in the affirmative, but forbade the opening of those belonging to certain people. It appeared that most of the granaries belonged to these people. When the Amir-e Nezam wanted to open the other granaries, he was informed that those belonged to friends of the crown-prince. The Amir-e Nezam who could not break this bread ring because of the influence of the olama involved, then organized a bread riot. On 24 August 1898 he sent soldiers to one of the greediest hoarders, the Nezam al-Olama, first *mojtahed* of Tabriz, who had hoarded about 70,000 *kharvar* of wheat (about 21,000 ton). The demonstration resulted in an attack on the Nezam al-Olama's house after the *mojtahed*'s servants had fired on the soldiers. These then attacked the *mojtahed*'s house and that of his brothers and plundered them. The mob plundered his house and that of five sayyeds, who had killed a few people defending the Nezam al-Olama's house. The *mojtahed* had to flee the city, but despite all this, the people still had to wait some time before the price of bread dropped.[38] According to the British Consulate in Isfahan, the mullahs' role in bread rings was facilitated when locusts arrived and the Iranian peasant, "led by his Moollahs, who are chiefly the great holders of the stores of grain in the place, and do not regard this advent of the locust as an unmixed evil, says it is the Divine will, and that Providence will provide the remedy."[39] Thus it happened that in Isfahan there had been two good harvest years in succession, but in 1898 bread was still scarce as a result of hoarding.[40]

However, not only religious leaders, but also those who claimed to defend the interests of the people, heroes of the Constitutional Revolution, fell victim to the seduction of enrichment through hoarding and selling wheat at high prices. A sad and notorious case is that of Tabriz in 1909. "During the siege of Tabriz, when the famine reached its height, so that the poor were to be seen dying in the streets and the town was in the last straits for food, the Persian leaders of the defence [Sattar Khan and Baqer Khan] retained large warehouses full of grain, for which they had not paid a penny, and refused to sell except at ruinous prices which they had fixed for their own profit."[41] Matters became so deperate that in April 1909, one month before the Russian occupation of the city, the chief of the committee in charge of the bread supply of Tabriz, Haji Qasem Aqa, was attacked by a group of furious women. They accused him of "being a corn forestaller," i.e., of hoarding grain. He fled into the telegraph office, where the women followed and manhandled him; "they attacked him savagely with the iron heels of their shoes, tearing out his beard and gouging out his eyes." He was finally killed by some men who came to help the women. He was then undressed and hung naked by his feet in the town's Artillery Square.[42]

---

37. Gordon 1896, p. 24.
38. Greenfield 1904, pp. 130-31; Gordon 1896, p. 24. In 1905, there was a grain ring once again in Tabriz, the leaders of which were the *Imam-Jom`eh* and Sa`d al-Molk, the mayor, while it was believed that the crown prince was their sleeping partner. Bratislaw 1923, p. 53.
39. DCR 1662, p. 6.
40. DCR 2260, p. 13.
41. Moore 1914, p. 147, see also pp. 22-23.
42. De Lorey 1910, p. 317. A similar event occurred in Isfahan on 16 March 1911, when due to drought there was a shortage of bread, which led to a demonstration by women. They went to the Municipality building, which they attacked and looted, while they also killed the head of the Municipality and hung his corpse in the Meydan-e Shah. Thereafter they attacked government offices and freed the prisoners from the prison. The governor then ordered soldiers to fire at the demonstrators as a result of which some were wounded after which they scattered. Aqeli, vol. 1, p. 204.

The government's relative disinterest in the condition of the population resulted in the absence of a well-defined policy towards the food problem, while its execution was ineffective. Even after things got out of hand, when steps were taken to bring some order to the chaotic state of urban provisioning, these measures were on an ad hoc basis and of an incidental nature. It was a common occurrence for government officials to allow a bread ring to create a near famine, and then under public pressure to take measure to restore conditions to normal. These measures largely consisted of ordering bakers to lower their prices. The latter would complain that they had bought grain at high prices and could not sell for lower prices. The government would take a firm stand against the bakers who either would stop baking or tamper the quality of the bread. The government would retaliate by either flogging some bakers or clipping their ears, or, in extreme cases have a baker burnt in his own oven. The bakers' guild would strike and eventually reach a compromise with the government. Soon prices would rise again, and the population would have to pay.[43]

The formulation of an efficient government policy was furthermore hampered by the fact that the central government was not really aware of the financial and economic state of the country or of its possibilities. In spite of the fact that the government's main task was the collection of taxes and that the country's main source of wealth was land and its produce; some areas were over-assessed, while others were under-assessed.[44] This ignorance explains why Naser al-Din Shah was able to ban the export of wheat nation-wide when bread was scarce, without realizing the consequences of such a ban. Since his action was dictated by fear of further rioting and concern about the swindling prestige of the regime, it is not surprising it had harmful consequences. Such governmental measures often had results contrary to what was intended.

Frequently, the prohibition of wheat exports was declared for Iran as a whole, but this was not beneficial for the needs and possibilities of a local situation. In those areas where there was no scarcity, local authorities allowed export of wheat, but imposed higher illegal duties. For the cultivators the embargo meant "that their grain was either unsalable or only fetched a price sufficiently low to enable the exporters to pay what the local governor demanded for it to be exported."[45] Therefore, cultivators were not inclined to sow more grain than needed locally, and in some parts of Iran famines were caused because farmers changed from wheat to cash crops. In any case, the effect of the restriction of wheat cultivation was more apparent when there was a local crop failure.[46] Moreover, wheat embargos were occasionally imposed solely to increase the income of the local governor; e.g., "imports from India to Bushire (but in very small quantities and leading to a heavy loss) have been made, in order to show the central authorities that the embargo was necessary."[47]

The taxation system was the third factor which proved to be disadvantageous to the food situation. Because of the poor transportation system, a barter economy prevailed in much of Iran. And it entailed the payment of officials and of taxation in kind to a great extent. In itself the practice was useful, for it enabled the government to dispose of a quantity of grain sufficient to guarantee the supply of food in the cities. However, these taxes, paid in kind, were converted immediately into cash at fixed rates; this conversion was known as *tas'ir* and took place for two reasons.[48] In the first place, transportation was so difficult and involved so many people that it was easier for the Iranian bureaucracy to have these taxes directly converted

---

43. Wills 1886, pp. 37-38.
44. Lambton 1953, p. 152; Floor 1999.
45. FO 60/586, (report dated 27 April 1897).
46. Wilson 1932, p. 168; FO 60/611, (letter 31 July 1899); FO 60/613, (letter 11 July 1899).
47. FO 60/586, (report dated 27 April 1897); Wills 1886, pp. 313-14.
48. Floor 1999, pp. 265, 342.

into cash.⁴⁹ This tendency was accelerated by the fact that towards the end of the nineteenth century the central government increasingly needed more money to pay for travels of the Shah and the upkeep of the army and administration.⁵⁰ The demand for money was accentuated by a serious depreciation of the Iranian currency. Taxation, therefore, was used to provide the government with ready cash.⁵¹

Tamam-e 'omr-e khod zahmat kashidam
pas andaz-e mara bad hava bord
Mara az mal-e donya bareh'iy bud
keh anra ruz rowshan kadkhoda bord
Khorsui dashtam ruzi mobasher
gereft anra va dar zir-e 'aba bord
Gelim-e kohneh zir andaz-e man bud
shabi Amniyeh amad jabeja bord
Do man gandom keh nan-e khaneh am bud
z man arbab-e ghafel az khoda bord
Az an kasht va az an kharman cheh mandeh
dar in deh az baraye man cheh mandeh?

تمام عمر خود زحمت کشیدم
پس انداز ما را باد هوا برد
ما را از مال دنیا برّه ای بود
که آنرا روز روشن کدخدا برد
خروسی داشتم روزی مباشر
گرفت آنرا و در زیر عبا برد
گلیم کهنه زیر انداز من بود
شبی امنیه آمد جا بجا برد
دو من گندم که نان خانه ام بود
ز من ارباب غافل از خدا برد
از آن کشت و از آن خرمن چه مانده؟
در این ده از برای من چه مانده؟

I toiled for my whole life and all I saved was swept away by the wind
Amongst worldly good I had a lamb which was taken away by the bailiff in broad daylight
I had a cloak; one day the agent seized it and carried it away under his cloak.
There was an old blanket which I used as carpet. One night the road guard came and removed it.
The two maunds of wheat which were the food of my house were seized by the ungodly landlord
What has remained of that sowing and harvest? What is left to me in this village?⁵²

According to Curzon, the conversion rates in 1889/1890 "were as a rule from fifteen to twenty-five percent lower than the current prices, obtainable in the market."⁵³ This, however, was a very conservative estimate, since other sources show that corrupt officials made more substantial profits. Around 1900 the conversion rates in Khorasan were fifty percent lower than the market price, according to Yate.⁵⁴ A more tangible example is given by Kosogovski. The governor of Ormiyeh had to pay five thousand tumans yearly in cash and one thousand *kharvar* of cereals in kind. When the officials sent to fix the conversion rates were bribed, they fixed a lower rate, half or even one-third of the market value. If the real value had been nine tumans per *kharvar* the governor would only pay three thousand *tumans* and store the grain in his granary. In winter, when the roads were impassible or during harvest time, when prices rose, he would sell the grain for nine *tumans*.⁵⁵ Sometimes even lower rates were paid in the late 1890s around Tabriz. According to the British consul, in the villages of origin, wheat was converted at 2-4 *tumans* per *kharvar*, while during 1896-98 the price

---

49. Shuster 1912, p. 171.
50. Issawi 1971, p. 338.
51. Avery and Simmons 1974.

52. Poem by Aby Turab Jali, reproduced in Ricks 1984, p. 196.
53. Curzon 1892, vol. 2, p. 480. For an example of its impact on the poor, see Mirza Ebrahim 2535, p. 170.
54. Yate 1900, p. 83.
55. Kosogovski 1341, pp. 211-12.

in Tabriz had been 10 *tuman*s per *kharvar* for wheat at 6-7 *tuman*s for barley.[56]

The policy of selling and transferring crown lands (*khaleseh*), which was implemented after 1885, further weakened the already ineffectual government bread policy. The object of these sales was to supply the government with cash. As a result, large quantities of wheat and barley fell into the hands of private persons, while the quantities in the state granaries fell. The consequences of this policy were aggravated by the sales of grain from the state granaries to provide money for the court. The policy of selling crown lands may have resulted in improved output of these lands, but in practice it led to severe food shortages, while the available quantities of grain were sometimes twice as much as required for local consumption. The oligopolistic position of the big grain holders enabled them to fix their own price in the absence of a strong government policy concerning the urban food situation. Moreover, these big grain holders preferred to let their grain rot rather than sell it at low prices.[57]

New but failed policy after the 1871 famine

As if the above-mentioned structural problems were not enough for the Iranian bureaucracy, it also had to deal with periodic droughts, which ravaged parts of the country every three to five years. The subsequent famines caused much damage to the population and to the economy of the country. Although Iran had experienced some major famines in 1814 and 1835, while there had been serious bread riots in Tehran itself during the famine of 1861, the government had continued to deal with the bread situation as it had done since time immemorial. Band aid was given, some people were punished, and the population had to hope for a better harvest in the next year and starve until then.

The drought of 1871-73, which ravaged all of Iran, lasted in some areas until 1873 and was the worst famine in Iran for two hundred years. Because of insufficient nourishment, subsequent epidemics carried off a large portion of the population.[58] As to the situation in Shiraz, Wills reported:

> The famine was now setting in Persia seriously-*for two years not a drop of rain had fallen*; the crowds of professional beggars were reinforced by really hungry people, thefts from shops became common. In the corn-chandlers' shops very small supplies if grain were seen, and these much adulterated by the addition of dust, stones, etc. The bakers baked as little bread as they could, mixing their dough in as small quantities and as slowly as possible; the loaves became gradually worse and worse, though the price remained nominally the same. The coarse barley-bread ceased to be baked altogether, and at last the bakers refused to sell to the crowds which formed at their shop doors unless they were their regular customers, and then only for ready money, and a small loaf to each person, selling by weight being discontinued altogether. All who had enough ready money laid in a store of grain and flour.[59]

In May 1871, Mounsey arrived at the village of Mayin, near the Band-e Amir, which was "so miserably poor that bread was scarcely to be had, and many of its inhabitants were reduced to eating half-matured ears of barley."[60] In 1881, Stack reported that "Our guide on this march showed me bread

---

56. FO 60/598 (letter 20/09/1898).
57. Floor 1999, pp. 340-42; Issawi 1971, p. 208; DCR 2260, p. 13.
58. Issawi 1972, chapter two.
59. Wills 1895, p. 251. Italics in the original. For the situation in Isfahan, see Wills 1886, pp. 37-38. For another contemporary eye-witness account of the impact of the famine in a large number of locations in Iran, see Brittlebank 1873.
60. Mounsey 1872, p. 255.

made of green herbs, which he said had been the food of the poor people for many months."[61] At that time the price of bread in Kashan was one tuman for one *man* (3 kg) of bread, which meant that bread prices had increased twenty times above normal. A contemporary source depicts this period in the following words: "The time when cannibalism was normal was the year 1288 (1871). Moslems ate dead Moslems, nay even dead Jews. People took their houses apart and sold the wood so that they could obtain something edible; one Tabriz *man* (3 kg) of bread was bought at one half *methqal* (2.3 g) of gold."[62] In Mashhad people fled the city in the hope to be captured by Turkmen, preferring the crust of bread of slavery to the indifferent rule of their governor, who did nothing to alleviate their lot, although he posted guards to prevent this.[63] During that time the olama of the Imam Reza shrine in Mashhad fed some 500 people daily, which represents 1 percent of the population of Mashhad and was far below the percentage represented by the poor in that town and about the same number of people that they fed during normal times.[64]

After the severe famine of 1871 Naser al-Din Shah took steps to prevent similar calamities. Orders were issued to establish large state granaries that together would hold reserves sufficient to feed the population of Tehran for at least six months. The wheat was to remain in storage until the next harvest, when it was sold to the bakers and new grain was stored. This new policy was not only intended as a hedge against calamities of an unforeseen nature such as droughts, but also to act as a check on bread rings. An adequate reserve of grain in the state granaries would deter them from driving up wheat prices in a bad year, for the government would sell grain at normal prices, and thus act as a stabilizing factor in the grain market. Although in principle it was a well-intentioned policy, it was difficult to implement with a corrupt bureaucracy. Kosogovski knowingly remarked: "On the one hand this policy seemed an advantage; on the other hand it was a source of income."[65]

To implement the new bread policy Naser al-Din Shah decided to build a big new granary in Shah Abdol-Azim to store wheat from the rural areas around Tehran. Within the Ministry of Finance a new office was created to serve as the granary office (*edareh-ye anbar-e ghalleh-ye dar al-khelafeh*) and placed under the direction of a court official.[66] In the first year of operation, wheat from the state granary was sold at five *tuman*s per *kharvar*. Bread had to be sold at eight *shahi*s per *man* (3 kg). Bakers could buy two to three *kharvar* (600-900 kg) of government wheat per day; they had to buy the remainder in the market. Because the granary office tampered with the quality of the wheat and also because the governors fleeced the bakers with several imposts, the bakers themselves started selling adulterated and short-weight bread. Naturally, the population did not benefit from such measures, the more so, since the bakeries mainly served the lower classes. The middle and higher classes had their dough prepared at home from their own unadulterated wheat and then baked

---

61. Stack 1882, vol. 1, p. 230.
62. Naraqi 1345, p. 264.
63. Bellew 1999, p. 344. Anonymous 1873, pp. 8 (terrible impact on Gilan and Isfahan, where 27,000 people died, and negative role of central government), 32 (240 deaths in Tabriz daily), 64 (slaving expeditions by Afghans who captured 40,000 people, while in Mashhad 8,000 died, while central government refuses aid from Russia and Britian), 168 (entire districts depopulated), 204-05 (impact on the country is devastating, including for the nomads, who also lost much of their herds).
64. Goldsmid 1876, vol. 1, p. 364; Chanykov 1862, p. 99; Bassett 1887, p. 226; Vambery 1867, p. 323; Eastwick 1864, vol. 2, p. 213.

65. Kosogovski 1341, p. 171; Mostowfi n.d., vol. 2, p. 43.
66. Millspaugh 1925, p. 77 ("The huge ambar or granary with a capcity of four hundred thousand bushels."); Sani` al-Dowleh 1306, appendix, p. 27. 400,000 bushels is about 11,000 tons. 1 bushel wheat = 60 lb US (35.24 l) and 61.3 lb Imperial (36 l) 1 bushel barley = 48 lb US (28.2 l) and 49 lb Imperial (28.8 l).

in bakeres-for-hire (*mozdi-paz*). Matters became worse when the government gave permission to the bakers to raise the price of bread from eight *shahi*s to ten, then to twelve and finally to fourteen *shahi*s. When the price of government wheat was raised from five to six *tuman*s per *kharvar*, yielding an additional income of three hundred *tuman*s per day, the bakers were allowed to raise bread prices to sixteen *shahi*s per *man*. Two years later (1875) the government added another tuman per *kharvar* to the price of its wheat and the price of bread rose to 18 *shahi*s. When people started to protest, Naser al-Din Shah ordered the bread price lowered, but he did not agree to lower the price of government wheat, which was then eight *tuman*s per *kharvar*. Then bakers then went on strike. Finally they received permission to sell bread of one *man* weight minus five *sir*s (about 2.5 kg), so that the effective bread price remained at fourteen *shahi*s per *man*.[67]

Although one cannot deny that there was some improvement in the bread situation in Tehran – bread was available in sufficient quantities, although at high prices- corrupt government practices made it an incomplete and ineffective policy. In the provinces, where most governors made only half-hearted attempts to copy the Tehran policy, the situation remained mostly as before and bread scarcity was as common as corruption.[68] In Isfahan, there seems to have been a change, be it that it was temporary. When discussing the bakers guild, Mirza Hasan Khan Tahvildar wrote in 1890, "Formerly, on account of the great number of inhabitants in the province, they tampered a little with the bread, but, nowadays, because there is no price fixing and the government is well organized, bread is fine and of good quality everywhere."[69]

How fragile the policy framework was is clear from the situation in, for example, Azerbaijan, which only seven years after the introduction of the new bread policy suffered a severe famine. The British consul in Tabriz reported that in Ormiyeh in May 1880: "Dying men, children thrown into the streets to die, half eaten by dogs, are common sights. In one village three women were taken in the act of eating a child. With a few exceptions no mercy or care was shown by the Khans or wealthy and nothing was done by the Government."[70] Vakil al-Molk the governor of Kerman, was one of the few officials who dealt effectively with the bread situation. He designed a scheme to relieve beggars in winter

> and issued so many hundreds of lithographed tickets monthly, and each of these entitled the recipient to so many pounds of bread, which was made at a certain bakery in the town. To prevent abuse as far as possible, the Prince sent his officers down to the shop to take bread from it by haphazard daily, and insisting on having this mixture of millet and barley-flour on his own table. He furthermore forced all his suite and the gentry of Kerman to buy tickets from him for distribution, telling each man how many *tomans*' worth he was expected to take.[71]

The elite, who had met considerable financial reverses as the result of the famine and the subsequent economic crisis, was seriously affected by the

---

67. Kosogovski 1344, pp. 171-72.
68. For an example how the occurrence of famine and subsequent high bread prices was dealt with in 1866 in Shiraz, see Busse 1972, pp. 356-58. For details on the scarcity of foodstuffs in Shiraz between 1884 and 1898, see Sirjani 1361, p. 787 (index). Even at faraway Sarakhs a government food warehouse was built. Monshi 2536, p. 39. For other parts of Iran, see Nezam al-Saltaneh Mafi 1361, vol. 1, pp. 24-26, 70,161-62, 231, 234-37, 258; vol. 2, pp. 143, 145,227-35, 239-40.

---

69. Tahvildar 1342, p. 118. For more information on this craft, see Wulff 1966, pp. 291-95; see also Benjamin 1887, pp. 95-96.
70. FO 60/431, (letter 3 May 1880 - "Although the local authorities banned the export of rice and grain, different kinds of produce were daily being shipped at Bandar-i Giz.")
71. Sykes 1898, p. 184. For another, be it temporary example, see Ala al-Molk 1364, pp. 26-27, 29.

Fig. 37: Kerman bread coupons (Sykes 1898, frontispiece).

crisis in the Iranian monetary system in the 1890s. "Those who had a stake in the economy, merchants, courtiers, notables, divines, fought by all means, fair and foul, to protect their economic interests."[72] An era of bread riots began, which lasted well into the twentieth century. Notwithstanding the rising prices, wages hardly increased, while their real purchasing power fell, because they were paid in copper money of uncertain and falling value. When the government occasionally intervened by fixing the price the rate of the silver *qeran* and copper money, it had a beneficial influence on the supply of bread. However, such measures were of an incidental nature; more often than not the government, because of its misdirected interest in the official rate, often varied this rate, sometimes even demanding taxes to be paid in silver *qeran*s.[73]

The year 1896, the Jubilee of Naser al-Din Shah's reign, was to be celebrated by a variety of festivities. Although there was no reason for it, for the condition of the country was slowly deteriorating. Food was scarce and prices were correspondingly high. Transportation of provisions to Tehran had been stopped, because robbers made the roads unsafe. Meanwhile, meat and rice prices in Tehran had risen due to speculation by both municipal authorities and private individuals. Of the latter the most obnoxious were the middlemen (*dallal*), mostly soldiers, who met the drivers bringing the sheep from Qazvin halfway. Many of these *dallal*s were servants of the governor of Tehran, Na'eb al-Saltaneh, the shah's son. They would buy the sheep at half or a third of the market price under the pretext that the import of sheep into Tehran had been banned. The price of meat not only rose because of these corrupt practices, excessive taxation of the butchers by the governor of Tehran accounted for about 40 percent of the increase of meat prices, according to Kosogovski. When the latter was put in charge of tax collecting, meat prices fell from 25 to 15 *shahi*s per *man*.[74]

When in April 1896 the bakers and butchers were exempted from paying taxes, it was expected that this measure would have a beneficial effect on food prices in the city. Instead it had the opposite effect. Instead of a price reduction, the population was confronted with a sharp rise in prices. The shepherds refused to come with their sheep to Tehran, because the butchers owed them 12,000 *tuman*s, which they were unable to pay as a result of excessive taxation. Even when the supply of sheep was resumed (grand vizier Amin al-Soltan paid the butchers' debt to ease the situation), meat remained expensive, because of Na'eb al-Saltaneh's interference in the market.[75]

---

72. Avery and Simmonds 1974, p. 294; Kasravi 1319, vol. 1, p. 193.
73. DCR 2260, p. 7; Kosogovski 1341, p. 88.

74. Kosogovski 1344, p. 181. There also were bread problems in Tabriz at that time. Bigham 1897, p. 103.
75. Kosogovski 1344, pp. 47-48. For the text of the *farman*, see Rezvani 1349, p. 262, photo 5.

This was the situation facing Mozaffar al-Din Shah when he acceded to the throne in April 1896. This weak ruler only made things worse with his policy of *pul mikhvaham* (I want money) for his European travels, which led to accelerated sales of crown lands and a growing public debt. Prices of wheat and thus of bread remained abnormally high during 1896-99 and no steps were taken to improve and increase supply. Because of a severe winter in 1897-98 the harvest of 1898 was not good, and although flour was imported from Russia, it was insufficient to bring relief. Foreign Legations, to feed their own staff and dependents, either bought large quantities of grain, had it milled and baked bread on the Legation's premises or with an order from the government were assigned to a baker to supply it with quality bread. The latter method did not work well, for in the case of the US Legation the arrangement fell apart and its staff had to look out for themselves.[76]

In 1898 there was another major famine in Azerbaijan, the granary of Iran. On 15 August 1898 out of some 90 bakeries that generally supplied the public needs in Tabriz only eight were working. Bread cost 35 *shahi*s per *man*; in September the cost of one *kharvar* of government wheat supplied to the public bakeries was eight *tuman*s as opposed 12 to 18 *tuman*s sold according to the quality in the market. In general, prices of life necessities had doubled and even tripled. A week later prices lowered when new supplies were brought from the well-stocked districts surrounding Tabriz. But prices were still beyond the means of most people, who usually ate bread of various mixtures costing 16 *shahi*s per *man*. The need for road improvement and the abolition of the conversion rates was never more clearly indicated than by the disparity in prices between Tabriz and the villages that supplied that city. Thus, the price per *kharvar* during the past three years in Tabriz had been 10 *tuman*s, while in the villages during the same period it was sold at two to four *tuman*s.[77] The bread riots and plundering of some notorious hoarders showed that large quantities of grain, which could easily have ended the bread scarcity had been hoarded in Tabriz itself.[78]

The 1899 harvest was also inadequate and as a result there was scarcity of bread of an indifferent quality. Moreover, there was a suspicion that the wheat market was manipulated by speculators and hoarders.[79] The central government finally took action when a royal order dated 5 Rajab 1317 AH/9 November 1899 was issued that ordered the following:

> Not later than 5 Sha`ban (9 December) anybody, high and low, who hoards grain has to offer this for sale in the square or any other place and to sell it at a price that is reasonable at that time. After one month, if somebody has not offered his grain for sale and does not heed the government's order and has kept stores of grains he will have his hoarded grain confiscated without further ado that will be sold at any price offered. Those who have dependents may only keep 10 kharvar of flour for their own domestic use, and have to sell the quantity that exceeds this.[80]

However, this belated and ineffective government intervention did not prevent Mozaffar al-Din Shah's reign being marked by manipulation of the food market by his governors and other officials on an unprecedented scale. In 1905, bread was expensive again in Tehran. According to the French diplomat de Lorey:

---

76. US Consular Reports 1900, pp. 168-69; `Eyn al-Saltaneh 1376, vol. 2, pp. 1050, 1131-33, 1211, 1222, 1269, 1328, 1333-34, 1341,1347, 1350, 1352-53, 1357-58, 1369, 1466-67, 1482, 1487, 1751.
77. FO 60/598 (letters 15 and 29 August, 12, 19 and 20 September 1898).
78. Kosogovski 1341, p. 240.
79. United States Consular Reports, 1900, pp. 168-69.
80. Rezvani 1349, p. 262, photo 4.

This year has been disastrous for Persia - no water, no bread, no money. The wheat has been 'cornered' by rich courtiers, so powerful that the Shah does not dare to make them disgorge. At this time last year its price was nine *tomans* and a half or ten *tomans* the *Khalvar*. This year it costs eighteen or nineteen *tomans* the *Khalvar*. The barley, which was sold ten years ago at from nine to eleven *krans* the *Khalvar*, and had mounted to five *tomans* the *Khalvar* last year, fetches to-day twelve *tomans*; and all these prices will augment considerably during winter."

Mozaffar al-Din Shah was confronted by demonstrating women when on 6 May 1905 he paid a visit to the shrine of Shah Abdol-Azim, south of Tehran. Eyn al-Dowleh, the prime minister, had received 1,000 *tumans* from the bakers allowing them to fix their own prices and to adulterate their bread with sawdust, saying it was Astrakhan flour. Because the shah shortly thereafter left for Europe the women started demonstrating in front of the crown prince's palace on 8 May 1905. He asked for some time to improve the situation and after four days bread became a little more plentiful, for a while. At the same time, the prime minister sold bad government wheat to the bakers. When the bread scarcity became serious in the second half of May, women demonstrated every day in front of the crown prince's palace, who promised improvement, but nothing changed, even when the governor of Tehran threatened the bakers with severe bodily punishment.[81] A Persian satirical journal produced recipe of dough in the manner of an elementary chemical manual.

> Mix in equal parts bran, small pebbles, sawdust, bean shells, and salt. Then one adds 2% of flour. One makes large flat pieces places them in the oven and takes them out immediately.
> Characteristics: solid body, flexible, consistency of leather, cannot be dissolved in solvents. In particular in stomach acids, bitter and salty taste, its density is that of silver.
> Physiological characteristics: it causes painter's colic, headaches, vertigo, and constipation. It is a violent poison.[82]

THE FIRST *MAJLES* AND THE BREAD PROBLEM

It is not surprising then that many people, especially the lower classes, believed that the fight for the Constitution was a fight for lower prices of life necessities. This belief was fostered by some propagandists, who even promised cheaper bread.[83] In fact, the constitution of a Parliament or *Majles* led to lower prices, for after the revolution no baker dared to sell under-weight bread to his customers. The *Majles* made a good start by abolishing the conversion rates on the crown lands in 1907. The objective of this decision was to increase the revenue both in cash and kind. However, the leaseholders of these crown lands refused to pay the higher taxes. A compromise was eventually reached.[84]

Other measures taken by the *Majles* were extensions of Naser al-Din Shah's decree of 1303 (1885), which like the law of 4 Dhu'l-Qa`deh 1325 (December 1907) was aimed at strengthening central government control. Articles 1, 6 and 4.48 of this law stipulated that above all the governors had to take the necessary steps to insure the food security of their province. Article 42 defined the task of governors more specifically. The governors were ordered to promote the development

---

81. Sepehr 1368, pp. 134, 146, 151, 208; Nazem al-Olama Kermani 1347, vol. 1, p. 57; Kasravi 1319, vol. 1, p. 22; Dowlatabadi n.d., vol. 2, p. 84.

82. Olmer 1906, p. 20.
83. Kasravi 1319, vol. 1, p. 22; Dowlatabadi n.d., vol. 2, p.
84. During the 1906 strike when thousands sought refuge at the British Legation, "A half-ton of bread was required daily to feed the crowds." Wishard 1909, p. 314.
84. Kasravi 1319, vol. 1, p. 227; Mostowfi n.d., vol. 2, p. 353.

of agriculture, especially in those areas where scarcity and famine could be expected. They were also charged with regulating the price of grain and other life necessities. Together with the municipal and police authorities, the governors had to take strong action against the use of false weights and the manipulation of the market. However, this law did not provide any punitive measures that could be taken against fraudulent or negligent governors. But, even if such measures had been provided, the central government could not have applied them, because it had neither the power nor the means to do so.[85]

Moreover, the *Majles* was not always working for the benefit of the population. The accusation that some interest groups in the *Majles* or in the provincial councils fixed prices that were advantageous to themselves, was justified. Through pamphlets, secret societies attacked the delegates and the authorities, drawing attention to their dubious activities. But these and other protests did not have any effect either on the authorities and the food situation.[86] People wrote poems and satirical prose decrying the speculation with the grain market. Browne quotes one such poem dealing with "*Ihtikar* or *Anbar-dari* (*i.e.* making a 'corner' in wheat or bread)" by Mirza Hoseyn Tabib-zadeh aka Kamal of Tabriz, which was recited for him by Mirza Mohammad Khan Ashrafzadeh from memory.

So long as the fingers of the bread-corners are on the bread
There is unrest in the world and ruin in the age.
That fair ascendant star of Justice is eclipsed;
That beauteous face of Equality is hidden.
O hungry child, cry not thus, or else
There will be slap on thy face from the hands of the bread corners!
O mother, surrender that ornament of thy embrace to the earth,
For a human life is cheaper than a mouthful of bread!
The pen is wearied of talking so much of bread;
The pages of the *Kamal* are dyed with blood: what hurt is there in this?[87]

A famous example of satirical prose is that by Dehkhoda in his wildly popular pieces called *Charand va parand* (Charivari) in the newspaper *Sur-e Esrafil* in which he derides the adulteration of bread flour and implicitly the acquiescence of the authorities with this practice.

> For example, when our great men consider that the people are poor and cannot eat wheaten bread, and that the peasant must spend all his life in cultivating wheat, yet must himself remain hungry, see what they do. On the first day of the year they bake the bread with pure wheat-flour. On the second day in every hundredweight (*kharwar*) they put a maund of bitter apricot stones, barley, fennel-flower, sawdust, Lucerne, sand-I put it shortly as an illustration-clods, brick-bats and bullets of eight *mithqals*. It is evident that in a hundredweight of corn, which is a hundred maunds, one maund of these things will not be noticed. On the second day they put in two maunds, on the third three, and after a hundred days, which is three months and ten days, a hundred maunds of wheat-flour have become a hundred maunds of butter apricot stones, barley, fennel-flower,

---

85. Demorgny 1913, p. 96.
86. Kasravi 1319, vol. 1, p. 320; RMM 15/1911, pp. 176-79; Archief Ministerie van Buitenlandse Zaken, letter 27 July 1908, no. 17353; de Lorey 1910, pp. 21, 25 (November 1906 bread riot by starving people).

87. Browne 1914, pp. 108, 299-300.

sawdust, chaff, lucerne and sand, and that in such a fashion that no one has noticed it, while the wheaten bread habit has entirely passed out of men's minds.
In truth intelligence and fortune are closely connected with one another![88]

THE BREAD SHORTAGE OF 1912

In the fall of 1911 the food situation was critical not only in Tabriz, but in northern Iran in general, and in Tehran in particular, where there was a severe bread scarcity. The harvest had been poor partially due to drought and partially due to destruction of crops caused by disorders in 1910, mainly through the incursion of Mohammad Ali, the ex-shah. The government asked Morgan Shuster, the Amercan Treasurer-General, to supervise the provisioning of Tehran. In the execution of his task, Shuster was obstructed by reactionary grandees, who were already making a bread ring to enrich themselves and embarrass the government, and it "was only by the most extraordinary means that I was able to gather five thousand to six thousand tons of wheat and barley." The assassination at the end of November 1911 of the head of the bakers' guild, one of the leading grain speculators, eased some of the difficulties in supplying food.[89]

The temporary improvement brought about by Shuster's brisk policy reverted, after his departure, to its former condition of wheat cornering. The winter of 1912 had been cold and the spring was rather dry. On New Year's Day, 21 March 1912, bread was scarce and the governor of Tehran ordered that the supply of Tehran be put under the supervision of J.J. Mornard, the new Belgian Treasurer-General. Mornard created a new office in the Treasury department and appointed Matin al-Saltaneh as its head. Because this official knew nothing about the problem at hand, he asked the heads of the bakers' guild Mashhadi Hoseyn Nanva and Haji Mohammad Hoseyn Razzaz, to advise him. Grain remained scarce throughout the harvest period and people were afraid that new supplies would not reach the city. There were riots, and a stream of pamphlets was published accusing the authorities of causing a willful and orchestrated famine. One pamphlet stated that this "famine is not natural, it is provoked. In fact, from 21 July until 8 August, six to ten hundred loads of grain entered Tehran regularly. After 8 August, in addition to the loads for the government, about 1,600 loads were brought in daily for private persons. It is interesting to note that in the second half of July one could buy bread without difficulty. However, during the first half of August, where there was plenty of grain in the market and prices should have fallen, they increased enormously, and bread was scarce and of inferior quality."[90]

The heads of the bakers' guild and Matin al-Saltaneh wanted to sell wheat from the state granary at harvest time, although these stores were to have been kept until the end of the year when stocks were very low. The bread at harvest had to be prepared from grain bought in the market. Mornard, however, hesitated to sell the government grain so early in the year. Therefore, the leaders of the bakers' guild created an artificial shortage of bread by closing their granaries. Mornard was deceived by this stratagem and gave orders to collect wheat from the districts around Tehran and to supply the two leaders of the bakers' guild daily with 300 *kharvar* of wheat from the state granary at low prices. This measure brought an end to the bread shortage. Mornard wanted to isolate the grain merchants by refusing to buy grain from them and forcing them to leave their grain to rot

---

88. Browne 1959, vol. 4, p. 473.
89. Shuster 1912, pp. 170-72, 206, 288.

90. Demorgny 1913, p. 102. It is probably at this time that new regulations were proposed to improve the bread situation of Tehran, of which certain parts were later implemented, see Afshar 1389, pp. 489-91.

in their granaries. Abdollah Mostowfi, then head of the Treasury Department within the Ministry of Finance and our main source of information for this period, pointed out that the state granary just did not have enough in storage to last until the next harvest. Mornard countered that according to the *omana-ye maliyeh* (members of the Treasury Board)[91] there was enough grain for two years. Mostowfi told him that this Board did not know the difference between wheat and barley and that what was actually available was 30,000 *kharvar* from crown lands and 45,000 *kharvar* from tax payments in kind. This quantity was in??sufficient to provide a four-month supply of bread for Tehran. "Moreover, now that the sale of government grain at harvest time has become known, things will get worse. Those who have grain will now hide their grain and will not give even one seed. They will wait until the end of the year when you will have to go to them. Then they will sell to you at whatever price they dictate. You will not make their wheat rot, but they will empty the Treasury."[92]

From the beginning of October 1912 the bread situation in Tehran became serious. It had become very difficult to provide the bakers with 300 *kharvar* of wheat. About one-third of the city remained without bread most of the time. The greater part of *taftani* bread was now prepared mainly with barley. Gradually barley was also used for preparing *sangak* bread that was like a thick quilt and inedible. The bakers did not only prepare bread of unsifted wheat and barley flour, but added old bran, which usually was sold to cattle owners. The wheat price had risen from 17 to 35 *tuman*s per *kharvar* and the price of barley from 10 to 25 *tuman*s. Under growing pressure of public opposition to his policy, Mornard sent armed wheat buyers to the villages around Tehran to procure wheat and barley. The grain owners, however, were alarmed by this action;

they were afraid that they would lose control over the market and refused to sell at prices even higher than the prevailing ones. It was then decided that Russian wheat would be imported. Because sweet-meat-sellers (*shirini forush*) were prepared to buy this wheat at high prices, the bakery office (*edareh-ye nanva'i*) ruled that the bakers should be given a mixture consisting of one-fourth Russian wheat, one fourth-Iranian wheat and one half barley. However, bread prepared from this mixture was bad and inedible. The bakers separated the better quality mixture from the inferior, baked good bread and sold it for high prices. They baked bread of poor quality from the inferior mixture and sold it at 32 *shahi*s per *man* (3 kg). In this way the Treasury lost five to six thousand *tuman*s each day on the sale of grain to the bakers.[93]

In November 1912, the bread situation deteriorated daily and Mornard asked Mostowfi to take charge of the bakery office. At that time there were four thousand *kharvar* of Russian flour, three thousand *kharvar* of barley and one thousand *kharvar* of wheat in the state granary. This quantity was sufficient to provide a 40-day supply of bread. Fortunately, Russian flour was bought and would be delivered in two weeks, while wheat and barley would arrive from areas around Tehran. Mostowfi then formed a committee of five people called the bread committee (*kumiteh-ye nan*). They divided the city into the following four areas, each of which was placed under the control of a different person.

Area	Person in charge
Mahalleh-ye Dowlat	Mirza Hasan Khan Baqa al-Dowleh
Majalleh-ye Sangalaj and Darvazeh-ye Qazvin	Mirza Homayun Khan Sayyah
Mahalleh-ye `Udlajan	Mirza Ali Akbar Khan
Mahalleh-ye Bazar	Fathollah Mostowfi

---

91. Mostowfi n.d., vol. 2, p. 385. On the *omana-ye maliyeh*, see Lambton 1953, p. 240.
92. Mostowfi n.d., vol. 2, p. 386.

93. Mostowfi n.d., vol. 2, pp. 392-93.

With the permission of Mornard the committee adopted various measures. First, it did not attempt to regulate the price of grain. Second, to improve the quality of bread it changed the mixture sold to the bakers so that it consisted of Russian flour (50%), local wheat (25%) and barley (25%). Furthermore, the committee decided that for every six shops there should be one inspector (*mofattesh*) in whose presence dough had to be prepared to avoid adulteration of the bread. The wages of the inspectors did not cost the Treasury more than about 300 *tuman*s per month. Regulations for the supervision of the bakers and a code of conduct for them were drawn up. Permits (*javaz*) stating amount, quantity, and name of the baker, his area, date of issue and duration were issued. The committee did nothing to control the financial relations between the state granary and the bakers who had to deal with the state granary by themselves.

The inspectors were in charge of controlling the incoming and outgoing quantities of flour, fuel, salt and bran of the bakery shops. They also sealed the granary and the coal bin. The baking of very crispy (*du atesheh*) bread was prohibited as were under-weight selling (*kam forushi*), half baked bread, foul water in the reservoir, and not sending away people queuing at the shop; each of these offenses had a specific fine, which was raised in case of repeat offenses. The chief inspector's office was located in the areas of which he was in charge. He had two police officers at his disposal to carry out his orders. Each night he would take a sample of bread from all the bakers in his area, on which a paper was pinned recording the name of the shop owner and would hand these to the chief of his area.

At an informal meeting with the bakers, Mostowfi told them that they no longer had a guild chief - *nanva bashi*; "I am your guild chief (*rish safid va kadkhuda*)" he told them. He explained that they would do business with the state granary and pay for the flour, which they would receive on showing the *javaz*. He showed them the new mixture and acquainted them with the new supervisory measures. He also bluntly informed them that he wanted bread on the counters.

According to Mostawfi, the bread situation improved considerably. The inspectors were so effective that there was no more under-weight selling. Also, under their supervision, faulty scales were checked, patched-up flour sacks replaced with new ones, and hygienic conditions strictly observed. Flour and water were mixed in the presence of the inspectors, who also checked the morning dough (*khamir-e sobh*). In each area there was also a designated bakery that the chief inspector himself inspected. Two weeks after the new rules were implemented the bread price had stabilized to such an extent that the income of a baker had dropped from four to five *tuman*s to two *tuman*s per day.[94]

As the supply of grain offered in the market increased daily the wheat price fell. This trend was encouraged because the bakers were not allowed to buy grain, while the government did not buy any because there was enough grain in the state granary to satisfy 40 days of consumption. Mostowfi proposed to begin buying when wheat and barley prices had fallen respectively to 20 and 15 *tuman*s per *kharvar*. His proposal was accepted because, as he pointed out, if prices fell lower, imports from Khamseh and Iraq districts would not find a market. He estimated the amount that the government lost on the price of bread was 12 *tuman*s per *kharvar*. The flour mixture cost 30 *tuman*s per *kharvar* and was sold for 18 *tuman*s to the bakers, who in turn sold bread at 32 *shahi*s. This loss would decrease by six *tuman*s when wheat prices fell and the price for bakers would go up by two to three *tuman*s, thus reducing their profit. His proposal was accepted by the government and the committee took steps accordingly. The result was that prices

---

94. Mostowfi n.d., vol. 2, pp. 396-401.

remained at the level of 22 and 15 *tuman*s for wheat and barley respectively until the beginning of the following year. When wheat from Varamin finally arrived in July 1913 the import of Russian flour was discontinued and bread prices fell to 15 and 20 *tuman*s for barley and wheat, which was less expensive than it had been two years previously.[95]

When the bread situation returned to normal by the summer of 1913, Mostowfi wanted to return to his old job. His did not like Mornard and their collaboration was marred by strained relations. Mostowfi objected to Mornard's interference in the work of the Bread Committee and claimed, "One year ago he didn't understand anything about the bread situation and now that I have informed him about all matters, he still doesn't know enough."As a result he interfered in a clumsy manner. The Belgians were unhappy with an independent-thinking Iranian and wanted instead a *mirza benevis* (a 'yes-man'). They believed that they were sufficiently informed to do the job, especially after I had told them that the harvest was good that year and production was one and half time the wheat needed by the country. So they no longer needed the bread committee." The government accepted both his resignation and his suggestion to make bread baking free, so that villagers could bring bread into Tehran and sell it. This last measure would act as a check on bakers who cheated.[96]

The 1917-18 Famine

Meanwhile, the bread situation of West Azerbaijan had become critical as a result of the Ottoman invasion in 1915. In Ormiyeh, Armenian and Assyrian refugees suffered starvation and only with the help given by American missionaries were their lives saved. The latter, financed by the American Committee of Armenian and Assyrian Relief, had organized a bread distribution as follows: until noon bread was sold, thereafter one sheet of thin bread was distributed to each needy person who had no money to buy bread or nothing to eat. To distribute the bread required 20-30 men over seven hours each day. In May 1915, demand was overwhelming; more than 3,000 bread tickets for 1 to 300 persons were issued and re-issued and these were updated regularly. On one day more than 5 tons of bread was distributed, but thereafter the need became less; fortunately bread was cheap at that time. An amount of $10,000 was sent from the USA and received in the fall of 1915. This kept 10,000 Assyrians and Armenians alive on rations of bread and salt only. In 1916, the situation did not change and hundreds of people had only one dry scrap of bread to eat. Even well-to-do people were begging bread, while bread became more expensive.[97]

Tabriz was not spared famine either. Disappointing rainfall in November 1916 and subsequent drought were harbingers of a bad harvest. To deal with the expected bread problem a local aid committee was established, which was dominated by members of the local Democratic Party. Lambert Molitor, the Belgian director of the Customs Administration in Tabriz, at first was only a member of this committee. However, when the food supply situation became problematic the government on 24 September 1971 put Molitor in charge of food supply of Tabriz. Despite the fact that Heynssens, the national head of the Customs Department had been reluctant to allow this, because "he was tired of Iranian intrigues and did not want his subordinate to get involved with another task than Customs," the cooperation between Molitor and the Democrats was excellent. Meanwhile, the price of

---

95. Mostowfi n.d., vol. 2, pp. 402-08.
96. Mostowfi n.d., vol. 2, pp. 430-32.

---

97. Rockwell 1916, pp. 17-18, 24-25, 35, 47, 67; *The Southern Workman* XLV/1916, 455-57 pictures of the American compound in Ormiyeh, the breadline, and refugees. In general, see Hellot-Bellier 2002, p. 339; Zirinsky 2002, pp. 359f; Shedd 1922.

bread in Tabriz had risen with 500%, while rice had become impossibly expensive. Every day there were about 100 deaths due to hunger, while children died in the streets. The main supply problem was that the large landowners kept their stock of grain hidden and they and others involved only looked after their own personal interests. After the Turks as well as the Democrats had been expelled from the city by the Russians, these confiscated grain and the draught animals, which the peasants needed to till the soil. The Russians established a plant to salt down meat, which was transported by rail to Tiflis for use by the Russian troops at Kars. Between 1914 and 1918 a total of 150,000 draught animals were confiscated, which, of course, worsened the prospects of good harvests. To face the dire situation Molitor rationed the supply of bread and put the bakeries under supervision, because he was convinced that there was enough food available in the province, but its distribution was inadequate. Furthermore, stocks of nuts and dried fruit were seized, which were distributed among the population likewise in a rationed manner. The situation in the winter 1917/18 threatened to become catastrophic when food supply came to a halt when camel transports were unable to cross the snow covered mountain passes. Molitor was able to induce the Bolsheviks, who had taken over control after the October Revolution, to supply Tabriz by rail with grain that was destined for the Russian army. To ensure the regular supply of food required constant negotiation, because the railway was also used to evacuate the Russian troops. It was also agreed that the salted meat for the Russian army stored in Azerbaijan would be sent to Tabriz. However, the Moslems refused the meat, because it had been handled by infidels, although the Armenian inhabitants of Tabriz gladly consumed it. In the Russian warehouses, situated at Sharafkhaneh, a village near Tabriz, not only food but also arms were stored. This attracted all kinds of unsavory elements, the more so, because the local political situation had become chaotic and politics prevailed over concern about the hungry population. Necessary steps to improve the food supply were not taken. Moreover, the transport situation worsened, because of frequent attacks on the railway, which caused that the Russians abandoned its maintenance. Also, fuel for the train was in short supply, and after a while the rail service to Tiflis was discontinued. The mojtaheds and Iranian troops who guarded the warehouses at Sharafkhaneh first served themselves, while they also terrorized the local population. Much of the equipment, including lorries, became defective. As a result of all these developments, many peasants fled to Tabriz to find food, which was ever more in shorter supply. The beef that until than had remained untouched now was much in demand. Because the rain in February 1918 had been good the harvest was good as well and the bread situation returned to more normal conditions. The same was not the case for the political situation, because on 8 June 1918 Tabriz was occupied by Ottoman troops, who caused new problems for the population.[98]

This dire situation was not limited to Azerbaijan. Towards the end of 1916 and the beginning of 1917 large areas of Iran were struck by drought and Varamin, an important grain producing village near Tehran, suffered from insects (*senn*). The price of wheat that had been 20 *tuman*s per *kharvar* in the spring of 1916 rose to 25 *tuman*s in the fall of 1916. The wheat price rose even more in the spring of 1917 and reached 30 *tuman*s per *kharvar*. When harvest time arrived wheat became even more expensive. Seham al-Dowleh was appointed *ra'is-e nanva* (chief of the bakery office). To assist him in his task a so-called *kumiteh-ye arzaq* (alimentation committee) was appointed; this committee consisted of seven or eight of the most important merchants who met daily. Due to World War I and the Russian October Revolution, wheat could not be imported from Russia or India. The committee

---

98. Laureys 1996, pp. 61-63.

advised the government to sell bread at two *qeran*s and two *abbasi*s per *man* (3 kg), which meant that it would suffer a daily loss of 32 *tuman*s per *kharvar*.⁹⁹

In October 1916, Mostowfi was appointed chief of the alimentation service (*ra'is-e edareh-ye arzaq*), which was part of the Ministry of Finance. This service had "a monopoly of the purchase and sale of grain in Tehran and adjoining provinces."¹⁰⁰ At that time nine months remained until the next harvest and Tehran needed 80,000 *kharvar* of wheat. Not even one-tenth of that quantity was available in Tehran or its vicinity, while the provinces had no grain surplus to send to Tehran. However, the rice harvest had been very good that year in Mazandaran. Because of the October Revolution, rice that normally would have been exported to Russia now remained in the hands of the farmers. Mostowfi, therefore, proposed to bring 30 to 40,000 *kharvar* of rice to Tehran to avoid people starving. The government agreed to this proposal. By that time it had become extremely difficult to secure 300 *kharvar* of wheat and barley daily, the quantity of grain needed to feed Tehran. The food crisis was intensified by the fact that in Tehran bread cost two *qeran*s and two *abbasi*s per *man*, while outside the city it rose to three to four *qeran*s. This led to the transfer of bread from Tehran. One of the members of the alimentation committee was the Armenian merchant Alexander Toumaniantz who had agents all over Mazandaran. He undertook to buy and transport 30,000 *kharvar* of rice to Tehran. Consequently, at the beginning of the winter this quantity of rice was safely stored in the state granary and the danger of famine was prevented.

As he had done in 1912, Mostowfi requested a few friends to supervise the implementation of the alimentation service's policy. The city of Tehran was now divided into the following three areas:

Fig. 38: Stamps benefiting the Alimentation Service (credit: Behruz Nassre).

Area	Supervisor
Mahalleh-ye Chaleh-ye Meydan	Ali Mansur
Mahalleh-ye Dowlat	Ali Dehkhoda
Mahalleh-ye Bazaar va Darvazeh-ye Qazvin	Fathollah Mostowfi

In addition to the three area chiefs, four chief inspectors and one inspector per six shops were appointed. Each day they checked the preparation of dough in the bakeries and the work of bakers in general. This led to a fall in under-weight selling, although the crowds made it impossible to prevent it altogether. Under-weight selling was very profitable for the bakers and they even sold half-baked

---

99. Mostowfi n.d., vol. 2, pp. 495-96; Shahri 1386, vol. 2, p. 396.
100. Millspaugh 1926, p. 25.

bread, for thus they could increase their income by 20 percent.[101]

Eyn al-Dowleh, who had been scheming to become grand vizier, finally achieved his objective on 28 December 1917. Under pressure from the bazaaris, Ala al-Saltaneh resigned and Eyn al-Dowleh was appointed in his stead, who, according to Mostowfi, was heavily indebted and intended to take advantage of the food situation to improve his financial situation. As a result, Mostowfi gradually had to close bakeries and instead of the normal 300 *kharvar* only 150 *kharvar* and on some days only 100 *kharvar* per day were supplied to the city. Each day, based on the state granary's stock, the price was fixed as were the number of shops that had to be open the next day in the various city quarters. But both the granary' stock and the number of working shops decreased; the latter were open by rotation. It was then decided to open the *dampokht pazi* kitchens and the people had no choice but to eat rice. With Mostowfi's agreement, Mokhber al-Saltaneh who was the Minister of Alimentation (*vazir-e arzaq*), decided to fix the price of a dish of steamed rice with fava beans (*dampokht pazi*) at 32 *shahi*s and readied the public kitchens. In November 1917 the food crisis worsened and more bakeries were closed. The preparation of *dampokht* was started, but the people preferred bread, despite the problems of obtaining it. Among the population this year of famine, therefore, was known as 'the year of steamed rice' or *sal-e dampokhtak*.[102] The already strained relations between Mostowfi and Eyn al-Dowleh broke down when the latter ordered the state granary to discontinue selling grain to the bakers. During the subsequent discussion between the two men, Eyn al-Dowleh ordered one of his servants to strike Mostowfi, who then resigned from his post as chief of the alimentation service. The next day, on 20 May 1918, Eyn al-Dowleh was dismissed. Mostowfi does not attribute his fall to their dispute, but he adds, "if it is coincidental it is strange."[103]

The bread situation in Tehran remained critical. Molitor, like all other Europeans, had been evacuated from Tabriz after the Ottoman occupation of that city. Arrived in Tehran at the beginning of July 1918 he was put in charge of the city's food supply by the end of that month with full powers and authority to act as he saw fit. He also became supervisor of the royal domains (khaleseh), because these supplied most of the grain needed for Tehran city and province. To prevent illegal export of grain, Molitor ordered the military to cordon off the city; he further confiscated all bakeries, mills and those grain stocks that were fiscal payments in kind. Molitor did not demand grain from villages that were owned by the shah, as a result much grain from other villages was transported there. Therefore, he finally demanded that grain from the royal villages, part of which was actually rotting, also become available for distribution. This was also necessary because in January 1919 Molitor still had great difficulty to obtain sufficient quantities of grain to supply Tehran. Thereafter, the situation improved, also because Molitor paid the those transporting the grain promptly and directly from Tehran. By the end of March 1919 the situation was such that Molitor obtained so much grain that he even had to find new storage for it. All these measures were much resented by landowners, speculators and other self-interested people, who intrigued to undermine his position. The newspapers slandered Molitor and the population of Tehran was incited to demand bigger rations, which according to Molitor were adequate. When he left in November 1919 on furlough to Belgium he was accused of taking millions of ill-gotten gains with

---

101. Mostowfi n.d., vol. 2, pp. 498-500; Kuhestani-nezhad 1381, p. 42.
102. Kuhestani-nezhad 1382, p. 40; Mostowfi n.d., vol. 2, p. 504.

103. Mostowfi n.d., vol. 2, pp. 504-06.

him. However, the government of Iran appreciated what Molitor had done and Vothuq al-Dowleh, the prime-minister, officially congratulated him in April 1919, while there even was talk among the population of Tehran to erect a statue for him. When Molitor returned in 1920, he was appointed national head of the Customs Department.[104]

The new prime minister was Mostowfi al-Mamalek, who limited the bakeries in Tehran to four and increased the price of bread to 4 *qeran*s and 6,000 *dinar*s. This was not enough to feed the city's population and, therefore, *dampokht* continued to be old at 32 *shahi*s per 3 kg to make up for the shortfall. The *dampokht* was rather watery, but it was food. Cooked rice (*berenj-e polow*) was not very expensive either, but still cost two to three times more than in normal years.[105] In March 1918, the price of wheat in Tehran was 120 *tuman*s per *kharvar*; all bakeries were closed and people had to get bread from the villages. Because rain was plentiful during winter time, the harvest was satisfactory and consequently the price of wheat fell to 36 *tuman*s per *kharvar* in July 1918.[106] According to Mostowfi, during this period no one died of hunger in Tehran. Those who died, about 100 to 200 per day, were victims of influenza. However, according to Sepahsalar Tonkabuni, 50 people died of hunger every day due to government neglect, "because we have no government."[107] He accused both the government and Ahmad Shah of selling their grain at high prices. The shah, therefore, was nicknamed Ahmad-e Allaf (Ahmad the grocer).[108]

Although this narrative is focused on Tehran worse conditions prevailed in western Iran, in particular in Tabriz, Ormiyeh, Salmas, Khoy, Hamadan and Kermanshah, due to the fact that in addition to famine conditions the people of that area also suffered from what is nowadays euphemistically called 'collateral damage' from the ongoing warfare between Ottoman, Russian, and British troops.[109] In fact, during the winter of 1917/18, thousands of people in Iran died of hunger and cold. This situation was further aggravated by hoarding and short-weight selling to customers by the bakers as well as the outbreak of the influenza pandemic.[110] To help the poor and destitute, Iranians organized some small relief operations (*kheyriyeh*) in various towns.[111] Unfortunately, these local actions fell far short of the needs, often serving not more than a few score of the poor. To raise money for these activities in Tehran, the local relief committee organized the performance of a number of theater pieces in the Grand Hotel the proceeds of which were donated for relief activities. Also, special stamps were issued with the overprint of "Alimentation Service (*edareh-ye arzaq*)" in cities such as Tabriz and Khoy, the proceeds of which likewise served to raise funds for the poor.[112] The main relief came from outside, in particular from the USA, where already in 1915 a committee was formed to provide relief, which was officially named Near East Relief in 1919.[113] The American committee had nothing to do with Tehran. When the Turkish troops left Tabriz, after having looted it, the Americans came back and brought relief to

---

104. Laureys 1996, pp. 63-65.
105. Mostowfi n.d., vol. 2, pp. 512-14.
106. Mostowfi n.d., vol. 2, pp. 512-14.
107. Mostowfi n.d., vol. 2, p. 513; Tafazzoli 1340, p. 534.
108. Forbes-Leith 1927, p. 150.

---

109. See, e.g. the description of the situation in the Kermanshah area by Forbes-Leith 1927, p. 21; Kuhestani-nezhad 1381, p. 43. For the situation elsewhere in Iran, such as in central Iran, Semnan, Isfahan, and Ardabil, see Ibid
110. Chaqueri 1978, pp. 7, 20. For a very biased and, in my view, misleading analysis of the 1917-18 famine, see Majd 2003. For a critical review of this book, see Floor 2005. Kuhestani-nezhad 1381, p. 40 also blames Russia and Great Britain for the various food crises between 1912 and 1918, without providing any factual evidence.
111. Post 1920, p. 71.
112. Kuhestani-nezhad 1381, p. 42; see pictures of stamps.
113. Barton 1930, (chapter 8 deals with Iran); Jackson, 1920.

25-50,000 people.¹¹⁴ This relief was mainly given in the form of food-for-work programs. Boys and men repaired streets, while women were employed weaving rugs, cloth, or spinning wool and cotton in return for "sufficient wages to provide for the minimum necessities of life." Furthermore, small orphanages were established at Tabriz, Hamadan and Kermanshah.¹¹⁵

In this last city at that time, Armenian refugees were living "on a dole of bread and a bowl of soup every day" from the Americans. There was plenty of food, but the shah, officials and merchants organized bread rings to their benefit. In Hamadan the Americans broke the bread corner by buying much grain, opening bakeries and distributing bread tickets.¹¹⁶ In the winter-spring of 1918 the price of bread rose 20-fold, but by the fall 1918 it had dropped to 10-fold. "The pre-war price of wheat was 60 cents; government offered to buy it at forced price of $7.50 per bushel, but we finally paid $8.85 per bushel." The Americans bought large quantities at that price and resold it at $4.85. For each ton the baker had to make 2,750 pounds of bread, to be sold at 6.5 cents per pound. This cheap bread (the going rate was 15-25 cents and the pre-war rate was 1.5 cents) was provided by 19 bakeries at 1 pound/p.p. Thus, bread for 25,000 people or 50% of the population of Hamadan was supplied, but only to ticket-holders, "which had been chosen by a house to house canvass" and only people who otherwise would have died. To compete, the Commission had to lower its price, but the harvest looked good."¹¹⁷ This forced local dealers to lower their prices and when they came down the Americans closed their bakeries and only to reopen them when the Iranian bakers raised their prices again. The shah benefited from the misery, where a few Europeans, Moslems and Zoroastrians did much to alleviate the situation.¹¹⁸ In November 1918 the British celebrated the Armistice in Europe by feeding 2,000 poor Kermanis, a gesture even appreciated by the anti-British Democrats in that town.¹¹⁹ By that time, in most parts of Iran the food situation had returned to normal.

It is an indication of the political importance of the bread situation that after the February 1921 coup d'etat by Ziya al-Din, the new prime-minister, and Reza Khan, the new Minister of War, one of the first acts of the former was to issue new regulations concerning the operation of bakeries. According to his proclamation, all shops had to open at sunrise and close at sunset except bakeries; the dough maker was allowed to start earlier. Furthermore, all shops needed to be closed on Fridays except bakeries. Furthermore, *nan-nakesh* (short-weight bread) was banned and dry *sangak* should not be lighter than 8 *sir* and fresh than 10 *sir*. Likewise dry *taftun* should not weigh less than 4 *sir* and fresh 5 *sir* leaving the balance. Each baker was responsible to build a tiled counter (*saku*) to put bread on that came from the oven, and bread should not be put on the floor. This was because it was customary to throw bread coming from oven on the ground in front of the customer to get rid of pebbles so that the buyers did not have to do so and to signal for whom the bread was intended. The counter of the bakery should be covered with a nice *methqal* cloth that had to be washed and changed each day. The interior of all foodshops had to be tiled; moreover, the dough had to be covered with clean cloth and to prevent bugs, stickly fly paper should be hung.¹²⁰

---

114. Post 1920, p. 71.
115. Barton 1930, p. 101.
116. Post 1920, p. 71.
117. Vaile 1919, pp. 11-14.
118. Post 1920, p. 71.
119. Skrine 1962, pp. 51 (details), 114. For details about the food situation in Kerman during the 1916-18 period, see Administration Report 1917, pp. 21-22 and Ibid., 1918, pp. 23-24.
120. Shahri 1371, vol. 1, pp. 259-61. Despite the ban of throwing bread on the ground, there still was often grit and pebbles in the bread, due to primitive method of grinding. Sykes 1910, p. 213.

In April 1921, as a result of this decree, the Municipality of Tehran started a so-called Hygienic and Assistance Service charged with the prevention of illness and of unhygienic conditions in the city. Amongst other things the new municipal body supervised the trade in foodstuffs and prohibited the sale of products unfit for consumption. Their control was directed toward butchers' and the bakers' shops in particular.[121] Although Ziya al-Din's decree remained a dead letter due to shortness of his government, his ideas were those of his contemporaries. Hence, subsequent governments pursued the same objectives and in fact made them happen over time.

The operation of the Alimentation Service (*edareh-ye arzaq-e 'omumi*) in Tehran was not discontinued. Although when the American Administrator-General Arthur Millspaugh took over the management of Iran's finances in 1922, he found the service was working at a loss. One of his first acts was to buy 198 motor trucks and 60 trailers for the transport of grain and thus he solved half of the bread problem.[122] He recognized the importance of government's interference with the price and quality of life necessities in the city, as "the conduct of the Alimentation Service is not merely a symbol of governmental efficiency, but also an indication of the political attitude of a government toward the people."[123]

In 1923, and probably earlier, bakers had to sign an agreement with the Alimentation Service. In this agreement the baker, who was identified by name and location, undertook to bake unadulterated bread with the flour or grain that he received from the state granary, within a period of 24 hours, and to sell the bread at the weight (4 *sangak* bread were about 3 kg) at a price fixed by the government. He further undertook not to close his shop without permission and not to sell bread to ambulant sellers (*nan-forushan-e dowreh-gerd*).[124] Nevertheless, the activities by the Alimentation Service hardly affected the bakers' guild, for as late as 1923 they retained "unsanitary methods and an age-old reputation for skull-duggery."[125] In 1927, the American Mission was severely criticized by members of the Majles, who opposed its role and its continuation. Pointed questions were asked by these delegates about the losses sustained by the Alimentation Service, which became known and somewhat of a scandal after the Budget Commission disclosed the findings of its investigation. The losses were estimated at 1.5 million tumans due to mismanagement. The scandal undoubtedly had an impact on the negotiations about the renewal of Millspaugh's contract, which broke down in July 1927. As a result, Millspaugh left the country, while the other Americans served out their contract.[126]

The bread problem under Reza Shah

From 1921 to 1929 on average 30,000 tons of flour per year was supplied to bakers in Tehran, excluding private households and the military. The grain was obtained from tax payments in kind and *khaleseh* revenue and purchases in the market.[127] Later in that decade the Alimentation Service was renamed Alimentation and Guild Service (*servis-e*

---

121. RMM 47, pp. 125-26.
122. Millspaugh 1925, p. 78; Ibid., 1926, p. 25. On the costly procurement of the lorries and its parts, see FO 416/81, Memorandum Mismanagement Alimentation Service by E.R. Lingeman. 02/07/1927. It seems that in other cities similar organizations existed, such as in Khuy where in 1917 an Alimentation Commisison (*kumisiyun-e arzaq*) was created. Aghasi 1350, p. 425. On the savings in time and cost due to the use of motorized transport, see Clawson 1993.
123. Millspaugh 1925, p. 78.

124. Rowghani 1385, pp. 41-43.
125. Millspaugh 1926, p. 103.
126. FO 416/81, Memorandum Mismanagement Alimentation Service by E.R. Lingeman. 02/07/1927
127. Baladiyeh-ye Tehran 1310, pp. 200-03.

arzaq va asnaf) and was part of the municipality of Tehran. A circular letter by that service to all bakers dated 23 Mordad 1309/14 August 1930 informed them of new regulations, including the payment of a fee of 10% for the upkeep of the Service. It further contained detailed instructions how the interior of the bakery had to arranged, with tiled oven, walls, and white-washed ceiling. Also, there had to be a separate basin for water, the flour storage areas had to have a white-washed ceiling and cemented walls. The Alimentation Service was in charge of supplying bakers with 60,000 *kharvar* of flour during six months, which it bought at 15 *tuman*s per *kharvar* (300 kg) and resold it to the bakers' guild, which had to repay the sum in 12 installments. The bakers' guild was responsible for the internal distribution of the grain among its members and was also responsible for the repayment. From this quantity the volume needed for the military and police was deducted. After the 60,000 *kharvar* had been supplied the bakers were free to buy and sell grain. To prevent hoarding and price increases, bakers had to apply the government's fixed prices.[128]

The *sangak, lavash* and *taftun* bakers who formed a guild were divided into 10 sections or *jowqeh*, and each section was responsible for (i) the purchase of one-tenth of the municipal wheat; (ii) for five percent of the daily wheat consumption of Tehran; and (iii) the rapid daily sale of good quality bread throughout the year. Each section had to appoint a representative. These ten representatives were jointly responsible to the Alimentation and Guild Service and for their members for one year. Within two weeks all bakers had to sign an undertaking promising to adhere to the various rules. A baker who did not sell good bread that days' bread would be all given to the orphans and poor. Fuel had to be distributed among members in an equitable manner. The price of bread was fixed at 9 *abbasi* per *man*. If they could not bake good bread they had to buy good wheat at whatever cost, while the price of bread remained unchanged.[129]

---

128. Rowghani 1385, pp. 53-55; Baladiyeh-ye Tehran 1310, p. 194.

129. Rowghani 1385, pp. 56-57.

Table 9.1: Estimated daily expenses of a standard *sangak* bakery in Tehran 1930

Item Description	Workers' Pay		Tobacco Pay (*pul-e tutun*)	Cost of Materirals			Total Cost	
	Tuman	Qeran	Qeran	Per	Qeran	Dinar	Qeran	dinar
Shater	1	7	1	1 man	1	800	19	800
Nan-gir	2	1	1	0.5 man	-	900	13	900
Atesh-andaz	-	6		Charak	-	450	6	450
Padu dast besikh	-	5		-	-	-	5	-
Khamirgir	-	8	1	0.5 man	-	900	9	900
Vardast	-	5		-	-	-	5	-
Ardgir	-	6		Charak	-	450	6	450
Padu-ye buteh gozar	-	4		-	-	-	4	-
Padu-ye miyaneh	-	3		-	-	-	3	-
Dokkandar	-	10		-	-	-	10	-
Mirza	-	4		-	-	-	4	-
Lighting and dung	-	3		-	-	-	3	-
Lunch shater, khamirgir and ateshandaz	-	2		-	-	-	2	-
Water carrier	-	2		-	-	-	2	-
Nan-e khur (12 persons)	-	-		3 man	5	400	5	400
Average shop rent	1	-		-	-	-	10	-
Milling fee 2 kharvar	4	-		-	-	-	40	-
Fuel	2	-		-	-	-	20	-
Salt	-	3		-	-	-	3	-
Sieving 2 kharvar	1	2		-	-	-	12	-
Porterage to storage	-	4		-	-	-	4	-
Weighbridge fee 1 kharvar	-	5		-	-	-	5	-
Office fees	3	-		-	-	-	30	-
Subtotal	-	-		-	-	-	223	950
Cost of 1 kharvar granary wheat	-	-		-	-	-	150	-
Cost of 1 kharvar good quality wheat	14	-		-	-	-	140	-
Total expenditure and cost of 2 kharvar wheat	-	-		-	-	-	513	950
Cost of 3 kharvar bread	-	-		-	-	-	450	-
Aver. profit per 2 kharvar baked	-	-		-	-	-	27	-

Source: Rowghani 1385, p. 85. One *kharvar* = 300 kg. Each *man* of bread is sold at 9 *abbasi*.

In the following years the operating rules for bakers were refined and reinforced. In 1933, the municipality of Tehran issued new rules that included among other things that bakers were not allowed to sell cold *sangak* or *taftuni* bread near another bakery. Both the number and sales area of bakeries was determined by the municipality; the owner of a bakery was not allowed to have a baker's permit unless he was a baker or had been in the past, nor was he allowed to own more than one shop; opening hours had to be respected, unless permission was given to close earlier and the shop could not be closed without permission; the bakery workers had to keep the premises clean; women and children had to be given priority in selling bread; only the type of bread for which the permit was given was to be baked. The time to begin baking was determined by the municipality and adjusted by season; non-compliance was punishable. Four pieces of *sangak* bread had to weigh 1 *man* (3 kg) and *do atesheh* bread should not weigh less than 8 *sir* (60 g), while no more than 4 pieces of *do atesheh* could be baked at one time in an oven. The fuel for all bakeries was distributed by the municipality and they had to buy it at the designated distribution centers; it was prohibited to buy it elsewhere, or to sell surplus fuel. In case of fuel shortage the municipality would adjust its distribution. It was not allowed to ask more than the fixed price in case the bread was sprinkled with poppy-seed (*khashkhash*). Each baker should have fuel and salt sufficient for one month. Also, there were some labor related rules concerning time-off for workers, hygiene related issues, each worker needed a health certificate and no bakery worker who was ill was allowed to be hired - the wages of the workers were fixed by the municipality and the baker was not allowed to pay them extra; and the man who places the dough in the oven (*shater*) had to work quickly so that customers would not have to wait. Finally, each baker had to make a downpayment of an amount of 500 riyals (*lavashi*), 1,000 riyals (*taftuni*), or 1,500 riyals (*sangaki*) as security.[130]

In 1937 further rules were issued by the Ministry of the Interior, which substantially did not differ from the ones issued in 1933, but they applied nationwide and not only to Tehran. In some cases rules were made more specific, e.g., the days when bakeries were allowed to close were listed (10 Moharram; 21 Ramazan, 28 Safar), and flour should not contain foreign substances. *Khoshkeh-pazi, shirmal-pazi, komaj-pazi, mozdi-pazi* bakers and the like did not need to make a down-payment as security.[131] Bakers obtained their grain from the *edareh-ye koll-e ghalleh va nan*, which was created in 1935 and had the monopoly for the distribution of grain.[132] To facilitate its task Reza Shah built "a large concrete grain elevator, called in Persia the Silo, which also housed a flour mill, equipped with modern machinery," which was the main source of flour for Tehran.[133] In July 1935, the government also formed a Company for the Stabilization of Prices of Cereals for buying and selling grain domestically before the harvest, and if need be to sell the surplus abroad if need be. It further fixed grain prices annually with a view to capture more revenues as well as to prevent hoarding and other supply problems. On 9 September 1936 the export of wheat became a government monopoly, while in 1937 the Company became a department under the Ministry of Finance.[134] Because of rising inflation this government price was always too low for the peasants, be it that it kept urban bread prices also low.[135]

However, these measures did not resolve the problem of local crop failures that still occurred

---

130. Rowghani 1385, pp. 59-62.
131. Rowghani 1385, pp. 64-68.
132. Yakta'i 1340, pp. 410-14.
133. Millspaugh 1945, p. 100. In fact, eight of these silos were built.
134. Gray 1938, p. 17.
135. Skrine 1962, p. 174.

throughout the country resulting in local scarcity of bread. The difference with the Qajar past was that under Reza Shah, both the central and local governments did more to address such situations. For example, in the Bushire area there was a complete crop failure and water shortage in 1932 and animals died by the thousands. The governor petitioned to make Tehran act and allow a relaxing of the monopoly trade restriction for wheat and fodder. Tehran assisted the governor, for "The Government had sent 5000 tons of grain from Mohammerah to be used as food and seed, the Governor of Bushire had requisitioned money from the few wealthy of Bushire and had brought 2,000 tons of wheat from Basra, 2,000 from Kermanshah, and from other places had come 2,000 tons of wheat and 1600 of barley. Water, too, had been brought down from Mohammarah to be distributed to the people in skins." Nobody died of starvation, but there were many thin people. "It was pitiful to see the old people and the animals."[136] It of significance to note that due to better roads and motorized transportation it was possible without any major problem and at relatively low cost, to transport wheat from a surplus to a deficit area, something that had been very difficult before 1922.[137]

Nevertheless the monopoly role of the state as a buyer and keeping crop prices artificially low had a negative impact on the rural population. For the peasants were forced to subsidize the urban consumers, and in particular the urban elite, by sacrificing their own desire for better and increased consumption. Peasants were penalized by the (i) difference in the government price of wheat, barley and other grains and those prevailing in the free market and (ii) disregard for the local needs that were considered secondary to that of the big cities.[138] Moreover, the manner in which this policy was implemented made its impact even more negative. Furthermore, landlords and those in the supply chain were upset by the (i) oppressive behavior of the government's collection agents; and (ii) the late or non-payment of the delivered grains.[139] The result of this policy of monopolies and exactions was that even people in fertile lands such as around Kermanshah had been reduced to a state of semi-starvation. This was due to the above four points, but in particular peasants were discouraged from planting grains given the too low a price the government was willing to pay. This trend coincided with a drought in 1939 and as a result there was not enough in the state granaries, as landlords were unwilling to sell and hoarded their grain.[140]

The bread crisis during World War II

In August 1941, Anglo-Soviet troops invaded Iran; Reza Shah abdicated and by coincidence this occupation was followed by famine, which was worsened due to hoarding. The *Times* correspondent reported from Kermanshah at the end of August 1941 that "large stocks of grain had been found by the advancing troops and that local scarcities were "evidently due to faulty distribution," as he put it euphemistically. Nevertheless bread riots occurred there in 28 October 1941 as well as in Shiraz.[141] Immediately after the invasion of Iran, the Allied troops delivered wheat to alleviate the local food situation. For example, the British landed 13,500 tons of wheat at the Persian Gulf ports in November 1941, while another 15,000 tons were en route.[142] At the time of the invasion, the food situation was already troublesome, which was worsened by the departure of Reza Shah, because it became more difficult to collect grain that in the past due to fear of the shah's despotic power. Because this

---

136. Merritt-Hawkes 1935, p. 4.
137. On this issue, see Clawson 1993.
138. Katouzian 1981, p. 133.
139. Tayarani 1372, pp. 20-21 (with examples).
140. Azari 1371, p. 4.
141. Skrine 1962, p. 79, 94.
142. Azimi 1989, pp.41, 45; Skrine 1962, p. 94-96, 117.

fear and power was gone, the political and administrative system was in disarray, and therefore, it became much more difficult to supply the cities, the more so because transportation had been disrupted because of the occupation, as 50% of Iran's public and privately-owned trucks were seized. This made it very difficult to transport food supplies from surplus to deficit areas, and, according to Millspaugh "transport accounted for at least half of the food problem." A contributing factor, be it a minor one, was that although the occupation troops were supposed to bring their own supplies they also drew on local resources. This was in particular the case in the Russian zone, which housed most of the occupation troops. Russia allegedly used 50% of Azerbaijan's grain harvest, the main supply source for Tehran's needs, for its own troops. Between March 1942–1943 it only allowed 300 tons of Azerbaijani wheat to be shipped to Tehran, whose population had increased by some 200,000 refugees from the Russian zone of occupation. Also at that time, food imports were difficult as imports had practically come to a standstill due to the war.[143]

The shah's abdication also had an adverse effect on the bread situation in Mashhad where the harvest had been not bad, but landowners hid as much of their grain as they could; the officials of the Economy (afterwards Food) Ministry squeezed it out of them by force or bribery, then hoarded it themselves; speculators, including officials, gambled in wheat futures, while bakers under contract to the government adulterated the rationed bread they baked and used the flour saved to make white bread for the 'free' market. "At Meshed in 1942 it was common to see shivering bread-queues waiting in the street for their dole of an indigestible grey substance composed chiefly of bread, poppy seeds and grit while round the corner the 'free' shops sold fine cakes and pastries to those who could afford them." While the British were distributing 3,000 tons from famine-stricken India (50% for road labor; 25% Zahedan; 20% Berjand, and 5% Mashhad) government officials, to prevent a drop in prices, took control of the first consignment. In this way, people would not learn that there was additional flour available. The British took steps to prevent furher interference and distributed the remainder of the flour that was later imported. However, the Iranian authorities protested against the British bypassing the local authorities. The British embassy in Tehran therefore told Skrine, the British Consul-General in Mashhad, to make use of the Ministry's local staff and only act in an advisory function. The result was continued hoarding by what Skrine called "the Gang of government officials, industrialists and profiteering contractors."[144] However, according to American officials the amount of wheat supposedly hoarded by landowners was much less than than intimated by the British. In fact, the British were forced to double their estimate of Iran's food needs in 1942 taking the lower estimated of hoarded stocks into account.[145]

In Mashhad and other cities, bread was adulterated with barley (which was officially permitted, be it that the official maximum was always exceeded), millet, bran and poppy-seed, because everybody in the supply line (grain-collector, transport owners, millers, and bakers) all wanted their 'cut' of the good wheat. Because the Red Army would suppress any riot, whether out of starvation or not, the Iranian authorities in charge of the food situation felt unhampered in their manipulation of the market. According to official figures, the city of Mashhad consumed 14,700 tons of food grains

---

143. Haas 1946, p. 226; Gol Mohammadi 1371, vol. 1, p. 298; Millspaugh 1945, pp. 44-45, 99; Skrine 1962, p. 173; Azari 1371, pp. 4-5 re trucks; the Russians commandeered them and thus wheat could not be transported; they also refused to make available their own trucks to help alleviate food situation; the British at times also were obstructing the food supply. Ibid., p. 5.

144. Skrine 1962, pp. 117-18, 121-22.
145. McFarland 1985, p. 53.

during March 1941-1942. One thousand tons of wheat came from India, 250 tons of barley from Russia, and the rest or 13,450 tons were collected by the Iranian officials. However, only 5,050 tons were made available at the low government rate for the bread ration, while 8,400 tons were sold by these officials at 1.5 to 3 times the government rate.[146]

In 1942 inflation, which had already increased significantly since 1938, had raised the cost of living 3 times compared to 1941, while in December it had already risen to almost 8 times.[147] In 1942, the official purchase price of wheat was one-third to two-thirds lower than the price in the 'free' market. The farmers lost considerably under these circumstances and thus made a deal with the government officials to buy part their wheat at the official price and another part at the 'free' market rate.[148] To address this issue the government decided to transfer the collection of grain from the Ministry of Finance to the new Ministry of Food. This could not have happened at a worse moment, because in 1942 there was a partial crop failure. Moreover, the government bureaucracy was ill-equipped to deal with the food problem in an efficient manner, and both the Russian and British ambassadors expressed their worry to prime-minster Soheyli in May 1942 about his inability to do so. He resigned three months later and was succeeded by Qavam, whose sole political program was to improve the food shortages.[149]

There was disagreement between the British and Americans how to assist the government of Iran in this respect. The British believed that there was enough food in the country, but it was hoarded, while the American ambassador, Louis

Fig. 39: Grain silo near Tehran (Shahri 1367, vol. 2, p. 405).

Dreyfus, disagreed and believed that the Iranians were only "one jump ahead of a bread shortage," which in Iran was "tantamount to starvation."[150] This attitude was clear from the assessment by Skrine, the British Consul-General in Mashhad, who submitted that the food situation was made worse by bread corners, while state granaries were empty leading to a short period of famine and months of semi-famine. One *kharvar* of wheat of 15 *tuman*s cost 400 to 450 or more and there was no bread to be had in the public market. This combination of internal and external factors caused shortages in the major cities, so that in 1942 bread became 30 times more expensive than normal. To give vent to their despair people demonstrated and/or rioted to protest the high prices of bread or its non-availbility, as many bakeries had closed. These events took place in Ashtiyan, Rasht (July), Borujerd (August), Malayer, Qazvin (September), Darab, Golpeygan (October), Arak (November), and Tabriz (February 1943), some of which were

---

146. Skrine 1962, pp. 175-76; on suppression of bread riots by the Russian army, see Tayarani 1372, pp. 21, 23.
147. Skrine 1962, p. 173-74; see also table 9.2. For the causes of the rise in inflation and the devastating economic impact of the occupation, see e.g. Katouzian 1981, pp. 142-43.
148. Skrine 1962, p. 175.
149. Azimi 1989, pp. 58-59, 67; Millspaugh 1945, p. 45.

150. Azimi 1989, p. 71.

put down by the Soviet army. Sometimes, these bread riots were put down with the use of arms, resulting in the loss of life. In Arak, the demonstration lasted longer than anywhere else, from August until 18 November 1942.[151] In Khorasan in 1942, people in Mashhad rioted against the government's decision to transport the alleged surplus of grain to Tehran. Merchants and landlords sent telegrams to the PM to protest as well. The situation became so serious that the *Majles* representative of Bojnurd warned his colleagues that a revolt might break out in the province. Protests were also heard from Khomeyn (near Isfahan) at that time.[152] Also, it led to serious bread riots in Tehran in early December 1942, which could only be put down with the help of the occupation forces. The result was more than 20 people killed, 700 wounded, 150 arrested, and 150 stores sacked and burned. To deal with the bread situation, state bakeries were established and the Allies helped with the import of grain, but it took time before these measures had an impact.[153]

Meanwhile, a large portion of the urban population suffered from undernourishment and malnutrition as food was insufficient and bad. Nevertheless, a protracted famine "had been averted only by reduction of rations, heavy adulteration of the flour, and Allied help in bringing in of grain and provision of transport."[154] In 1942, a total of 72,000 tons of wheat were imported by the British by sea representing one-fifth's of Iran's needs. Furthermore, 3,000 tons was promised to be sent to East Iran, where due to hoarding there were bread-queues at Zahedan and Khwash. Skrine, the Consul-General at Mashhad arranged for the immediate import of 100 tons of flour from Nok Kundi, which was commandeered by the Revenue Department on the instructions from Tehran (Ministry of Food and Economics). It refused to buy the flour itself, because its price was considered too high, and therefore, the flour was offered at an even higher price to the Indian community at Zahedan, which bought it immediately. To avoid being seen favoring the Indians over their own population the Revenue Department made available some of their hoarded wheat stock to the inhabitants of Zahedan.[155] There were many other issues that unnecessarily aggravated the food situation, some of which had unintended consequences that were not helpful to resolve the issue.[156]

Some Iranian scholars maintain that the occupying powers demanded the food surplus for their own troops, thus aggravating an already deficit food situation. However, Millspaugh and others maintain that this was not the major problem. In fact, in Mashhad in 1942, "The Russians released for the market all they could spare from military stocks of petrol, oil, wheat, flour, sugar and barley, but this did not help the outlying towns and villages, which existed as best they could on hoarded stocks."[157] It is true that on some occasions,

---

151. Skrine 1962, p. 173; Tayarani 1372, pp. 21(Mashhad) 22 (Darab/Fars; Rasht), 23 (Borujerd, Ashtiyan, Qazvin, Golpeygan, Malayer, Arak), 24 (Tabriz). Under the Foroughi cabinet (August 1941-March 1942) the Minister of Agriculture, "who had a vital task given the food shortages, was an ailing and incompetent person." Azimi 1989, p. 48.
152. Tayarani 1372, p. 21. According to Skrine 1962, p. 136, there was indeed a local rebellion at Bakharz near the Afghan border by Sowlat al-Saltaneh Hezara'i, whose real object was "to blackmail the Government in restoring valuable irrigated estates in the Fariman district ... that had been confiscated by the late Shah."
153. McFarland 1985, p. 51; Tayarani 1372, pp. 21, 24-25 (detailed description of the vents in Tehran); Azimi 1989, pp. 72-73; Haas 1946, p. 226; Gol Mohammadi 1371, vol. 1, p. 298; Millspaugh 1945, pp. 44-45, 99; Skrine 1962, p. 169 (incl. an attack on the house of PM Qavam, who shortly thereafter resigned); Farrokh 1347, pp. 435-47 (situation in Fars). Shahri 1386, vol. 2, p. 396 called it an artificially engineered famine. For a literary fiction description of famine in a village, see Ricks 1984, p. 355.
154. Haas 1946, p. 226; Gol Mohammadi 1371, vol. 1, p. 298; Millspaugh 1945, pp. 44-45, 99; Skrine 1962, p. 169 (incl. an attack on the house of PM Qavam, who shortly thereafter resigned).
155. Skrine 1962, p. 94-96, 117; Azimi 1989, p. 56.
156. See McFarland 1985 for a thorough analysis of all factors contributing to the food crisis.
157. Azari 1371, p. 4; Skrine 1962, p. 108. In 1943, the

Allied forces, in particular the Soviet army, helped themselves to local food supplies, as pointed out above, but these were incidents rather than regular occurrences. Later their help in collecting and transporting food was essential in resolving the food crisis. A constraining factor remained that wheat from the Russian occupied territory hardly reached other parts of Iran.[158]

To resolve part of the food problem of Tehran state bakeries were established, one of which was at the Silo. "An American supply officer suggested that it would be a good idea to establish a big central bakery in Tehran and to close down many small local bakeries." Kampsax, a Danish-Swedish company that had built the Trans-Iranian Railway and was providing technical assistance to the government of Iran, built the big bakery quickly. However the Iranian bakers went on strike. Moreover, the bread was the same as the bread made in Ohio and Minnesota, and not as the people were used to. "They consider the bread to be white as maggots and with a consistency of a mushroom; they would simply not eat it."[159] Not only was this new development disliked by the Iranian consumers, but the bakers also disliked this as it threatened their own position, and, therefore, "they not only sabotaged their own output in order to discredit the Silo flour but also instigated sabotage in the Silo bakery."[160] However, hunger does wonders for taste and food preference, for according to Koelz, an American anthropologist working in Iran:

During the war, a loaf in form and size like the American one appeared and was sold to the starving population. It had the advantage of permitting the use of any kind of flour and adulteration and was surely one of the most repulsive concoctions that ever appeared in the bread line in any country. The Persian usually likes a thin white bread and often displays with pride its whiteness. To make it thus, his wheat bread must have a good gluten content.[161]

The war bread was indeed not very attractive or tasty. The flour that the government sent to Tehran was known as 'silo,' (*nan-e silow*) for obvious reasons. It was not known what its ingredients were. Bread baked with this flour had such a bad color and taste and was dry and hard, that under normal circumstances hardly anyone would have bought it. However, people had no choice. Some prepared bread from barley and millet flour, which was better than silo flour bread. However, barley bread had the disadvantage that one hour after baking it became so hard and dry that it became inedible, even after it had been sprinkled with water. Again, millet bread only remained fresh for two hours. The mouth's saliva was so absorbed by it that a person almost choked on the bread.[162] Arthur Millspaugh, the government-appointed American Adminstrator-General of Finances, who was responsible for the bread supply, admitted that "the silo bread was of disgracefully poor quality-heavy, soggy, with a cement-like crust, containing not only a more than ordinary percentage of barley, but also bits of straw, small stones, and sand."[163]

Bread was not only scarce for urban dwellers, but also for workers in out-of-the-way places such as those working on the Trans-Iranian Railway

---

Russians offered 25,000 tons of wheat. Azimi 1989, p. 88.
158. Azimi 1989, pp. 46, 57 (there was a widespread belief in 1942 that the Allies were responsible for the food shortages).
159. Kampsax/Kurt, p. 55. It was Sheridan, US advisor the Ministry of Food, who took that decision. Millspaugh acknowledged that the bread produced was indeed not to the taste and customs of the Iranian consumer. Millspaugh 1945, p. 100.
160. Millspaugh 1945, p. 101; Shahri 1386, vol. 2, p. 397.

161. Koelz 1983, p. 165-66.
162. Gol Mohammadi 1371, vol. 1, pp. 298-99; Millspaugh 1945, p. 100.
163. Millspaugh 1945, p. 108.

that was built by the Danish-Swedish company Kampsax. Kurt Olsen, a Kampsax engineer reported that his company employed a number of purchasers to buy wheat from farmers. In addition it was in charge of food distribution to its contractors and Kampsax' own working staff. At that time, prices for the said commodities on the black market was 8 – 10 times that of the official prices, while many of the farmers were reluctant to sell. It was a hard life for the road maintenance crew and they were more interested in being supplied with bread than being paid.[164] Another Kampsax engineer, Ole Didrik Lærum, narrates a story during the construction of the southern line. It was winter and Kampsax had arranged for a transport of flour to Keshwar by a big caravan of mules, which should pass the mountain at Najun. Unfortunately, it had perished due to a snowstorm. As a result, there was a great risk for a famine among thousands of workers along the line. The workers had already suffered from scarcity of bread because the supplies had not come through for some time. Messrs. Blach and Furuholmen Jenssen of Kampsax, who were on their way to Khorramabad to obtain some assistance, unexpectedly met a large camel caravan. Mr. Blach didn't think twice, he jumped out of the car and bought the whole caravan on the spot. It was diverted to Khorramabad, where it was loaded with flour. Fortunately the camels made it through the snow in the pass. The caravan was received with great rejoicing. Many of the workers had already given up hope.[165]

On 4 May 1943 the *Majles* passed a law that gave Millspaugh (who had arrived in January 1943) extensive powers with regard to the food supply, albeit in collaboration with the Minister of Food. Rather than fixing the situation by fixing the prices of food products, Millspaugh decided to try to procure grain and other foodstuff in larger quantities, ration and distribute them on a fair basis, and sell them at low prices, which would not only have a stabilizing effect on household's cost of living, but also on inflation that was galloping.[166] Although the harvest of 1943 was very good the bread situation

Table 9.2: Cost of Living Index according to the Bank Melli Bulletin (1936-1947)

Year	Food	Lodging	Fuel and Light	Clothing	Sundries	General Index
March 1936-March 1937	100	100	100	100	100	100
March 1937-March 1938	120.3	119.5	121.5	121.1	131.3	121.1
March 1938-March 1939	127.8	147.3	126.4	129.9	162.5	132.5
March 1939-March 1940	133.4	159.8	137.1	146.6	191.1	142.7
March 1940-March 1941	151.7	193.9	138.3	167.5	211.7	161.9
March 1941-March 1942	251.8	218.4	184.9	255	271.2	243.1
March 1942-March 1943	522	360	344	500	449	476
March 1943-March 1944	1,081	724	769	1,112	924	1,003
March 1944-March 1945	1,029	972	653	1,295	989	1,030
March 1945-March 1946	768	1,111	584	916	950	882
*March 1946-March 1947	710-859	945-1176	424-558	706-799	8-5-881	726-831

* Only monthly figures available. Source: Roberts 1948, p. 42.

---

164. Kampsax/ Olsen, pp. 55, 68.

165. Kampsax/ Lærum, p. 38.

166. Millspaugh 1945, p. 97, 273-74 (the English text of the

grew more troublesome. There were new bread demonstrations in 1943 at Najafabad, Kermanshah, Zanjan, Sanandaj, and again in Tabriz. None were reported in the war years thereafter.[167] The selfish behavior of provincial governors and officials, who ignored instructions from the central government, as well as the inefficient and corrupt performance of the Ministry of Food, made the supply to the cities uncertain. Various groups of people involved in the bread situation committed all kinds of hanky-panky (*kupon-bazi*) with bread coupons that were issued by the government. Were it not for British help in collecting grain and British and Russian assistance in transporting it, the situation of semi-famine might have continued, for "lack of transportation had been at the heart of the difficulties in grain collection, as well as in the distribution activities." The government had increased the price of grain 2.5 times in 1942, but did not raise the price of bread. This subsidization of bread consumption weighed heavily on the budget and, therefore, in 1943, Millspaugh proposed to raise the price of bread in Tehran, which was approved. In August 1943 he was asked to take over the remaining functions of the Ministry of Food.[168] The hoarders complained about this price rise, because it would cause more inflation. However, their main worry was the narrowing of the difference between the government price and that of the 'free' market. Moreover, they took advantage of the new situation and merely charged higher prices.[169]

After Millspaugh had taken charge of the entire food administration there was political pressure to allow private transportation of grain into the cities and relax the government monopoly. As in the past, wealthy households could ensure their own supply of grain. Millspaugh, although sympathetic to such a change, refused to do so as there was no reserve in the state granaries, or the certainty that he could supply Tehran during the coming winter. Also, it would make his collection of grain more difficult given the high black market price of grain at that time. The result was a newspaper campaign against Millspaugh and political pressure to revoke his powers as well as threats to his person. To make matters worse there were long lines in front of the private bakeries leading to disturbances. Millspaugh then appointed an independent administration to supervise the bakeries led by Col. Saffari. At the same time, steps were taken to improve the quality of the flour. The result was that both the bread and the situation at the bakeries improved and by the end of 1943 there were hardly any complaints from the *Majles*.[170] The British Legation also assisted in this effort with a wheat collection and bread distribution scheme in the central and southern provinces. It also helped out governors with transport facilities, who since May 1943 were in charge of the grain collection. This upset black market transporters, of course.[171] However, the rich who normally ate *sangak* bread, prepared dough at home during the war years from the best local wheat flour and every morning their servants could be seen taking it to the bakeries, who were paid for their trouble (*mozdi-pazi*). This bread was popularly known as *nan-e khasseh*.[172]

Meanwhile, the bread situation improved significantly. Grain collection was better than ever before. Whereas on 23 October 1943 there was less than 11,000 tons in the Silo of Tehan, one year later it stored 30,000 tons. Not only did this allow an adequate supply to the cities, but also nationwide there were 154,000 tons in store or six month's supply. In the summer of 1944, Millspaugh therefore allowed the private transportation of grain

---

so-called Full Powers Law); Skrine 1962, pp. 171-72; Azimi 1989, pp. 84-85.
167. Tayarani 1372, p. 24 (with details).
168. Millspaugh 1945, pp. 100-01; Shahri 1386, vol. 2, p. 397.
169. Skrine 1962, p. 176.

170. Millspaugh 1945, pp. 108-09.
171. Skrine 1962, pp. 181, 197.
172. Gol Mohammadi 1371, vol. 1, pp. 298-99.

into the cities and intended to abolish the grain monopoly one year later. The grain reserve was a buffer against a famine and constituted a stabilizing factor in the grain market. Nevertheless, there was growing pressure from the *Majles* to immediately liberalize the market and introduce rules that were more to the liking of the landlords. To prevent this leading to actual legislation, Millspaugh made concessions and further relaxed some of the existing rules.[173] The improvement in the bread situation was not much appreciated by the food hoarders. In fact, they protested such as in Ahvaz in mid-November 1943 where they organized a riot in favor of more expensive bread!

> So much good bread had been sold by the Consular Liaison Officer at the low official price that the bakers found themselves being undersold and losing money, so they paid a couple of rials each to a number of bazaar loafers to make a *shullugh* (row) in favour of high-priced 'free' bread as against the cheap rationed article. The mob leaders took *bast* (sanctuary) in the telegraph office, and sent telegrams to the Minister of Food, then smashed up the instruments. Meanwhile, the bakers' representatives rushed up to Tehran to lay their case before the Cabinet, and now [the British] Legation are expecting any day to hear that they will be sent back to Ahvaz with orders to the Ostandar [governor] in their pocket to restore the black market in bread![174]

This was a positive development, because the distribution of monopoly goods (of which food was one) did not reach the entire population. The distribution officials claimed larger quantities than they actually distributed and sold the difference in the black market. Although this was known to the government it took no action, despite continuing scandals about its implementation.[175] According to British consuls the situation in early 1945 was as follows in selected provinces:

> Isfahan: Official 1.5 million, estimate for distribution of monopoly goods 800,000.
> Shiraz: One million tribes, 500,000 settled (indications are that the nomadic tribes do not receive monopoly goods).
> Bandar Abbas: Estimated 242,000 only; 15,155 coupons for monopoly goods issued.
> Zahedan: Population estimated 330,000, out of these only 62,000 have been issued with coupons for monopoly goods. Accurate population figures not possible owing to Central and Southern Mekran being inhabited mostly by nomadic tribes, the majority of whose members have not taken out registration papers.
> Meshed: Total population of Khorasan given as 2,044, 081, considered exaggerated. Finance authority gives figure based on coupon distribution as 434,893. This only includes main towns.[176]

Fortunately, the Iranian cabinet became convinced that firm steps needed to be taken to put an end to the food and other rackets and appointed a commission that visited the various provinces "to investigate the wheat, sugar, cloth and other scandals." It led, among other things to the release of hoarded stocks from government warehouses thus torpedoing the black market.[177]

By 20 January 1945 there was more than 56,000 tons of grain in storage in Tehran, and nationwide more than 273,000 tons, sufficient for ten months consumption. At the same time, the transportation situation was almost back to normal and thus, it no longer constituted an impediment to efficient food supply. Price controls also had a positive impact

---

173. Millspaugh 1945, pp. 117-18; Skrine 1962, pp. 181-82.
174. Skrine 1962, p. 181.

175. Political Diaries, vol. 16, pp. 179-80, 201.
176. FO 922/273, MESC Representative Tehran to Director Food Supply, MESC, Cairo. 14 May 1945.
177. Skrine 1962, pp. 184, 215.

as the cost of living declined significantly in the second half of 1944.[178] When Millpaugh left Iran in January 1945, the bread situation had returned to normal.[179] Because Millspaugh had not introduced structural changes in the rules that governed the food supply that meant that the age-old problems continued to bedevil the supply to the cities. The bread situation continued to be a major problem and headache for future governments. For example, when in 1946, prime-minster Qavam, who had been ousted from office in December 1942 due to bread riots, was asked in an interview what his program consisted of, he picked up a piece of bread from his desk and said: "This is my program. If I can put bread of good quality in the hands of all Iranians, other problems will be easy to solve."[180]

As is clear from Table 9.2 the government still had a long way to go to improve the nutritional situation of the majority of the population as wages lagged behind inflation. Moreover, when wages were raised this invariably resulted in an immediate rise of prices of the staple food products, and thus, workers saw little or no benefit from their raise.

After 1950, there are no reports of famine in Iran due to a more effective government and an improved road network, but there still remained a nutritional problem. As noted in the previous chapter, in general, the average caloric intake henceforth was adequate for the population at large, but some 44% of the population was still undernourished. Still, there remained the urban problem of selling bread and other products at inflated prices, or selling them below weight, while adulteration nevertheless occurred. However, slowly but surely the diet of most people improved. In this connection it is telling to note that during the 1963 conference about the "Problems of Tehran" not one of the many serious social issues addressed concerned the bread situation.[181] Despite these improvements, there were times that bakers were, however, still up to their old game of cheating customers. Likewise the penalties in those cases were less harsh than in the past, but the following 1971 newspaper report is of interest: "Five bakers in Manjil near Rasht were convicted of overcharging their customers and sent to jail with shaved heads when they refused to pay fines of 1,500 rials each."[182]

Fig. 40: The government's main problem BREAD (Shahri 1367, vol. 2, p. 404).

---

178. Millspaugh 1945, pp. 130-31.
179. Gol Mohammadi 1371, vol. 1, p. 299; Skrine 1962, p. 216.

180. Atabaki 1993, p. 70.
181. Anonymous 1343.
182. *Kayhan*, International edition (weekly) vol. 3, no. 148, January 23, 1971, p. 3.

BREAD POLICY UNDER THE ISLAMIC REPUBLIC

Under both the Pahlavi regime as well as the Islamic Republic of Iran the government subsidizes food consumption, mostly wheat flour to ensure a low bread price. To that end the government monopoly buys wheat from the farmers at a fixed price that every year is revised by the National Economic Council. For example, in 1997, the government paid 480 rials/kg of wheat to the local farmer and provided it to the bakeries at the price of 40 rials/kg (less than one-tenth of the price paid to producers).[183] At the end of 2010, because food subsidies constituted almost 6% of GDP in 1997, the government decided to replace subsidies on bread, cooking oil, and meat, with targeted social assistance

(طرح یارانه ها هدفمندسازی).

This measure may have a negative impact on the nutritional value of people's diets as they are reportedly eating less meat and vegetables. However, it is too soon to determine whether this is the case or not.

---

183. [http://www.fao.org/DOCREP/004/Y1329E/y1329e07.htm]

BIBLIOGRAPHY

Archives

Archief Ministerie van Buitenlandse Zaken, dossier Perzië, letter 27 July 1908, no. 17353.

Kampsax Archives, Copenhaguen (nowadays the Company's name is Cowiconsult).

Kurt Olsen, *Storm over Mellemøsten* (Storm over the Middle East). He was employed in Kampsax Iran from 1933 to 1947.

Ole Didrik Lærum, *Ingeniøren og Eventyret* (The Engineer and the Adventure). He was employed in 1933 at Kampsax, head office. He stayed in Iran until 1944.

National Archives (Kew Gardens, London).

FO 248/191, Report on Gilan by McKenzie, 13/04/1860.

FO 60/196, Stevens to Hagee Meerza Mehmed Khan (Tabriz 18/02/1854).

FO 60/327 (1870).

FO 60/431, letter 3 May 1880.

FO 60/586, report by H.J. Tweedie, 27 April 1897.

FO 60/598, letters 15 and 29 August and 12, 19 and 20 September 1898.

FO 60/611, letter 31 July 1899.

FO 60/613, letter 11 July 1899.

FO 371/20830.

FO 371/40222.

Books and Articles

Abrahamian, E. 1974. "Oriental Despotism: The Case of Qajar Iran," *IJMES* 5, pp. 3-31.

Adams, Isaac 1900. *Persia by a Persian* n.p.

Adib al-Molk, Abdol-Ali. 1349/1970. *Dafe` al-Ghorur*. ed. Iraj Afshar. Tehran.

Administration Report = *Administration Report of the Persian Gulf Political Residency for the year (1873 to 1935)* in Government of India. *The Persian Gulf Administration Reports 1873-1947*, 10 vols., Gerrards Cross, Archives Editions, 1986.

Aelian, 1997. *Varia Historia* translated by Diane Orstrom Johnson. Lewiston NY: E. Mellen Press.

Aghasi, Mahdi 1350/1981. *Tarikh-e Khuy*. Tabriz.

Afshar, Iraj 1389/2010. *Daftar-e Tarikh, majmu`eh-ye asbad va manabe`-ye tarikhi*, daftar chaharom. Tehran, Bonyad-e Mahmud Afshar, pp. 489-91.

Afzal al-Molk, Gholam Hoseyn 1373/1994. *Safarnameh-ye Mazandaran va Vaqaye`-ye Mashruteh*. ed. Hoseyn Samadi. Tehran.

Ahsan, Muhammad Manazir 1979. *Social Life Under the Ababsids 170-289 AH (786-902 AD)*. London-New York: Longman.

Aitchison, J.E.T. 1890. "Notes on the products of Western Afghanistan and of North-Eastern Persia," *Transactions of the Botanical Society*. Edinburgh XVIII.

Ala al-Molk 1364/1985. *Safarnameh-ye Baluchistan*. Tehran: Vahid.

Alberts, Robert Charles 1963. *Social Structure and Culture Change in an Iranian Village* 2 vols. Ph.D. dissertation University of Wisconsin.

Al-e Ahmad, Jalal 1333/1954. *Owrazan*. Tehran: Danesh.

___ 1337/1958. *Tatneshinha-ye Boluk-e Zahra*. Tehran: Danesh.

Alexander, James Edward 2000. *Travels from India to England*. New Delhi.

Algar, H. 1969. *Religion and State in Iran 1785-1906*. Berkeley: University of California Press.

Amanat, Abbas ed. 1983. *Cities & Trade: Consul Abbott on the Economy and Society of Iran 1847-1866*. London, Ithaca.

Amir Khizi, Esma`il 1339/1960. *Qiyam-e Azarbaijan va Sattar Khan*. Tehran.

Amin al-Dowleh, Mirza Ali Khan. 1341/1962. *Khaterat-e siyasi*. ed. Hafez Farmanfarma'iyan Tehran: Ketabha-ye Iran.

Amory Jr., C. 1929. *Persian Days*. Boston/New York: Houghton-Mifflin Co.

Anderson, T.S. 1880. *My Wanderings in Persia*. London: James Blackwood & Co.

Ange de Saint Joseph 1985. *Souvenirs de la Perse safavide et autres lieux de l'Orient (1664-1678)*, translated by Michel Bastiaensen (Brussels, 1985).

Anonymous 1828, *Sketches of Persia, from the journals of a traveller in the East* 2 vols. London.

___, 1846. *Persia*. London Society for Promoting Christian Knowledge. London.

___, 1859. *Annual Report of the Board of American Commissioners for Foreign Missions*. Boston.

___, 1873. "The Famine in Persia," in *The Friend, religious and literary journal*, XLV/1873, Philadelphia, pp. 8, 32, 64, 168, 204-05.

___, 1910, "La situation agraire en Perse a la vieille de la revolution," *RMM* 12, pp. 616-25.

___, 1932. *Lands and Peoples. The World in Color*. Part 12: Persia-Iraq-Turkey. New York: The Grolier Society.

___, 1937. *Hudud al-`Alam. 'The Regions of the World.' A Persian geography 372 A.H.-982 A.D.* translated by V. Minorsky. London: Luzac.

___, 1343/1964, *Sokhananiha va gozareshha dar nakhostin seminar-e bar-rasi-ye masa'el-e ejtema`i-ye shahr-e Tehran*. Tehran: Daneshgah.

___, 1360/1981. *Ashpazi-ye dowreh-ye Safavi*. ed. Iraj Afshar. Tehran: Seda va Sima-ye Jomhuriy-ye Eslami-ye Iran.

___, 1389/2010. *Jame` al-Sanaye`*. ed. Iraj Afshar. Tehran: Mirath-e Maktub.

`Aqeli, Baqer. 1379/2000. Ruzshomar-e Tarikh-e Iran, 2 vols. Tehran.

Arbab, Mohammad Taqi Beg 2536/1977. "Ketabcheh-ye Tafsil-e Halat va Nofus va Amlak-e dar al-Iman-e Qom," ed. Hosein Modarresi Tabataba'i, in *Farhang-e Iran-Zamin* 22, pp. 67-206.

Asadi Tusi 1336/1957. *Loghat-e Fors*. ed. Mohammad Dabir-Siyaqi. Tehran: Tahuri.

Asaf, Mohammad Hashem 1348/1969. *Rostam al-Tavarikh*, ed. Mohammad Moshiri. Tehran.

Astarabadi, Mirza Mehdi Khan 1368/1989. *Tarikh-e Jahangosha-ye Naderi*. Tehran: Donya-ye Ketab.

Ashtor, E. 1968. "Essai sur l'alimentation des diverses classes sociales dans l'Orient medieval," *Annales ESC* Sept-Oct., pp. 1018-21.

___, 1970. "The diet of the salaried classes in the medieval Near East," *Journal of Asian History* 4, pp. 1-24.

___, *A Social and Economic History of the Near East in the Middle Ages*. London.

Atabeki, Touraj 1993. *Azerbaijan: Ethnicity and Autonomy in the Twentieth-Century Iran*. London, IB Tauris.

At`ameh, Abu Eshaq Boshaq Hallaj Shirazi 1360/1981. *Divan-e At`ameh*, ed. Kahel. Shiraz: Ma`refat.

Atkinson, James 1832. *Customs and Manners of Persian Women*. London: Oriental Translation Fund.

Aubin, E. 1907. *La Perse d' aujourd'hui*. Paris: Armand Colin, 1907.

P.W. Avery and J.B. Simmons 1974 "Persia on a Cross of Silver, 1880-1890," *Middle Eastern Studies* 10, pp.259-68.

Azari, Shahla 1371/1992. "Qahti va gerani-ye nan (1320-24 shamsi)," *Faslnameh-ye ganjihen-ye asnad* 2/1-2, pp. 4-17.

Azimi, Fakhreddin 1989. *Iran. The crisis of democracy 1941-1953*. London: IBTauris.

Back, Michael 1978. *Die sassanidischen Staatsinschriften*, Acta Iranica 18, Leiden: Brill.

Baladiyeh-ye Tehran 1310/1931. *Dovvomin Salnameh-ye Ehsa'iyeh-ye Tehran*. Tehran: Baladiyeh.

___, 1312. *Dovvomin?? Salnameh-ye Ehsa'iyeh-ye Tehran*. Tehran: Baladiyeh.

Ballantine, Henry 1879. *Midnight Marches Through Persia*. Boston: Lee and Shepard.

Barbaro, Josaphat 1873. *Travels to Tana and Persia by J. Barbaro and A. Contarini* 2 vols. Transl. Lord Stanley. London: Hakluyt.

Barton, James L. 1930. *Story of Near East Relief 1915-1930*. New York: MacMillan, 1930 (chapter 8 deals with Iran).

Basir al-Molk Sheybani 1374/1995. *Ruznameh-ye Khaterat*. Iraj Afshar and Mohammad Rasul Daryagasht eds. Tehran.

Bassett, James 1886. *Persia, the Land of the Imams* (New York: Charles Scribner's Sons.

Bast, Olivier ed. 2002. *La Perse et la Grande Guerre*. Paris/Tehran.

Bastiaensen, Michel 1985. *Souvenirs de la Perse safavide et autres lieux de l'Orient (1664-1678)*. Brussels: Editions de l'Universite de Bruxelles.

Batmanglij, Najmieh 1986. *Food of Life: Ancient Persian and Modern Iranian Cooking and Ceremonies*. Washington, DC: Mage Publishers.

Bazargan, Soghra 1989. "Beryani," *Encyclopedia Iranica* (on line edition; 15 December).

Bazin, Marcel 1970. *La vie rurale sans la region de Qom (Iran central)*. Paris: Association Langues et Civilisations

___, 1980. *Le Talech. Un region ethnique au nord de l'Iran*. 2 vols. Paris: IFRI,

Bazin, Marcel and Bromberger, Christian et al. 1982. *Gilan et Azerbayjan Oriental*. Paris: IFRI

Beck, Lois 1991. *Nomad. A Year in the Life of an Qashqa'i Tribesman in Iran*. Berkeley.

Bélanger, Charles 1838. *Voyage aux Indes-Orientales*. 2 vols. Paris: Arthus

Bellew, H.W. 1873. *Record of the March of the Mission to Seistan Under the Command of Major-General F. R. F.R. Pollock*. Calcutta: Foreign Department Press.

___, 1999. *From Indus to the Tigris*. Lahore: Sang-e Meel.

Benjamin, S. G. W. 1887. *Persia and the Persians*. London: John Murray.

Beyhaqi, Abu Fazl Mohammad b. Hoseyn 1324/1945. *Tarikh-e Beyhaqi* eds. Ghani and Fayaz. Tehran.

B. Isfandiyar, Mohammad b. al-Hasan 1905. *An abridged translation of the History of Tabaristan* by E.G. Browne. Leyden: E.J. Brill

Benn, Edith Fraser 1909. *An Overland Trek From India*. London: Longmans & Co.

Bienkowski, P.and Millard, Alan eds. 2000. *Dictionary of the ancient Near East*. Philadelphia: Univ. Pennsylvania Press.

Bigham, Clive 1897. *A Ride Through Western Asia*. London: Macmillan & Co.

Binder, Henry 1887. *Au Kurdistan*. Paris.

Binning, R.B. M. 1857. *A Journal of Two Years' Travel in Persia, Ceylon, etc.* 2 vols. London: Wm. H. Allen & Co.

Bird Bishop, Isabelle A. 1891. *Journeys in Persia and Kurdistan*. 2 vols. London.

Bleibtreu, J. 1894. *Persien: Das Land der Sonne und des Löwen*. Freiburg.

Bolukbashi, Ali 1347 /1968. "Vazheh-ye sangak o pishineh-ye sangakpazi dar Iran,"*Honar o mardom*, N.S., 74-75, pp. 31-42; 76, pp. 47-51.

___ 1348/1969. "Taftunpazi dar Tehran," *Honar o mardom*, N.S., 81, pp. 45-54.

Boré, Eugene 1840. *Correspondance et mémoires d'un voyageur en Orient*. 2 vols. Paris: Olivier-Fulgence.

Borhan, Mohammad Hoseyn b. Khalaf Tabrizi 1342/1963. *Borhan-e Qate`*. Ed. Mohammad Mo`in et al. 5 vols. Tehran: Ebn Sina.

Borhanian, Khosro 1960. *Die Gemeinde Hamidieh in Khuzistan*. Cologne University thesis.

Boyce, Mary 1975. *A Reader in Manichaean Middle Persian and Parthian*. Leiden: Brill.

___, 1968. "Middle Persian Literature," in B. Spuler ed. *Handbuch der Orientalistik* 4.2.1. Iranistik, Literatur. Leiden: Brill.

Bradley-Birt, F.B. 1910. *Persia, through Persia from the Gulf to the Caspian*. Boston: J.B. Millet.

Bratislaw, A. C. 1923. "Turbulent Tabriz," *Blackwood's Magazine*, 37-59.

Briant, Pierre 2002. *From Cyrus to Alexander: a history of the Persian Empire*. Winona Lake, Ind.: Eisenbrauns.

Brittlebank, William 1873. *Persia During the Famine*. London: Basil Montague Pickering.

Bromberger, C. 1974. "Habitations du Gilân," *Objets et mondes* 14, pp. 3-56.

Brosset, Marie-Félicité 1849-58. *Histoire de la Géorgie depuis l'antiquité jusqu'au XIX siècle*. 2 vols. St. Petersburgh.

___ 1979, *Collection d'Historiens Arméniens*. 2 vols. in one. Amsterdam: Philo Press.

Browne, E.G. 1914. *Press and Poetry of Modern Persia*. Cambridge: Cambridge UP.

____1959. *A Literary History of Persia*. 4 vols. Cambridge, CUP.

Brugsch, H. 1863. *Die Reise der K.K. Gesandtschaft nach Persien 1861-1862*, 2 vols. Berlin: J.C. Hinrichs.

Buckingham, J.S. 1829. *Travels in Assyria, Media and Persia*. London.

Bukhari, *al-Sahih*. [http://www.usc.edu/dept/MSA/reference/reference.html]; also [http://hadith.al-islam.com/Display/Display.asp?Doc=0&Rec=7607].

Busse, Heribert translator 1972. *History of Persia under Qajar Rule*. New York: Columbia UP.

Canard, M. 1959. "Le riz dans le Proche-Orient aux premiers siècles de l'Islam," *Arabica* 6, pp. 113-31.

CENTO 1968. *Conference on combating malnutrition in preschool children*.

Chanykov, N.V. 1862. *Memoire sur la partie meridionale de lAsie Centrale*. Paris.

Chaqueri, C. ed. 1978. *The Condition of the Working Class*. Florence: Mazdak.

Chardin, Jean 1811. *Voyages*, ed. L. Langlès, 10 vols. Paris.

___, 1927. *Travels in Persia*. ed. Sir Percy Sykes. London: Argonaut press.

Chelebi, Evliya. 2009. *Travels in Iran & the Caucasus in 1647 & 1654*. Translated by Hasan Javadi and Willem Floor. Washington DC: Mage Publishers.

Chirikov, E. I. 1989. *Putvoj zhurnal russkogo komissara-posrednika po turetsko-persidskomu razgranicheniyu* (St. Petersburg, 1875) translated into Persian by Abkar Masihi as *Siyahatnameh-ye Musyu Chirikuf*. ed. Ali Asghar `Omran (Tehran, 1358/1979) and partly translated into English as "Extracts from the Diary of Y. I. Tchirikof," in Schofield, Richard ed. 1989, 12 vols. *Iran-Iraq Border*, vol. 2, pp. 327-471.

Chodzko, Alexander 1842. *Specimens of the popular poetry of Persia*. London.

Choksy, Jamsheed 1995. "Dron," *Encyclopedia of Iran* (on line version).

Clawson, Patrick 1993. "Knitting Iran Together: The Land Transport Revolution, 1920-1940," *Iranian Studies* 26/3-4, pp. 236-50.

Coan, Frederick G. 1939. *Yesterdays in Persia and Kurdistan*. Claremont: Sauders Studio Press

Collins, E. Treacher 1896. *In the Kingdom of the Shah*. London: T. Fisher Unwin.

Conolly, Arthur 1834. *Journey to the North of India overland from England through Russia, Persia, and Affghaunistaun*. 2 vols. London: Richard Bentley.

Cooper, Merian C. 1925. *Grass*. New York: Putnam's Sons.

Curzon, G.N. 1892. *Persia and the Persian Question* 2 vols. London.

Dandamaev, M.A. and Lukonin, Vladimir 1989. *The Culture and Social Institutions of Ancient Iran*. Cambridge: Cambridge UP.

DCR or Diplomatic and Consular Reports, Government of Great Britain:

DCR 207, Report on a Journey from Tehran

DCR 1376, "Report for the Years 1892-93 and 1893-94 on the Trade, &c. of the Consular District of Ispahan. Report of a Journey made to Yazd, Kerman, and Shiraz, and on the Trade &c. of the Consular District of Ispahan by J.R. Preece (London 1894).

DCR 1662, Report on the Trade and Commerce of Ispahan and Yezd for the Year 1894-95 by Preece (London 1896).

DCR 1953, Report on the Trade and Commerce of the Consular District of Ispahan for the Year 1896 by Preece (London, 1897), pp. 1-16.

DCR 2260 Report on the Trade and Commerce of the Consular District of Ispahan for the Years 1897-98 and 1898-99 by consul Preece (London, 1899), pp. 3-21

DCR 3748, Report for the Year 1905-06 on the Trade of Ispahan and Yezd by Dr. Aganoor, acting consul-general (London, 1907), pp. 1-13.

DCR 5048, Report on the Trade of the Consular District of Ispahan for the Year ending March 20, 1912 by consul-general T.G. Grahame (London, 1913), pp. 1-54 (also includes the Yezd (43-51) and the Sultanabad trade report (52-54).

De Bode, Clement Auguste 1843. "Notes on a Journey, in January and February, 1841, from Behbahan to Shushter," *RGS* 13, pp. 86-107.

___, 1845. *Travels in Luristan and Arabistan*. 2 vols. London: J. Madden & Co.

Dehkhoda, *Loghatnameh*.

Della Valle, Pietro 1663-64. *Les Fameux Voyages* 4 vols. Paris: Gervais Clouzier.

De Lorey, Eustace & Sladen, Douglas 1907. *Queer Things About Persia*. Philadelphia-London: J.B. Lippincot Co.

___, 1910. *The Moon of the Fourteenth Night*. London: Hurst & Blackett.

De Morgan, Jacques 1894. *Mission Scientifique en Perse*. 5 vols. Paris.

Demorgny, G. 1913. *Essai sur l'Administration de la Perse*. Paris.

Denis, A. 1843. "Question de Perse. Affaire de Kerbela." *Revue de l'Orient*. I, pp. 129-42.

De Panisse, Comte 1867. *La Russie, la Perse, l'Inde. Souvenirs de voyage 1865-1866*. Paris: Jouaust.

De Rochechouart, Julien 1867. *Souvenirs d'un Voyage en Perse* Paris.

Desmet-Grégoire, H. 1980. "Le pain dans la région d'Hamadân," *Studia Iranica* 9, pp. 251-76.

___, 1989. "Bread," *Encyclopedia Iranica* (on line edition; 15 December).

De Windt, Harry. *A Ride to India across Persia and Baluchistan* (London: Chapman & Hall, 1891).

Digard, J. P. 1981. *Techniques des nomades Baxtyâri d Iran*. Paris.

Djirsara, Ali Akbar 1970. *Das Dorf Ahar (Iran). Die Bevölkerungs-, Sozial- und Wirtschaftsgeographische Struktur und Entwicklung*. Bonn: Rheinische Friedrich-Wilhelms University thesis.

Dowlat, Manizheh, Sa`edi, Gholam Hoseyn and Hazarkhani, Manuchehr 1352/1973. *Hashiyeh-neshinan-e Tehran. Taghdhiyeh va Behdasht*. Tehran:

Daneshgah (Mo'assesseh-ye Motale`at va Tahqiqat-e Ejtema`i) mimeograph

Dowlatabadi, Yahya n.d. *Hayat-e Yahya* 4 vols. Tehran.

Durand, E. R. 1902. *An Autumn Tour in Western Persia*. New York: E. P. Dutton & Co.

Dwight, H.G. 1917. *Persian Miniatures*. New York: Doubleday, Page & Co.

Eastwick, Edward B. 1976. *Journal of a Diplomate's Three Years' Residence in Persia*. 2 vols. Tehran: Imp. Org. f. Soc. Services, 1976.

Ebn Ebrahim, Mohammad 1343/1964. *Saljuqiyan va Ghozz dar Kerman*. Ed. Mohammad Ebrahim Bastani Parizi. Tehran: Tahhuri.

Encyclopedia Britannica 2009.

Elahi, Etrat 2010. "Kak," *Encyclopedia Iranica* (on line version; 8 November).

E`temad al-Saltaneh, Mohammad Hasan Khan 1345/1967. *Ruznameh-ye Khaterat*. ed. Iraj Afshar. Tehran: Amir Kabir.

E'tesam al-Molk 1351/1972. *Safarnameh-ye Mirza Khanlar Khan E'tesam al-Molk*. ed. Manuchehr Mahmudi. Tehran.

Ettinghausen, Richard 1965. *Turkish Miniatures* UNESCO.

Eyn al-Saltaneh, Qahraman Mirza Salur 1376/1997. *Ruznameh-ye Khaterat*. 10 vols. eds. Mas`ud Salur and Iraj Afshar. Tehran: Asatir.

Faramarzi, Ahmad 1379/2000. "Banader va jazayer-e khalij-e Fars," in eds. Iraj Afshar and Karim Esfahaniyan. *Pazhuheshha-ye Iranshenasi. Namvareh-ye doctor Mahmud Afshar*, vol. 12. Tehran: Bonyad-e Mahmud Afshar, pp. 576-696.

Faridi, H.A., Finney, P.L. and Rubenthaler, G.L. 1981. "Micro Baking Evaluationof Some US Wheat Classes for Suitability in Iranian Breads," *Cereal Chemistry* 58/5, pp. 428-32.

Farrokh (Mo`tasem al-Saltaneh), Sayyed Mehdi 1347/1968. *Khaterat-e Siyasi-ye Farrokh*. Ed. Parviz Lushani. Tehran: Amir Kabir,

Fateh, M.K. 1926. *The Economic Position of Persia*. London.

Feilberg, C.G. 1952. *Les Papis*. Copenhagen: Nordisk.

Fesharaki, Paridokht 2537/1978. *Abadiha-ye Hozeh-ye Abgir-e Lut-e Jonubi. Pazhheshi dar Joghrafiya-e ensani va eqtesadi*. Tehran: Daneshgah (Mo'assesseh-ye joghrafiya).

Flandin, Eugene and Coste, Pascal 1851. *Voyage en Perse*. 2 vols. Paris: Gide et J. Baudry.

Floor, Willem 1985. "The office of muhtasib in Iran," *Iranian Studies* 18, pp. 53-74.

___, 1998. *The Afghan Occupation of Safavid Persia 1721-1729*. Paris.

___, 1999. *The Fiscal History of Iran in the Safavid and Qajar Periods*. New York: Bibliotheca Persica.

___, 2000. *The Economy of Safavid Persia*. Wiesbaden: Reichert.

___ 2003 a. *Agriculture in Qajar Iran*. Washington DC: Mage Publishers.

___, 2003 b. *Traditional Crafts in Qajar Iran*. Costa Mesa: Mazda.

___ 2005. Review of Mohammad Gholi Majd, The Great Famine and *Genocide* in Persia, 1917-1919, in *Iranian Studies* 31/, pp. 192-96

___ 2009. *Guilds, Merchants and Ulama in Nineteenth Century Iran*. Washington DC: Mage Publishers.

Floyer, E.A. 1979. *The Unexplored Baluchistan*. Quetta: Nissa Traders.

Forbes, Frederick 1844. "Route fromTurbat Haidari, in Khurasan, to the river Heri Rud, on the borders of Sistan," *RGS* 14, pp. 145-92.

Forbes-Leith, F.A.C. 1927. *Checkmate, Fighting Tradition in Central Persia*. New York: Robert M. McBride & Company.

Fowler, George 1841. *Three Years in Persia* 2 vols. London: Colburn.

Fragner, Bert 1979. *Persische Memoirenliteratur als Quelle zur neureen Geschichte Iran*. Wiesbaden: Steiner.

Fraser, J.B. 1984. *Narrative of a Journey into Khorasan in the Years 1821 & 1822*. Delhi: Oxford UP.

___, 1826. *Travels and Adventures in the Persian Provinces and the Southern Banks of the Caspian Sea*. London: Longman, Rees, Orme, Browne and Greene.

___, 1840. *Travels in Koordistan, Mesopotamia*, 2 vols. London: Richard Bentley.

___, 1973. *A Winter's Journey from Constantinople to Teheran*, 2 vols. in one. New York: Arno.

Frazer, James George 1907. *The golden bough: a study in magic and religion*. 10 vols. London.

Frederiksen, Birthe 1996. *Caravans and Trade in Afghanistan. The Changing Life of the Nomadic Hazarbuz*. London: Thames and Hudson

Fryer, John 1909-15. *A New Account of East India and Persia Being Nine Years' Travels, 1672-1681*, 3 vols. London: Hakluyt.

Gabriel, Alfons 1940. *Weites Wildes Iran*. Stuttgart.

Ghirshman, Roman 1963. *Perse, Proto-Iraniens, Medes, Achéménides*. Paris: Gallimard.

___, 1977. *L'Iran et la migration des Indo-Aryens et des Iraniens*. Leiden, Brill.

Gignoux, Philippe 1984. *Le Livre d'Arda Viraz*. Paris.

Gmelin, Samuel Gottlieb 2007. *Travels through Northern Persia 1770-1774*, translated and annotated by Willem Floor. Washington DC.

Goldsmid, Sir Frederic J. 1876. *Eastern Persia, An Account of the Journeys of the Persian Boundary Commission 1870-71-72*, 2 vols. London: MacMillan & Co.

Gol Mohammadi, Mohammad Moqaddam 1371/1992 *Tuyserkan. Seyri dar owza`-ye-ye tabi`i, tarikhi va ejtema`i* 2 vols. Tehran.

Gordon, Thomas Edward 1896. *Persia Revisited*. London: Arnold.

Goulder, Jill 2010. "Administrators' bread: experiment-based re-assessment of the functional and cultural role of the Uruk bevil-rim bowl," *Antiquity* 84, pp. 351-62.

Government of Great Britain 1882, Astarabad 1881, *Accounts and Papers* 71.

Gray, F.A.G. 1938. *Report on Economic and Commercial Conditions in Iran during 1937*. London: HMSO.

Greenfield, J. 1904. *Die Verfassung des persischen Staates*. Berlin: Franz Vahlen.

Gudarzi-nezhad, Shapur 1352/1973. *Kangavar. Joghrafiya-e ensani va eqtesadi*. Tehran: Daneshgah (Mo'assesseh-ye joghrafiya).

___, 1354/1975. *Rustaha-ye Asadabad. Joghrafiya-e ensani va eqtesadi*. Tehran: Daneshgah (Mo'assesseh-ye joghrafiya).

Hajj Sayyah 1346/1967. *Khaterat-e Hajj Sayyah*. ed. Hamid Sayyah. Tehran: Ebn Sina.

Hall, Melvin 1947. *Journey to the End of an Era*. New York: Charles Scribner's Sons.

Hanway, Jonas 1753. *An Historical Account of the British Trade over the Caspian Sea*. London.

Harmatta, János 1953. "Three Iranian Words for Bread," *Acta Orientalia Academiae Scientiarum Hungarica* 3/3, pp. 245-83.

Harris, W.B. 1896. *From Batum to Baghdad*. Edinburgh: Blackwood.

Harris, D.R. 2010, *Origins of Agriculture in Western Central Asia: An environmental-archaeological study*. Philadelphia, Univ. of Pennsylvania.

Harrison, J. V. 1941. "Coastal Makran," *The Geographical Journal* XCVII/1, pp. 1-17.

___, 1946. "South-West Persia: A Survey of Pish-i Kuh in Luristan," *The Geographical Journal* 108, pp. 55-71.

Helbaek, Hans 1969. "Plant collecting, Dry-farming and Irrigation Apriculture in Prehistoric Deh Luran," in Frank Hole, Kent V. Flannery, James A. Neely eds. 1969, *Prehistory and Human Ecology of the Deh Luran Plain*. Ann Arbor, pp. 383-426;

Hellot-Bellier, Florence 2002. "La Premiere Guerrre mondiale a l'ouest du lac d'Urumiye," in Bast 2002, pp. 329-52.

Henning W.B. 1971. *A Fragment of a Khwarezmian Dictionary*. Ed. D.N. MacKenzie. London: Daneshgah

Herodotus, *Histories*.

Hoffmann, Birgitt 2000. *Waqf im Mongolischen Iran*. Stuttgart: Franz Steiner.

Hole, Frank 1969. *The Archeology of Western Iran*, Washington DC: Smithsonianj Institute.

Hole, Frank; Flannery, Kent V. and Neely, James A. eds. 1969. *Prehistory and Human Ecology of the Deh Luran Plain*. Ann Arbor: University of Michigan.

Höltzer, Ernst 2535/1976. *Persien vor 113 Jahren* ed. **Mohammad Assemi. Tehran: Vezarat-e Farhang va Honar.**

Homayuni, Sadeq 1353/1974. *Gushehha-ye az adab va rosum-e mardom-e Shiraz*. Shiraz.

Horne, Lee 1994. *Village Spaces. Settlement and Society in Northeastern Iran*. Washington DC: Smithsonian.

Ibn al-Balkhi 1912. *Description of the Province of Fars* translated by G. Le Strange London: Royal Asiatic Society.

Ibn Batuttah 1958. *The Travels of Ibn Battutta*. Tr. H.A. R. Gibb and C.F. Beckingham. 5 vols. Cambridge: Cambridge UP.

Ibn Fazlan 2005. *Ibn Fazlan's Journey to Russia*. Tr. by R.N. Frye. Princeton: Markus Wiener.

ILO 1937. "Récentes enquêtes en Iran." *Revue Internationale du Travail* 36, pp. 881-884.

Issawi, Charles 1971. *The Economic History of Persia*. Chicago: Chicago UP.

Ivanow W. 1926. "Notes on the Ethnology of Khurasan," *Geographical Journal* 67/2, pp. 143-58.

___, 1931. "Alamut," *RGS* 77, pp. 38-45.

Janab, Aqa Mir Sayyed Ali. 1303/1924. *Ketab al-Esfahan*. Isfahan (lithograph).

Jackson, Kate 1920. *Around the World to Persia- letters written while on the journey as a member of the American Persian Relief Commission in 1918*. New York.

Jackson, A.V. Williams 1910. *Persia Past and Present. A Book of Research and Travel*. New York: MacMillan.

___, 1911. *From Constantinople to the Home of Omar Khayyam*. New York: MacMillan.

Jahangiri 1367/1988. *Kandelus*. Tehran: Mo'asseseh-ye Farhangi-ye Jahangiri

Jaubert, P. Am. 1821. *Voyage en Armenie et la Perse*. Paris: Pélicier-Nepveu.

Jefferey, Arthur 2007. *The foreign vocabulary of the Qur'an*. Brill: Leiden.

Jenner, George. 1870. "Report by Mr. Jenner on the Condition of the Working Classes in Persia," *Accounts and Papers* 32 (LXVIII), 396-400.

Johnson, Greg Alan 1973. *Local exchange and early state development in southwestern Iran*. Ann Arbor, University of Michigan

Jones, Henry L. 1870. "Report by Consul-General Jones on the Condition of the Indstrial Classes in Tabreez," *Accounts and Papers* 32 (LXVIII), 417-22.

Kasravi, Ahmad 1319/1940. *Tarikh-e Mashruteh-ye Iran*. 3 vols. Tehran.

Katouzian, Homa 1981. *The Political Economy of Modern Iran 1926-1979*. New York: NY UP.

Kaempfer, Engelbert 1940. *Am Hofe des persischen Grosskönigs (1684-85). Das erste Buch der Amoenitates exoticae in deutscher Bearbeitung*, hrsg. v. Walter Hinz. Leipzig: K.F. Koehler.

___ 1976, *Amoenitatum Exoticarum Politico-Physico-Medicarum Fasciculi V*. Tehran.

Kempthorne, Lt. G.B. 1835. "Notes made on a survey along the eastern shores of the Persian Gulf in 1828," *JRGS* 5, pp. 263-85.

Keshavarzian, Arang 2007. *Bazaar and State in Iran*. Cambridge: Cambridge UP.

Kinneir, J. Mc. 1973. *A Geographical Memoir of the Persian Empire*. New York.

Klaproth, Julius 1814. *Travels in the Caucasus and Georgia performed in the years 1807 and 1808*. London: Henry Colburn.

Knanishu, Joseph 1899. About Persia and its People. Rock Island, Ill.

Koelz, Walter N. 1983. *Persian Diary, 1939-1941*. Ann Arbor Michigan.

Kosogovski, V.A. 1344/1965. *Iz Tegenrankovo Dnevnika*, translated into Persian by Abbas Qoli Jali, *Khaterat-e kulunel Kasakufski*. Tehran: Jibi.

Kotov, F.A. 1959. *Khozhenie kuptsa Fedota Kotova* ed. N.A. Kuznetsova (Moscow 1958), translated into English by P.M. Kemp, as *Russian Travellers to India and Persia [1624-1798] Kotov-Yefremov-Danibegov*. Delhi.

Kuhestani-nezhad, Mas`ud 1381/2002. "Sal-e dampokhtak; qahti-ye sal-e 1296 sh." *Faslnameh-ye ganjihen-ye asnad*, 12/1-2, pp. 40-52.

Ladjevardi, H. 1981. *Politics and Labour in Iran: 1941-49*. Syracuse: Syracuse UP.

Lamberg-Karlovsky et al. 1907 *Excavations at Tepe Yahya, Iran 1967-1969*, Progress Report I. Cambridge, Mass, Peabody Museum (Harvard).

Lambton, A.K.S. 1969. *Landlord and Peasant in Persia*. London: Oxford UP.

Landor, E. Henry Savage 1903. *Across Coveted Lands* 2 vols. New York: Scribners.

Laureys, Eric. 1996. *Belgen in Perzië 1915-1941, verwezenlijkingen, verhoudingen en attitudes*. Leuven: Peeters.

Layard A. H.1846. "A Description of the Province of Kuzistan," *RGS* 16, pp. 1-105.

___, 1971. *Early Adventures in Persia, Susiana, and Babylonia*. Westmead: Gregg Int.

Le Strange, Guy 1966. *The Lands of the Eastern Caliphate*. London.

Loeb, Lawrence 1977. *Outcaste - Jewish Life in Southern Iran*. New York.

Lindberg, K. 1955. *Voyage dans le Sud de l'Iran*. Lund: Gleerup.

Lycklama à Nijeholt, T.M. 1873. *Voyage en Russie, au Caucase et en Perse*. 4 vols. Paris-Amsterdam: Arthus Bertrand-C.L. van Langenhuysen.

MacGregor, C.M. 1879. *Narrative of a Journey through the Province of Khorassan and on the N.W. Frontier of Afghanistan in 1875* 2 vols. London: Wm. Allen & Co.

Mahmoodian, Saeed 2007. *Encyclopedia Larestanica*. Fishersville, VA.

Mahmudi, Farajollah 1352/1973. *Joghrafiya-ye Nahiyeh-ye Qorveh, Bijar, Divandareh*. Tehran: Daneshgah (Mo'assesseh-ye joghrafiya).

Mafi 1361/1982. *Khaterat va Asnad-e Hoseyn Qoli Khan Nezam al-Molk Nezam al-Saltaneh Mafi* 2 vols. ed. Ma`sumeh Nezam-Mafi and Sirus Sa`dvandiyan. Tehran.

Majd, Mohammad Gholi 2003. *The Great Famine and Genocide in Persia, 1917-1919*. Lanham, MD: University Press of America.

Malcolm, Napier 1905. *Five Years in a Persian Town*. London: John Murray.

Manuchehri 1326/1947. *Divan-e Ostad Manuchihri-ye Damghani*. Edited by Mohammad Dabir-siyaqi. Tehran: Do Esfand.

Marsh, H. C. 1877. *A Ride Through Islam*. London: Tinsley Brothers.

Martin, Vanessa 2005. *The Qajar Pact. Bargaining, Protest and the State in 19th-century Persia*. London: I.B. Tauris.

Massé, Henri 1938. *Croyances et Coutumes Persanes* 2 vols. Paris: Maisonneuve.

Matz, Samuel A. 1992. *Bakery Technology and Engineering*. New York: Springer.

Mazdapur, Kataviyun 1382/2003. "Tafa'ol-e Nowruz," in Behruz Vajdani ed., *Majmu`eh-ye maqalehha-ye dovvomin hamayesh-e mantaqeh'i-ye Nowruz*. Tehran, pp. 39-45.

McFarland, Stephen L. 1985. "Anatomy of an Iranian Political Crowd: The Tehran Bread Riot of December 1942," *International Journal of Middle East Studies* 17/1, pp. 51-65.

Mehrbani, Hoseyn 1343/1964. "Hazinehha-ye ghadha'i dar Tehran," in Anonymous 1343, pp. 357-368.

Meisami, Julie Scott 1991. *The Sea of Virtues (Bahr al-Fava'id) A Medieval Islamic Mirror for Princes*. Salt Lake City: Utah UP.

Merritt-Hawkes, O. A. *Persia – Romance & Reality* (London: Nicholson & Watson, 1935).

Meshkat al-Soltan, Ali Akbar 1367. "Meshkat al-Mosaferin," in *Mirath-Eslami-ye Iran* ed. Rasul Ja`fariyan 10 vols. Qom, vol. 5, pp. 11-118.

Mez, A. 1922. *Die Renaissance des Islams*. Heidelberg.

Migeod, Heinz-Georg 1990. *Die persische Gesellschaft unter Nasiru'd-Din ah (1848-1896)*. Berlin: Klaus Schwarz.

Mignan, Robert 1839. *A Winter Journey through Russia, the Caucasian Alps, Georgia etc.* 2 vols. London: R. Bentley.

Miller, Naomi 1992. "The Origins of Plant Cultivation in the Near East," in eds. C. Wesley Cowan and Patty Jo Watson, *The Origins of Agriculture, an international perspective*. Washington DC: Smithsonian, pp. 39-58.

Millspaugh, A.C. 1925. *The American Task in Persia*. New York.

___, 1926. *The Financial and Economic Situation of Persia*. New York, 1926.

___, 1945. *Americans in Persia*. New York: Brookings Institute.

Mirza, Youel B. 1920. *When I Was A Boy in Persia*. Boston: Lothrop, Lee and Shepard.

Mirza Ebrahim 2535. *Safarnameh-ye Astarabad va Mazandaran va Gilan*. ed. Mas`ud Golzari. Tehran: Bonyad-e Farhang-e Iran.

Mitford, Edward Ledwich 1884. *A Land March from England to Ceylon Forty Years Ago*. 2 vols. London: Allen & Co.

Mobasheri, Mahmubeh 1389/2009. *Farhang-e ejtema`i-ye `asr-e Mowlana*. Tehran: Sorush.

Molkara, 1325/1946. *Sharh-e Hal* ed. Abbas Eqbal. Tehran.

Monshi, Mohammad Ali 2536/1977. *Safarnameh-ye Rokn al-Dowleh*. ed. Mohammad Golbon. Tehran: Sahar.

Moore, A. 1914. *The Orient Express*. London: Constable & Comp.

Moore, Benjamin Burgess 1915. *From Moscow to the Persian Gulf*. New York: G.P. Putnam's Sons.

Morier, James 1812. *A Journey through Persia, Armenia and Asia Minor in the Years 1808 and 1809*. London: Longman, Hurst, Rees, Orme, and Brown.

Mortesen, Inge Demant 1993. *Nomads of Luristan*. London: Thames and Hudson.

Morton, Rosalie Slaughter 1940. *A Doctor's Holiday in Iran*. New York; Funk & Wagnalls Company.

Mostowfi, Abdollah n.d. *Sharh-e Zendegani-ye Man* 3 vols. Tehran: Zavvar.

Mounsey, Augustus H. 1872. *A Journey Through the Caucasus and the Interior of Persia*. London: Smith, Elder & Co.

Mumford, John Kimberley 1901. "Along a Persian Highway," *Harper's Weekly*, vol. XLV, no. 2298, January 5, pp. 10-11.

Mustawfi, Hamdallah 1919. *The Geographical Part of the Nozhat al-qolub*, ed. Le Strange. Leyden/London: Brill/Luzac.

Najm ol-Molk, Abdol-Ghaffar 1342/1963. *Safarnameh-ye Khuzestan*. ed. Mohammad Dabir-Siyaqi. Tehran: Elmi.

Naraqi, Ehsan 1345/1966. *Tarikh-e ejtema`i-ye Kashan*. Tehran.

Nashat, Guity and Beck, Lois eds. 2003. *Women in Iran. From the rise of Islam to 1800*. Chicago.

Nateq, Homa 1362/1983. "Sar-aghaz-e eqtedar-e eqtesadi va siyasi-ye molayan," *Alefba* 2/2, pp. 40-57.

Nazem al-Olama Kermani 1347/1968. *Tarikh-e Bidari-ye Iraniyan* 3 vols. ed. Sa`id Sirjani. Tehran: Bonyad-e Farhang-e Iran.

Nirumand, Mostafa and Ahsan, Majid 1351/1972. *Hashiyeh-neshinan-e Bandar `Abbas*. Tehran: Daneshgah (Mo'assesseh-ye Motale`at va Tahqiqat-e Ejtema`i).

Nizam al-Mulk 1960, *The Book of Government or Rules for Kings* translated into English by Herbert Darke. London.

Norden, Hermann n.d. *Under Persian Skies*. Philadelphia: McCrea Smith.

O'Donovan, Edmond 1882. *The Merv Oasis*. 2 vols. London: Smith, Elder & Co.

Okazaki, Shoko 1986. "The great Persian famine of 1870-71," *BSOAS* XLIX/1, pp. 183-92.

Olearius, Adam 1971. *Vermehrte newe Beschreibung der moscowitischen und persischen Reyse*, ed. D. Lohmeier. Tübingen: Max Niemayer.

Olmer, U. 1908. "L'Industrie Persane," *Nouvelles Archives des Missions Scientifiques et Littéraires*, 16, pp. 1-110.

Orsolle, E. 1885. *Le Caucase et La Perse*. Paris: E. Plon, Nourrit & Co.

Pellat, Ch. "Khubz," *Encyclopedia of Islam*2.

Perkins, J. 1843. *A Residence of Eight Years in Persia*. Andover: Allen, Morrill & Wardwell.

Pigulevskaia, N. *Les Villes de l'Etat Iranien aux epoques Parthe et Sassanide*. The Hague-Paris, 1963.

Planck, Ulrich 1962. *Die sozialen und ökonomischen Verhältnisse in einem iranischen Dorf*. Cologne – Opladen: Westdeutscher Verlag.

Polak, J.E. 1862, "Beitrag zu den agrarischen Verhältnissen in Persien", *Mittheilungen der K.-K. Geogr. Gesellschaft* VI, pp. 107-43.

___, 1865. *Persien, das Land und seine Bewohner*. 2 vols. Leipzig: F.A. Brockhaus.

Political Diaries of the Persian Gulf 1904-1947, 17 vols. n.p. Archive Editions, 1990.

Polo, Marco 1993. *The Travels of Marco Polo*. Henry Yule and Henri Cordier eds. 2 vols. New York: Dover.

Post, Wilfred 1920. "The Forty-Ninth Star," *The New Armenia* XII/May, pp. 69-72.

Potts, Daniel T. 1997. *Mesopotamian Civilization: the material foundations*. London: Athlone Press.

___, 1999. *The Archeology of Elam: formation ands transformation of an ancient Iranian state*. Cambridge, Cambridge UP.

___, 2009. "Bevil-Rim Bowls and Bakeries: Evidence and Explanations from Iran and the Indo-Iranian Borderlands," *Journal of Cuneiform Studies* 61, pp. 1-23.

Preedy, Victor R.; Watson, Ronald Ross and Patel, Vinood 2011, *Flour and Breads and Their Fortification in Health and Disease Prevention*, p. 266.

Pybus, William 1810. *A Manual of Useful Knowledge*. Hull.

Quintus Curtius Rufius 1883. *Life and Exploits of Alexnder the Great*. ed. William Henry Crosby. New York: Appelton & Comp.

Rabino, H.L. and Lafont, F. 1910 and 1911. "La culture du riz en Guilan (Perse) et dans les autres provinces du sud de la Caspienne," *Annales de l'ecole nationale d'agriculture de Montpellier*, N.S. vol. 10, pp. 130-63 and 11, pp. 1-51.

Rakhsh Khurshid, Aziz et al. 1346. *Bamadi. Tayefeh'i az Bakhtiyari*. Tehran: Mo'assesseh-ye Motale`at va Tahqiqat-e Ejtema`i,

Reineggs, Jacob 1807. *A general, historical, and topographical description of Mount Caucasus*, tr. Charles Wilkinson. 2 vols. London.

Reinhold, John G. 1972. "Phytate Concentrations of Leavened and Unleavened Iranian Breads," *Ecology of Food and Nutrition* 1, pp. 187-92.

Renfrew, E.F. 1994 "Vegetables in the ancient near eastern diet," in *Civilizations of the Near East* eds. J.M.Sasson et al., 4 vols. New York.

Rezvani, Mohammad Esma`il 1349, "A`lanha va `alamiyehha-ye dowreh-ye Qajar," *Barrasiha-ye Tarikhi* 5/2, pp. 253-92.

Rice, Clara Colliver 1923. *Persian Women & Their Ways*. London: Seeley, Service & Co.

Rich, Claude James 1836. *Narrative of a Residence in Koordistan ... and of a visit to Shirauz and Persepolis*. 2 vols. London: James Duncan.

___, 1839. *Narrative of a Journey to the Site of Babylon ... with a Narrative of a Journey to Persepolis*. London: Duncan and Malcolm.

Richard, Francis ed. 1995. *Raphael du Mans, missionnaire en Perse au XVIIe s*. 2 vols. Paris: L'Harmattan.

Ricks, Thomas ed. 1984. *Critical Perspectives on Modern Persian Literature*. Washington DC: Three Continent Press.

Ristvet, Lauren; Baxshliyev, Veli and Ashurov, Sefer 2011. "Settlement and Society in Naxçivan: 2006 Excavations and Survey of the Naxçivan Archeaeological Project," *Iranica Antiqua* 46/2011, pp. 1-53.

Rivadeneyra, Adolfo 1880. *Viaje al interior de Persia*. 3 vols. Madrid.

RMM = *Revue du Monde Musulmane*.

Roberts, N. S. 1948. *Iran, economic and social conditions*. London: HMSO.

Rockwell, William Walker 1916. *The Piitful Plight of the Assyrian Christians in Persia and Kurdistan*. New York, American Committee for Armenian and Assyrian Relief.

Rosen, Friedrich 1926. *Persien in Wort und Bild*. Leipzig: Franz Schneider.

Rowghani, Sayyed Da'ud 1385/2006. *Nan-e Sangak*. ed. and intr. by Javad Safi-nezhad. Tehran.

Rumlu, Hasan 1349/1970. *Ahsan al-Tavarikh* ed. 'Abdol-Hoseyn Nava'i. Tehran: Babak.

Sadid al-Saltaneh 1342/1963. *Bandar `Abbas va Khalij-e Fars*. ed. Ahmad Eqtedari. Tehran: Amir Kabir.

Safinezhad, Javad 1345/1966. *Talebabad*. Tehran: Daneshgah.

Salzman, Philip Carl 1994. *Black Tents of Baluchistan*. Washington DC: Smithsonian.

Sana'i Ghaznavi, Abu'l-Majd Majdud b. Adam 1380/2001. *Divan*. Ed. Modarres Razavi. Tehran: Entesharat-e Sana'i

Sani` al-Dowleh 1306/1889. *Ketab al-Ma'ather va'l-Athar*. Tehran (lithograph).

Schindler, A. Houtum. *Eastern Persian Irak* (London: Murray, 1898),

Schwarz, Paul 1993. *Iran im Mittelalter nach den Arabischen Geographen*. 9 parts in 4 vols. Frankfurt am Main: Institute for the History of Arabic-Islamic Science (reprint of the 1896-1936 edition).

Schwartz, Benjamin ed. 1942. *Letters from Persia written by Charles and Edward Burgess 1828-1855*. New York: NY Public Library.

Sen Gupta, P.N. 1968. "Food Policy and Planning Based on Household Food Consumption & Nutrition Survey - Report to the Government of Iran." Rome, FAO (mimeo).

Sepehr, Abdol-Hoseyn 2536/1977. "Mokhtasar-e Joghrafiya-ye Kashan," ed. Iraj Afshar in *Farhang-e Iran Zamin* 22, pp. 430-58.

___, 1368/1989. *Yadashtha-ye Malek al-Mo'arrekhin*. ed. Abdol-Hoseyn Nava'i. Tehran.

Shahri, Ja`far 1367/1988. *Tarikh-e ejtema`i-ye Tehran dar qarn-e sizdahhom*. 6 vols. Tehran: Rasa.

___, 1371/1992. *Tehran-e Qadim*. 5 vols. Tehran: Mo`in.

Shedd, Mary Lewis 1922. *The Measure of a Man. The Life of William Ambrose Shedd Missionary to Persia*. New York: George H. Doran.

Sheil, J. "Notes on a Journey from Tabriz, through Kurdistan, via Van ... in July and August 1836," *RGS* 1838, pp. 54-101.

Sheil, Lady 1973. *Glimpses of Life and Manners in Persia*. New York: Arno.

Shokurzadeh, Ebrahim 1346/1967. *`Aqayed va Rosum-e `Ammeh-ye Mardom-e Khorasan*. Tehran: Bonyad-e Farhang-e Iran.

Shuster, W.M. 1912. *The Strangling of Persia*. New York: The Century.

Shwartz-Be'eri, Ora. *The Jews of Kurdistan*. Jerusalem 2000

Sirjani, Sa`idi 1361/1982. *Vaqaye`-ye Etefaqiyeh*. Tehran: Nashr-e Now.

Skrine, Sir Clarmont 1960. *World War in Iran*. London: Constable & Company.

Smith, Sydney. 1871. "Report by Major Smith, Assistant Resident at Bushire on the Condition of the Working Classes in Bushire [sic; Lingah]," in *Accounts and Papers* 32 (LXVIII), pp. 400-08.

Soltykoff, Alexis 1851. *Voyage en Perse*. Paris: L. Curmer et V. Lecou.

Southgate, Horatio. *A Tour Through Armenia and Mesopotamia*, 2 vols. (New York: D. Appleton & Co, 1840).

Speelman, Cornelis 1907. *Journaal der reis van den gezant der O.I.Compagnie Joan Cunaeus naar Perzië*. Ed. A. Hotz. Amsterdam: Johannes Müller.

Speer, Robert E. 1900. "Wayside Views in Persia," *Frank Leslie's Popular Monthly Magazine*, pp. 248-63.

Spuler, Bertold. 1952. *Iran in Früh-Islamischer Zeit*. Wiesbaden: Steiner.

Stack, Edward 1882. *Six Months in Persia*. 2 vols. New York: G.P. Putnam's Sons.

Stark, Freya 2001. *The Valley of the Assassins*. London: John Murray.

Stöber, Georg 1978. *Die Afshar. Nomadismus in Raum Kerman (Zentraliran)*. Marburg/Lahn: Geographischen Institut der Unversität Marburg.

Stocqueler, J.H. 1832. *Fifteen Months' Pilgrimage through untrodden tracts of Khuzistan and Persia*. London: Saunders and Otley.

Strabo, *Geography*.

Stratil-Sauer, Lotte and Gustav 1934. *Kampf um die Wueste*. Berlon: Reimar Hobbing.

Steingass, F.J. *A Comprehensive Persian-English Dictionary*.

Sundermann, W. 1984. "Ein weiteres Fragment aus Manis Gigantenbuch," in *Orientalia Jacques Duchesne-Guillemin Emerito Oblata*, Acta Iranica 23, pp. 491-505.

Sykes, Ella 1901. *Through Persia on a Side-Saddle*. London.

___, 1910. *Persia and its People*. London: MacMillan.

Sykes, Percy M. 1902 a. *Ten Thousand Miles in Persia or Eight Years in Iran*. New York: Charles Scribner's Sons.

___, 1969. *The History of Persia*. 2 vols. London: MacMillan.

Tahbaz, Sirus 1342/1963. *Yush*. Tehran: Mo'assesseh-ye Motale`at va Tahqiqat-e Ejtema`i.

Tafazzoli, Mahmud, 1340/1961 "Yaddashtha-ye chap nashodeh-ye Sepahsalar-e Tonkabuni," *Rahnama-ye Ketab* 4/5-6, p. 530-38.

Tahvildar, Mirza Hoseyn Khan 1342/1963. *Joghrafiya-ye Esfahan*. ed. Manuchehr Setudeh. Tehran: Daneshgah.

Tavernier, Jean-Baptiste 1930. *Voyages en Perse*. ed. Pascal Pia. Paris: Editions du Carrefour.

The Southern Workman XLV/1916.

Thevenot, J. de 1971. *The Travels of M. de Thevenot into the Levant* 3 vols. in one. Westmead: Gregg Int.

Tayarani, Behruz 1372/1993. "Jang-e jahani-ye dovvom, qahti va vakoneshha-ye mardomi dar qebal-e an 132-24," *Faslnameh-ye ganjihen-ye asnad* 3/9, pp. 20-31.

Tonkabuni, Mirza Mohammad 1364/1995. *Qesas al-Olama*. Tehran: Entesharat-e `Elmi-yer Eslamiyeh.

Torabi, Soheyla. "Nagahi beh vazi`at-e arzaq dar Iran dar salha-ye jang-e jahani-y avval," *Faslnameh-ye ganjihen-ye asnad*, pp. 24-33.

United Nations 2001. Economic and Social Commission for Asia and the Pacific. *Social Development Management Information Systems (SOMIS)*. Bangkok.

US Army 1963. *Area Handbook for Iran* (Washington DC).

US Consular Reports 1900. Herbert W. Bowen, "Scarcity of bread in Persia," vol. LXII , 1 November 1899.

US Department of Agriculture 1961 a, *Foreign Agricultural Service*.

___, 1961 b. *Economic Research Service*, Issues 64-118.

US Government 1971. *Area Handbook for Iran*. Wshington DC: USGPO.

Vaile, Roland S. 1919. "Breaking a Wheat Corner in Persia," *Pomona College Quarterly Magazine*, vol. VIII/1 October, Claremont, California, pp. 11-14.

Vambery, A., 1867. *Meine Wanderungen und Erlebnisse in Persien*. Pesht.

Vaziri, Ahmad Ali Khan 1346/1967. *Joghrafiya-ye Kerman*. ed. Bastani Parizi, Tehran: Farhang Iran Zamin.

Von Freygang, Mme. 1823. *Letters from the Caucasus and Georgia*. London: John Murray.

Von Haxthausen, Baron 1854. *Transcaucasia. Sketches of the Nations and Races between the Black Sea and the Caspian*. London: Chapman and Hall.

Von Kremer, Alfred 1890. "Studien zur vergleichenden Culturgeschichte vorzüglich nach arabischen Quellen. I. Brot und Salz," *Sitzungberichte der Philosophisch-Historischen Classe der kaiserl. Akademie der Wissenschaften in Wien* vol. 120, pp. 1-34.

Von Soden, Wolfram 1994. *The ancient Orient; an introduction to the ancient Near East*. Grand Rapids, Mich: Wm. B. Eerdmans.

Währen, Max 1967. *Brot und Gebäck im Leben und Glauben des Alten Orients*. Bern.

Waines, David 1987. "Cereals, Bread, and Society. *JESHO* 30/3, pp. 255-85.

Weston, Harold F. 1921. "Persian Caravan Sketches," *National Geographic Magazine* 39/4, pp. 417-68.

Wieshöfer, Josef 2001. *Ancient Persia*. London: IB Tauris.

Wilbraham, Richard 1839. *Travels in the Transcaucasian Provinces of Russia*. London: John Murray.

Williams, E. Crawshay 1907. *Across Persia*. London: Edward Arnold.

Wills, C. J. 1886. *Persia As It Is*. London: Sampson Low, Marston, Searle & Rivington.

___, 1893. *In the Land of the Lion and the Sun*. London: Ward, Lock & Bowden.

Wilson, S.G. 1895. *Persian Life and Customs*. New York: Fleming. H. Revell.

Wilson, A. T. 1932. *Persia*. London.

Wishard, John G. *Twenty Years in Persia. A Narrative of Life under the Last Three Shahs* (New York: Fleming H. Revell, 1908).

Wright, Henry T. *An Early Town of the Deh Luran Plain. Excavations at Tepe Farukhabad*. Ann Arbor 1981, pp. 227-30;

Wulff, Hans 1966. *Traditional Crafts of Persia*. Cambridge, MIT.

Xenephon, 1896. *Fist Five Book of the Anabasis*. Translated by J.S. Watson. Philadelphia: David Mckay.

Yakta'i, Majid 1340/1961. *Tarikh-e Dara'i-ye Iran*. Tehran.

Yate, C .E. 1900. *Khurasan and Sistan*. London: William Blackwood & Sons.

Zavosh, H.M. 1370. *Tehran dar Gozargah-e Tarikh-e Iran*. Tehran: Eshareh.

Zirinsky, Michael 2002. "American Presbyterian Missionaries at Urmia during the Great War," in Bast 2002, pp. 353-74.

INDEX

A
acorns 25
Alexander 160
apples 103
asiyaban 31
Azerbaijan 111

B
Bacchus 98
bakers 50, 51, 52, 122, 144, 156
Bakhtiyaris 25
Baluchistan 19, 21
barley 18, 19, 20, 21, 103, 110, 116
Boir-Ahmadi 25
bread 16, 23, 50, 71, 97, 98, 103
butchers 52, 122, 144
butter 84, 103

C
Caspian 115
Chardeh Kalateh 18
cheese 103
Choghadak 116
Christians 52
Churak 98
coffee 98
corn 20, 26, 110, 111
cotton 19, 21, 71, 114

D
dates 20
diet 103, 106, 108, 114, 115

F
Fars 25
fish 20
flour 19, 21, 25, 103, 111
fodder 18
food from the bazaar 53

G
goats 111
grocers 122

H
Haji Molla Rafi` 124
harvest 114
Helmand 19, 21

I
India 19
Isfahan 20

J
jarchi 122

K
Kerman 161
Khisht 112
Khorasan 26, 111
Khuzestan 165
Kurdistan 18, 25

L
luffa 26, 111
lul tree 116

M
Mamasani 25
masons 52
Meimand 111
milk 103
millet 19, 20, 21, 114
Mirza Javad Aqa 124
Morghab 19, 21
mulberry 26, 111
mules 18
musicians 98

N

nanva-bashi 52, 121
Nezam al-Ulama 125
notables only cook at home 53

O

oleaster 111

P

painters 52
pastry 86

Q

quinces 103

R

rice 19, 20, 22, 23, 110, 115

S

sheep 20, 111
Shiraz 25
singers 98
sorghum 19, 21, 110
soup 86

T

tahhan 31
tanners 52
tanning 25
tas`ir-e ajnas 122
tea 98
Tehran 112
tobacco 21, 110
trade 17
trees 26, 111

W

wheat 19, 21, 103, 110, 112
women 25, 115

Y

Yazd 19, 20, 114

Z

Zagros 25

www.ingramcontent.com/pod-product-compliance
Lightning Source LLC
Chambersburg PA
CBHW080806300426
44114CB00020B/2854